Lady in Waiting

Lady in Waiting

My Extraordinary Life in the Shadow of the Crown

ANNE GLENCONNER

HODDER &
STOUGHTON

ZULEIKA

First published in Great Britain in 2019 by Hodder & Stoughton
An Hachette UK company
By joint imprimatur with Zuleika

3

A CIP catalogue record for this title is
available from the British Library

Hardback ISBN 978 1 529 35906 0
Trade Paperback ISBN 978 1 529 35907 7
eBook ISBN 978 1 529 35908 4

Typeset in Celeste by Palimpsest Book Production Limited,
Falkirk, Stirlingshire

Printed and bound in Great Britain by Clays Ltd, Elcograf S.p.A.

Hodder & Stoughton policy is to use papers that are natural,
renewable and recyclable products and made from wood grown
in sustainable forests. The logging and manufacturing processes
are expected to conform to the environmental regulations
of the country of origin.

Hodder & Stoughton Ltd
Carmelite House
50 Victoria Embankment
London EC4Y 0DZ

Zuleika
Thomas House
84 Eccleston Square
London SW1V 1PX

www.hodder.co.uk
www.zuleika.london

For my children, grandchildren and great-grandchildren

Contents

PROLOGUE

One morning at the beginning of 2019, when I was in my London flat, the telephone rang.

'Hello?'

'Lady Glenconner? It's Helena Bonham Carter.'

It's not every day a Hollywood film star rings me up, although I had been expecting her call. When the producers of the popular Netflix series *The Crown* contacted me, saying that I was going to be portrayed by Nancy Carroll in the third series, and that Helena Bonham Carter had been cast as Princess Margaret, I was delighted. Asked whether I minded meeting them so they could get a better idea of my friendship with Princess Margaret, I said I didn't mind in the least.

Nancy Carroll came to tea, and we sat in armchairs in my sitting room and talked. The conversation was surreal as I became extremely self-aware, realising that Nancy must be absorbing what *I* was like.

A few days later when Helena was on the telephone, I invited her for tea too. Not only do I admire her as an actress but, as it happens, she is a cousin of my late husband Colin

Tennant, and her father helped me when one of my sons had a motorbike accident in the eighties.

As Helena walked through the door, I noticed a resemblance between her and Princess Margaret: she is just the right height and figure, and although her eyes aren't blue, there is a similar glint of mischievous intelligence in her gaze.

We sat down in the sitting room, and I poured her some tea. Out came her notebook, where she had written down masses of questions in order to get the measure of the Princess, 'to do her justice', she explained.

A lot of her questions were about mannerisms. When she asked how the Princess had smoked, I described it as rather like a Chinese tea ceremony: from taking her long cigarette holder out of her bag and carefully putting the cigarette in, to always lighting it herself with one of her beautiful lighters. She hated it when others offered to light it for her, and when any man eagerly advanced, she would make a small but definite gesture with her hand to make it quite clear.

I noticed that Helena moved her hand in the tiniest of reflexes, as if to test the movement I'd just described, before going on to discuss Princess Margaret's character. I tried to capture her quick wit – how she always saw the humorous side of things, not one to dwell, her attitude positive and matter-of-fact. As we talked, the descriptions felt so vivid, it was as though Princess Margaret was in the room with us. Helena listened to everything very carefully, making lots of notes. We talked for three hours, and when she left, I felt certain that she was perfectly cast for the role.

Both actors sent me letters thanking me for my help,

Helena Bonham Carter expressing the hope that Princess Margaret would be as good a friend to her as she was to me. I felt very touched by this and the thought of Princess Margaret and I being reunited on screen was something I looked forward to. I found myself reflecting back on our childhood spent together in Norfolk, the thirty years I'd been her Lady in Waiting, all the times we had found ourselves in hysterics, and the ups and downs of both our lives.

I've always loved telling stories, but it never occurred to me to write a book until these two visits stirred up all those memories. From a generation where we were taught not to over-think, not to look back or question, only now do I see how extraordinary the nine decades of my life have really been, full of extreme contrasts. I have found myself in a great many odd circumstances, both hilarious and awful, many of which seem, even to me, unbelievable. But I feel very fortunate that I have my wonderful family and for the life I have led.

CHAPTER ONE

The Greatest Disappointment

HOLKHAM HALL COMMANDS the land of North Norfolk with a hint of disdain. It is an austere house and looks its best in the depths of summer when the grass turns the colour of Demerara sugar so the park seems to merge into the house. The coast nearby is a place of harsh winds and big skies, of miles of salt marsh and dark pine forests that hem the dunes, giving way to the vast stretch of the grey-golden sand of Holkham beach: a landscape my ancestors changed from open marshes to the birthplace of agriculture. Here, in the flight path of the geese and the peewits, the Coke (pronounced 'cook') family was established in the last days of the Tudors by Sir Edward Coke, who was considered the greatest jurist of the Elizabethan and Jacobean eras, successfully prosecuting Sir Walter Raleigh and the Gunpowder Plot conspirators. My family crest is an ostrich swallowing an iron horseshoe to symbolise our ability to digest anything.

There is a photograph of me, taken at my christening in the summer of 1932. I am held by my father, the future 5th Earl of Leicester, and surrounded by male relations wearing solemn faces. I had tried awfully hard to be a boy, even weighing eleven pounds at birth, but I was a girl and there was nothing to be done about it.

My female status meant that I would not inherit the earldom, or Holkham, the fifth largest estate in England with its 27,000 acres of top-grade agricultural land, neither the furniture, the books, the paintings, nor the silver. My parents went on to have two more children, but they were also daughters: Carey two years later and Sarah twelve years later. The line was broken, and my father must have felt the weight of almost four centuries of disapproval on his conscience.

My mother had awarded her father, the 8th Lord Hardwicke, the same fate, and maybe in solidarity, and because she thought I needed to have a strong character, she named me Anne Veronica, after H. G. Wells's book about a hardy feminist heroine. Born Elizabeth Yorke, my mother was capable, charismatic and absolutely the right sort of girl my grandfather would have expected his son to marry. She herself was the daughter of an earl, whose ancestral seat was Wimpole Hall in Cambridgeshire.

My father was handsome, popular, passionate about country pursuits, and eligible as the heir to the Leicester earldom. They met when she was fifteen and he was seventeen, during a skiing trip in St Moritz, becoming unofficially engaged immediately, he apparently having said to her, 'I just know I want to marry you.' He was also spurred on by being rather frightened of another girl who lived in Norfolk and had taken a fancy to him, so he was relieved to be able to stop her advances by declaring himself already engaged.

My mother was very attractive and very confident, and I think that's what drew my father to her. He was more reserved so she brought out the fun in him and they balanced each other well.

Together, they were one of the golden couples of high society and were great friends of the Duke and Duchess of York, who later, because of the abdication of the Duke's brother, King Edward VIII, unexpectedly became King and Queen. They were also friends with Prince Philip's sisters, Princesses Theodora, Margarita, Cecilie and Sophie, who used to come for holidays at Holkham. Rather strangely, Prince Philip, who was much younger, still only a small child, used to stay with his nanny at the Victoria, a pub right next to the beach, instead of at Holkham. Recently I asked him why he had stayed at the pub instead of the house, but he didn't know for certain, so we joked about him wanting to be as near to the beach as possible.

My parents were married in October 1931 and I was a honeymoon baby, arriving on their first wedding anniversary.

Up until I was nine, my great-grandfather was the Earl of Leicester and lived at Holkham with my grandfather, who occupied one of the four wings. The house felt enormous, especially seen through the eyes of a child. So vast, the footmen would put raw eggs in a bain-marie and take them

7

from the kitchen to the nursery: by the time they arrived, the eggs would be perfectly boiled. We visited regularly and I adored my grandfather, who made an effort to spend time with me: we would sit in the long gallery, listening to classical music on the gramophone together, and when I was a bit older, he introduced me to photography, a passion he successfully transferred to me.

With my father in the Scots Guards, we moved all over the country, and I was brought up by nannies, who were in charge of the ins and outs of daily life. My mother didn't wash or dress me or my sister Carey; nor did she feed us or put us to bed. Instead, she would interject daily life with treats and days out.

My father found fatherhood difficult: he was strait-laced and fastidious and he was always nagging us to leave our bedroom windows open and checking to make sure we had been to the lavatory properly. I used to struggle to sit on his knee but because I was too big he would push me away in favour of Carey, whom he called 'my little dolly daydreams'.

Having grown up with Victorian parents, his childhood was typical of a boy in his position. He was brought up by nannies and governesses, sent to Eton and then on to Sandhurst, his father making sure his son knew what was expected of him as heir. He was loving, but from afar: he was not affectionate or sentimental, and did not share his emotions. No one did, not even my mother, who would give us hugs and show her affection but rarely talked about her feelings or mine – there were no heart-to-hearts. As I got older she would give me pep talks instead. It was a generation and a class who were not brought up to express emotions.

But in many other ways my mother was the complete opposite of my father. Only nineteen years older than me, she was more like a big sister, full of mischief and fun. Carey and I used to shin up trees with her and a soup ladle tied to a walking stick. With it, we would scoop up jackdaws' eggs, which were delicious to eat, rather like plovers'. Those early childhood days were filled with my mother making camps with us on the beach or taking us on trips in her little Austin, getting terribly excited as we came across ice-cream sellers on bicycles calling, 'Stop me and buy one.'

The epitome of grace and elegance when she needed to be, she also had the gumption to pursue her own hobbies, which were often rather hands-on: she was a fearless horse-woman and rode a Harley-Davidson. She passed on her love of sailing to me. I was five when I started navigating the nearby magical creeks of Burnham Overy Staithe in dinghies, and eighty when I stopped. I used to go in for local races, but I was quite often last, and would arrive only to find everyone had gone home.

Holkham was a completely male-oriented estate and the whole set-up was undeniably old-fashioned. My great-great-grandfather, the 2nd Earl, who had inherited his father's title in 1842 and was the earl when my father was a boy, was a curmudgeon and so set in his ways that even his wife had to call him 'Leicester'. When he was younger, he apparently passed a nurse with a baby in the corridor and asked, 'Whose child is that?'

The nurse had replied, 'Yours, my lord!'

A crusty old thing, he had spent his last years lying in a truckle bed in the state rooms. He wore tin-framed spectacles, and when he went outside, he would go around the park in a horse-drawn carriage, with his long-suffering second wife, who sat on a cushion strapped to a mudguard.

Influenced by the line of traditional earls, Holkham was slow to modernise, keeping distinctly separate roles for the men and women. In the summer, the ladies would go and stay in Meales House, the old manor down by the beach, for a holiday known as 'no-stays week' when they quite literally let their hair down and took off their corsets.

From when I was very little, my grandfather started to teach me about my ancestors: about how Thomas Coke, 1st Earl of Leicester in its fifth creation (the line had been broken many times, only adding to the disappointment of my father at having no sons), had gone off to Europe on a grand tour – the equivalent of an extremely lavish gap year – and shipped back dozens of paintings and marble statues from Italy that came wrapped in *Quercus ilex* leaves and acorns, the eighteenth-century answer to bubble wrap.

He told me all about when the *ilex* acorns were planted, becoming the first avenue of *ilex* trees (also called holm oak, a Mediterranean evergreen) in England. My grandfather's father had sculpted the landscape, pushing the marshes away from the house by planting the pine forests that now line Holkham beach. Before him, the 1st Earl in its seventh creation became known as 'Coke of Norfolk' because he had such a huge impact on the county through his influence on farming – he was the man credited with British agricultural reform.

Life at Holkham continued to revolve around farming the land, all elements of which were taken seriously. As well as dozens of tenant farmers, there were a great many gardeners to look after the huge kitchen garden. The brick walls were heated with fires all along, stoked through the night by the garden boys, so nectarines and peaches would ripen sooner. On hot summer days I loved riding my bike up to the kitchen gardens, being handed a peach, then cycling as fast as I could to the fountain at the front of the house and jumping into the water to cool down.

Shooting was also a huge part of Holkham life, and really what my father and all his friends lived for. It was the main bond between the Cokes and the Royal Family, especially with Sandringham only ten miles away – a mere half an hour's drive. Queen Mary had once rung my great-grand-mother, suggesting she come over with the King, only for my great-grandfather to be heard bellowing, 'Come over? Good God, no! We don't want to encourage them!'

My father shot with the present Queen's father, King George VI, and my great-grandfather and grandfather with King George V on both estates, but it was Holkham that was particularly famous for shooting: it held the record for wild partridges for years and it's where covert shooting was invented (where a copse is planted in a round so that it shelters the game, the gun dogs flushing out the birds grad-ually, allowing for maximum control, making the shoot more efficient).

It was also where the bowler hat was invented: one of my ancestors had got so fed up with the top hat being so imprac-tical that he went off to London and ordered a new type of hat, checking how durable it was by stamping and jumping on it until he was content. From then on gamekeepers wore the 'billy coke', as it was called then.

There were other royal connections in the family too. It is well documented that Edward, Prince of Wales, later King Edward VIII, had many love affairs with married, often older glamorous aristocrats, the first being my paternal grandmother, Marion.

My father was Equerry to the Duke of York and his sister, my aunt Lady Mary Harvey, was Lady in Waiting to the Duchess of York after she became Queen. When the Duke of York was crowned King George VI in 1937, my father became his Extra Equerry; and in 1953 my mother became a Lady of the Bedchamber, a high-ranking Lady in Waiting, to Queen Elizabeth II on her Coronation.

My father especially was a great admirer of the Royal Family and was always very attentive when they came to visit. My earliest memories of Princess Elizabeth and Princess Margaret come from when I was two or three years old. Princess Elizabeth was five years older, which was quite a lot – she was rather grown-up – but Princess Margaret was only three years older and we became firm friends. She was naughty, fun and imaginative – the very best sort of friend to have. We used to rush around Holkham, past the grand pictures, whirling through the labyrinth of corridors on our trikes or jumping out at the nursery footmen as they carried huge silver trays from the kitchen. Princess Elizabeth was much better behaved. 'Please don't do that, Margaret,' or 'You shouldn't do that, Anne,' she would scold us.

In one photograph we are all standing in a line. Princess Elizabeth is frowning at Princess Margaret, suspecting she is up to no good, while Princess Margaret is staring down at my shoes. Years afterwards, I showed Princess Margaret the photo and asked, 'Ma'am, why were you looking at my feet?'

And she replied, 'Well, I was so jealous because you had silver shoes and I had brown ones.'

In the summer the Princesses would come down to Holkham beach where we would spend whole days making sandcastles, clad in the most unattractive and prickly black bathing suits with black rubber caps and shoes. The nannies would bundle us all into the beach bus, along with wicker picnic baskets full of sandwiches, and set up in the beach hut every day, whatever the weather – the grown-ups had a separate hut among the trees at the back. We had wonderful times, digging holes in the sand, hoping people would fall into them.

Every Christmas, my family would go to a party at Buckingham Palace, and Carey and I would be dressed up in frilly frocks and the coveted silver shoes. At the end of the parties, the children would be invited to take a present each from the big table in the hall near the Christmas tree. Behind the table stood the formidable Queen Mary, who was quite frightening. She was tall and imposing, and Princess Margaret never warmed to her because every time she saw her, Queen Mary would say, 'I can see you haven't grown.' Princess Margaret minded frightfully about being small all her life, so never liked her grandmother.

Queen Mary did teach me a valuable life lesson, however. One year Carey rushed up to the table and clasped a huge teddy bear, which was sitting upright among the other presents. Before I chose mine, Queen Mary leant down towards me. 'Anne,' she said quietly, 'quite often rather nice, rather valuable things come in little boxes.' I froze. I'd had my eye on another teddy bear but now I was far too frightened to choose anything other than a little box. Inside it was a beautiful necklace of pearl and coral. Queen Mary was quite right. My little box contained something that is still appreciated to this day.

Our connection to the Royal Family was close. When I was in my late teens, Prince Charles became like a younger brother to me, spending weeks with us all at Holkham. He would come to stay whenever he had any of the contagious childhood diseases, like chickenpox, because the Queen, having never gone to school, had not been exposed to them. Sixteen years younger than me, Prince Charles was nearer in age to my youngest sister Sarah, but all of us would go off to the beach together.

My father taught him how to fish for eel in the lake, and when he got a bit older, my mother let him drive the Jaguar and the Mini Minor around the park, something he loved doing, sending great long thank-you letters telling her he couldn't wait to return. He was such a kind and loving little boy and I've loved him ever since – the whole family have always been deeply fond of him.

As soon as I was old enough to ride, I made the park at Holkham my own, riding past the great barn, making little jumps for Kitty, my pony. When we were a bit older, Carey and I would follow one of the very good-looking tenant farmers, Gary Maufe, on our ponies. Many years later I became a great friend of his wife, Marit. He used to gallop across the park on a great big black stallion, and after him we would go on our hopeless ponies, giddying them up, desperately trying to keep up.

It wasn't just my family who were part of Holkham but everybody who worked on the estate, some of whom had very distinctive characters. Mr Patterson, the head gardener, would enthusiastically play his bagpipes in the mornings whenever my parents had friends to stay, until my mother would shout, 'That's quite enough, Mr Patterson, thank you!'

My early childhood was idyllic, but the outbreak of war in 1939 changed everything. I was seven, Carey was five. My father was posted to Egypt with the Scots Guards so my mother followed to support him, as many wives did. Holkham Hall was partly occupied by the army, and the temple in the park was used to house the Home Guard, while the gardeners and footmen were called up, and the maids and cooks went off to work in factories to help with the war effort.

Everybody thought the Germans would choose to invade Britain from the Norfolk coast, so before my mother left for Egypt, she moved Carey and me up to Scotland, to stay with my Great-aunt Bridget, away from Mr Hitler's U-boats.

When she said goodbye, she told me, 'Anne, you're in charge. You've got to look after Carey.' If we had known how long she was going to be away, it would have been even harder, but no one had any idea how long the war would last and that, in fact, she and my father would be gone for three years.

CHAPTER TWO

Hitler's Mess

WE WENT TO live with our Ogilvy cousins in Downie Park, one of the Ogilvys' shooting lodges in Angus: their main house, Cortachy Castle, had been requisitioned and was being used as a hospital for Polish officers.

Although Carey and I were unsettled by the separation from our parents, going to Scotland felt like an adventure. I loved my Ogilvy cousins. There were six of them, and the three youngest – David, Angus and James – were all about the same age as me and Carey. We knew them well because every summer they would come and stay at Holkham, having great fun together, exploring and making up games. We watched as the boys played endless rounds of cricket on the terrace, wearing their special linen kilts that Carey and I wished we had. Our nanny wasn't quite so keen on them all because the best fruit – a valuable treat in those days – was kept for them and she would say they had come to 'take over'.

They were all very welcoming at Downie Park, and I was especially fond of David, whom I followed everywhere. I adored their mother, my Great-aunt Bridget, who was born Lady Alexandra Coke and was my grandfather's sister.

Great-aunt Bridget was a Christian Scientist – a nineteenth-century religion established by Mary Baker Eddy, which, during the First World War, cut a swathe through the aristocracy, converting many to it. It operates on the belief that sickness is an illusion that can be corrected by prayer. This provided comfort for Great-aunt Bridget and her husband, my Great-uncle Joe, the Earl of Airlie, because he, like many men, was suffering from the effects of the Great War. Great-aunt Bridget practised her beliefs and passed on many useful pieces of advice to me. Perhaps the advice that stuck with me most is 'Things have a habit of working out, not necessarily in the way you expect, and you must never force them.' Her grounded approach served Carey and me well, because we both found it very disconcerting to be away from our parents, with the outbreak of war.

On 3 September 1939, Great-aunt Bridget brought us down to the drawing room in Downie Park, where we listened to Neville Chamberlain's declaration of war on the ancient wireless. There was something heavy and serious in the Prime Minister's voice, which mirrored the atmosphere in the room. I stared at the carpet as I listened, not really knowing what was happening, wondering when we would be able to go home.

There was a very different atmosphere when, in 1940, Princess Elizabeth directly addressed the children of Britain. Again, we sat on the carpet in the drawing room, huddled round the wireless craning our necks towards Princess Elizabeth's voice, excited that we all knew her. It felt as if she was talking directly to us. At the end, Princess Elizabeth said, 'My sister is by my side and we are both going to say goodnight to you. Come on, Margaret.' And Princess Margaret responded, 'Goodnight, children.' We all answered back, thinking they could hear us, somehow imagining they were *in* the wireless. The Princesses were our heroines. So many children of our parents' friends had been sent off to America in order to escape the war and there were the two Princesses, still in England, in as much danger as us all.

The war meant that Carey and I and the Princesses were no longer in Norfolk together and the only time we saw them was when Carey, the Ogilvys and I visited Glamis Castle – Queen Elizabeth the Queen Mother's family estate, where Princess Margaret had been born.

Glamis is said to be the most haunted castle in Scotland and Princess Margaret knew every nook, cranny and ghoul. As we were exploring the grounds, she told us stories about the ghosts, the grey lady who is said to haunt the chapel and the tongue-less lady who runs across the lawn. The Ogilvys relished the stories and told their own, all about how there was a ghost at Cortachy, who would beat a drum whenever someone in the family died, leaving me relieved that Cortachy had been requisitioned. Just before we left, Princess Margaret took us down to see the train, which puffed along the edge of the grounds, standing on the bridge over the railway line, being enveloped in steam.

Apart from that, we didn't see them and life was quite limited. With no petrol and living in a big house far from the nearest town or city, we stayed within the grounds of Downie Park, only once going to Dundee when Uncle Joe took us to the theatre.

In the winter we would skate on the frozen lake, and when we weren't having lessons with our governess, we would do our 'war work', collecting sphagnum moss for the Red Cross, who used it to help to dress wounds, knitting gloves for the sailors on the mine sweepers, and entertaining the Polish officers at Cortachy Castle by playing snakes and ladders on their beds and putting on amateur dramatics for them.

Every afternoon, we would take our fresh air and exercise by walking down the long drive, then return to the house where a man from the nearby town of Kirriemuir would teach us to dance. Carey and I put on our black dancing shoes and in the vast dining room, with our cousin James, who was the same age as Carey and always wore a kilt, learnt how to do the Highland Fling and the Sword Dance.

James was not always so beguiling. He and Carey would regularly gang up on me. This might have been because I spent a great deal of time, rather pathetically, hugging trees, climbing up them and pretending they were my friends. Once up them, however, I would be too frightened to come down, so Carey and James would stand below, teasing me with their particular catchphrase: 'Cowardy, cowardy custard!' I had arrived at Downie Park a rather shy child, but I gradually came out of my shell. Being in a big pack of Ogilvys and part of a boisterous group soon toughened me up.

My parents had sent our own governess to Downie, my mother telling me before she left for Egypt: 'You're now too old to have a nanny, so Daddy and I have chosen a governess for you called Miss Bonner and she is very nice, and you will be very happy with her.' Well, it turned out that Miss Bonner was not very nice. She was fairly all right with Carey, but really cruel to me. Every night, whatever I had done, however well I had behaved, she would punish me by tying my hands to the back of the bed and leaving me like that all night. I was too frightened of Miss Bonner to ask Carey to untie me, and Carey would have been too frightened to do it anyway. Both Carey and I suffered badly through this. I wanted to protect Carey, fearing Miss Bonner might do the same to her, so neither of us told anyone. While Miss Bonner did not do the same to my little sister, Carey witnessed this inexplicable behaviour towards me and felt powerless that there was nothing she could do. Her distress would manifest itself in high temperatures linked to no specific illness.

Because my mother had chosen Miss Bonner, I thought she knew what the governess was doing to me and didn't mind, or even thought it was good for me. It caused me terrible confusion because I couldn't understand why my parents would want me to be treated like that.

Fortunately, Great-aunt Bridget's Christian Science saved me. Eventually, Miss Bonner was sacked, not because of her ill-treatment of me (which I am sure Great-aunt Bridget knew nothing about) but for being a Roman Catholic and taking me to Mass. There was nothing worse than Catholicism, as far as Great-aunt Bridget was concerned. When Miss Bonner left, I made a big fuss, pretending to be really upset that she was going, fearing she might somehow blame me and do something even more horrible.

Miss Bonner left an invisible scar on me. To this day, I find it almost impossible to think about what she did to me. Years later, she sent me a card congratulating me on my engagement, which triggered the most unpleasant rush of memories and made me physically sick.

Luckily, Miss Bonner was replaced with Miss Billy Williams, who was wonderful, although she looked rather daunting with a nose that was always running and one leg longer than the other so she had a limp. But she twinkled with kindness.

The minute Billy Williams set foot in Carey's and my lives, everything changed, and within days, we were devoted to her. I think she realised I'd had a difficult time with her predecessor, because she often gave me treats, taking me on fun days out. One of my favourite places was an Ogilvy shooting lodge, which was tucked into the hillside, surrounded by heather. She'd take us all off, walking along a pretty stream that ran through the bottom of the garden, stopping for a picnic, during which we would roll heather in a piece of newspaper and pretend to smoke it. We thought that was frightfully dashing.

As the months turned to years we became more aware of the horrors of the war, overhearing conversations referring to the increasing attacks on Britain. Even though we had been sent up to Scotland to get away from danger, we weren't far from Dundee, which was targeted heavily. In fact, there were more than five hundred German air raids on Scotland so we would probably have been safer staying in Norfolk. Once a German plane was shot down just above Tulcan lodge and, as a 'great treat', Billy Williams took me up to the wreckage to have a look. It was still smoking, although we saw no body, and I still have a piece of map I took from the plane, which was scattered in the heather.

As Carey and I absorbed more information, mostly through the wireless that James's nanny listened to tirelessly, we became convinced that Hitler and all his henchmen would come to England and each choose a stately home to live in. We had some idea that Hitler was going to Windsor and presumed, rather grandly, that either Himmler or Goering would choose Holkham. We weren't far wrong. It transpired that the Nazis had indeed planned to take over the country estates, although Hitler had his sights on Blenheim.

Carey and I, I suspect like many other imaginative children of the time, felt helpless in the face of the war. Knitting gloves and playing board games with Polish officers somehow didn't feel helpful enough. Our father was fighting and our mother, we had been told, was doing 'war work', but we were doing nothing to stop Hitler.

Discussing the dire situation, Carey and I became convinced Hitler was bound to visit Holkham at some point, so we decided that, somehow, we would go back there to kill him. In preparation for the assassination, we created a poison that we called 'Hitler's mess', a collection of jam jars containing anything really disgusting – scraps of food and medicine, muddy water and bits of fluff from the carpet. We hid it under our beds until it became so smelly that Billy Williams made us throw it away and, determined, we were forced to start again.

We had decided to make Hitler fall in love with us, which, when I think about it now, was rather like the Mitfords. But, then, we were going to kill him – which, I suppose, was rather unlike the Mitfords. Of course, we had no real understanding of the situation and even less control over our own lives. That was why we devised our plan. We had heard he liked the Aryan look and we were both fair-haired, especially Carey, who was the blondest little thing with huge blue eyes. We thought we must take advantage of this in order to save Britain.

We used to practise by pretending our teddy bear was Hitler, sidling up to him and saying things like, 'How lovely to see you. We're so pleased you've come to Holkham,' and 'Do you enjoy staying here? We've got a lovely drink for you, Mr Hitler – we've been saving it especially for you.' We didn't quite think through what would happen if we did actually manage to kill Hitler, but then I suppose we didn't get that far. We were absolutely convinced, however, that we could and would do it.

In 1943, when I was ten and Carey was eight, our parents returned from Egypt and we returned to Norfolk. It was an underwhelming reunion – our parents were like strangers to us and, instead of a warm embrace after so many years, Carey and I clung to Billy Williams, hiding behind her, out of sight. It was only a day or so before our mother won back our affection, but it took longer to build a rapport with our father, who wasn't as open and friendly and never hugged us like our mother.

By then my great-grandfather had died and my grandfather had become 4th Earl of Leicester. For a little while we lived in the Red House in the village at Holkham, with one ancient maid nicknamed Speedy because she moved so slowly. Carey and I enjoyed living there, playing with the village boys in the wood near the house – we called it 'the donkey wood'.

Then we moved into the family wing at Holkham. It was the first time, apart from holidays, I had ever lived in the big house and it felt very exciting to know that it was now our official home.

My grandfather liked to interest me and, wanting to teach me about Holkham's treasures, put me in charge of airing the Codex Leicester, Leonardo da Vinci's seventy-two-page manuscript, a study on water and stars. Once a fortnight, I would retrieve it from the butler's pantry, where it was kept in a safe along with the Coke jewels and a Bible picture book.

I used to lick my finger and spin through the pages, frowning down at Da Vinci's mirror handwriting, studying the little drawings and diagrams with interest. Bought on the 1st Earl's grand tour, it belonged to my family for at least two hundred and fifty years before, very sadly, my father had to sell it, needing money for the upkeep of the estate. Acquired at Christie's by an American businessman, Armand Hammer, in the eighties, it was then sold on to Bill Gates in 1994 for $30.8 million, a record sum, making it the most valuable book in the world – and covered with my DNA.

Life soon settled down at Holkham. My father continued his duties with the Scots Guards and my mother became head of North Norfolk's Land Girls. Carey and I spent a lot of time playing in the house, making dens in the attic out of a collection of Old Masters deemed too louche for the walls of the state rooms, oblivious to the value and the subject.

But the estate wasn't the same as it had been before the war. There was a prisoner-of-war camp in the park, first for Italians, then Germans, and the gamekeepers helped guard them. Carey and I were very curious and whirled around the outside of the camp on our ponies, spying on the prisoners. The Italians were charming, always waving and smiling, and became friends with my mother who, after the war, employed some of their sisters to work at Holkham: a lot of them decided to settle in England.

The Germans weren't so friendly, and Carey and I were terrified of them. They wore patches on their legs and arms – shooting targets should they escape – which the game-keepers longed for them to do so they could put in their game book: '14 pheasants, 6 partridge, 1 German'. As far as I know, the prisoners never tried to escape – the Germans were far more frightened of the keepers than they were of the official guards.

Holkham beach wasn't the same either. We couldn't picnic on the dunes because they were being used as a military practice ground, and the beach was covered with London buses and taxis on which the Royal Air Force practised airstrikes. At the end of the war, the buses and taxis were just left there. There is a big sand dune now where they were, and I expect most people have no idea they are still under it, rusting away in their sandy tomb.

The military also practised drills all the way along the woodland near the sand dunes and on the marsh. There was a pond at the edge of the marsh where a wall was built for training the soldiers who, throwing smoke bombs in front of them, had then to jump blindly over the wall and into the pond. Carey and I would take great delight in watching and, getting carried away, we would shout, 'Go on, jump, you cowardy cowardy custards! It's not at all deep. It's only a bit of water.' Within moments, a furious sergeant major would rush up, red in the face, yelling, 'What are you doing, girls? Will you get away? You're ruining my training!' at which point, we'd grab our bikes and scamper off, giggling.

My childhood was a curious mix of carefree adventure in beautiful surroundings and a pressing fear of the war. By the time I was eleven, long days of playing with Carey were swapped for boarding school. In the autumn of 1943, holding a single leather trunk with my name on it, off I went by train to Downham – a small school in Essex for girls. Because of the war, most of the teachers had been called up or moved into jobs to help with the war effort. Left with the halt and the lame, I was hardly likely to learn anything at all.

The school was in a big old house where we all had to sleep in the cellars for the first few terms because of the doodlebugs, which, overshooting London, would land very close to where we were:, the plaster would fall from the ceiling into our bunks. It was terribly frightening, and after a strike, I would check to see if I was in one piece. None of our parents seemed very concerned.

I felt rather alone and unsure. I had been away from my parents for three years and suddenly I was without them once more, and also without my governess, Billy Williams, and Carey, both of whom I adored. Gradually I did settle in, though, making friends, who included a girl called Caroline

Blackwood, later the writer, and wife of Lucian Freud, who used to walk with me to lessons and lived in a perpetual daydream. The older I got, naturally, the easier the five years of boarding school became, and after two years, Carey joined me, which was a comfort.

The headmistress, Mrs Crawford, had a gung-ho attitude and, despite having a husband, lived with another teacher, Miss Graham. Having played cricket for Scotland, Mrs Crawford tried to teach us girls to play. I hated it – I was always fielding a long way out, praying the ball didn't come near and dreading the shout, 'Quick! Catch, Anne!' whereupon I would inevitably drop it. The ball was so hard it hurt if it hit you. I did, however, enjoy lacrosse. A most aggressive game, it seemed to be made up of us all rushing about bashing people's teeth out with our sticks.

Our games mistress was called Ma P., though I thought she was really half-man. She was always blowing her whistle, whether to her dog or to us we never quite knew. She was the one who would get us into the swimming pool. It was always freezing cold but from 1 June, like it or not, we would 'jolly well get in'. I quite liked swimming and got some medals, including one for life-saving, which involved Carey volunteering to be the body, wearing clothes and being dragged halfway along the pool underwater. I passed and she survived.

Just before the end of the war, when I was twelve, my sister Sarah was born. Carey and I had known our mother was pregnant but when my father's sister Aunt Silvia rang us at school to tell us the news, we burst into tears. We knew how desperately my father had wanted a son and heir, and with my mother almost dying in childbirth, there was no chance of them having any more children, marking the end of my father's particular line of Cokes.

Despite the huge disappointment for the family, we all adored Sarah, whom we doted on, treating her like a doll. It was great fun to have another sister although Carey's and my childhood was separate from Sarah's because she was so much younger than us. Once the school term had finished, we would rush home to see her, our mother proudly showing off the rabbit-skin coat she had made for Sarah. She obviously hadn't cured it properly because the coat was completely stiff, so Sarah would sit in her pram, her arms stuck straight out, rather as if she was in a straitjacket.

When we were home, my mother took charge, organising every day with something active and fun that she would do with us all, an attitude that was rare. My school friends would remark on how amazing they thought she was, saying things like 'I wish I could have a mother like yours. My mother never plays with me.' But after the holidays, Carey and I would return to school on the train, waving goodbye to our mother, knowing it would be months before we saw her again.

In those days parents only came down to the school once a year, in the summer. There would be things like a 'fathers' cricket match' and a 'mothers' tennis match'. At one of these parents' open days, after the assembly, the headmistress summoned all the girls to her study. Looking extremely cross, she said, 'Something very serious happened during assembly, and unless the girl owns up, you will all be punished. A parent, Sir Thomas Cook . . .' the founder of the package holiday, incidentally '. . . was squirted in the back of the neck with a water pistol.'

There was silence as everybody looked at each other, wondering what would happen next. But then Caroline Blackwood put her hand up rather slowly and said, 'Well, actually, it was my mother who did it.'

Her mother, Maureen, Marchioness of Dufferin and Ava, had been wearing a hat with a sculpture of a duck in a pond with water in it. Every time she put her head down, the duck dipped its beak into the pond and, as she moved her head, the water sprayed the unfortunate Sir Thomas. Her hat was not the only extraordinary thing she wore: her shoes had see-through plastic heels with fish in them. They weren't real, thank goodness, but no wonder Caroline was so eccentric.

I was at school for two years before, in 1945, when I was thirteen, the war finally came to an end. I felt the most enormous sense of relief, although the atmosphere stayed tense. The nation had lost another generation of men and, with the economy taking a huge hit, there wasn't a feeling of jubilation, only an awareness that life would continue being hard.

Most of the staff from Holkham didn't return after the war and suddenly my parents were left wondering how they would pay for the upkeep of the estate. My father was a very capable man, but the war had changed him. He had fought in the Battle of El Alamein and managed to survive malaria as well as escaping death back in London: on the morning of 18 June 1944, a migraine stopped him going to the Sunday service held at the Guards' Chapel he often attended with his friends from the Scots Guards.

During the service the chapel took a direct hit, killing 121 people, including a lot of his friends. It was the most serious V1 attack on London during the war and it added to my father's burden of loss. His brother David had fought in the Battle of Britain and survived, only to die of thirst in North Africa when his plane was shot down in the desert.

After the war, my father was even more anxious and easily stressed. At the end of his life, he was plagued by traumatic visions of his time in Egypt.

Although the fighting had ended, my father was posted to Vienna to work with the Allied forces, and in the school holidays Carey and I were put on a train, organised by the Women's Institute, with labels round our necks, and sent to Vienna. We had to pass through the Russian zone and were told not to look the Soviet soldiers in the eye when they inspected the carriages. I was utterly petrified of those men, holding my breath as I stared at the hems of their moth-eaten greatcoats and their black boots, shuddering as they loomed over us, speaking in Russian.

We stayed in the British quarter in a house that had been requisitioned by Allied forces. By a strange coincidence the house belonged to Austrian friends of my parents, so my father had managed to allow them to stay in their own house, even though they had to move down to the basement.

Rationing was strict and parts of Vienna were lawless. The Soviet soldiers patrolled the streets, hurtling down the wide avenues in horse-drawn carriages, piled high with belongings they had looted. The only good thing about being there was that my mother managed to charm some American officers into allowing her to buy dairy products and sugar – something that English people had hardly seen for years – from their PX stores in the American quarter.

Despite the unrest, Sarah's nanny would walk me and my sisters, with my father's army batman, to Hotel Sacher, which was famous for its cakes, especially its 'Sacher Torte', a chocolate cake with apricot filling. We had our fresh ingredients hidden in Sarah's pram, and when we got to the hotel, I would hand the butter and eggs to the pastry chef, who would bake pastries for us that we then collected, hiding them in the pram until we got back to the house. To taste fresh, sweet pastries, especially as a child during a time when that sort of food was extremely rare and coveted, was wonderful. For those moments all the frightening Soviet soldiers were forgotten and what remained was simply the delicious taste – a huge and precious treat.

Once we were back in England, I returned to school for a few more years, which were particularly tough because the winter of 1946–7 was so cold: temperatures in England dropped to as low as -21 degrees Celsius. With no heating in the school or at Holkham, we all got the most terrible chilblains that would swell and pop, the pain stopping us sleeping.

In 1948, when I was sixteen, I finished school. It wasn't even a consideration that I should go on to university. Neither did I go abroad because there was no money for that – so, like all of my friends, I was sent to the first of my two British finishing schools, Powderham Castle. It was owned by the Earl and Countess of Devon, who had set up a scheme whereby twenty-five girls per year were taught how to run a big house – their big house – under the guise of what was called 'domestic economy'.

We were put on fortnightly rotations, shadowing different members of the household, and soon came to know which were bearable and which were not. We loved our time with the butler because he would let us drink the dregs of the wine that we had served guests, who were often our parents' friends. They would peer up at us, amazed to see the daughters of friends pouring them more wine. The more we poured the more they drank, and the more they drank the more we got to finish off. The butler taught us how to clean silver, which was really hard work – all by thumb, rubbing and rubbing with pink vinegar paste. Our thumbs got terribly sore, but the silver looked wonderful afterwards.

I didn't mind shadowing the cook as a scullery maid – occasionally we were allowed to make drop scones or chocolate cake – or the stint with the gardener, as I enjoyed the flower arranging. But I didn't like being with the housekeeper because she was an absolute stickler for making beds with hospital corners. I went with my friend Mary Birkbeck, who didn't really like people, much preferring dogs and horses. We weren't very interested in being taught social graces. Nor were we focused on finding out how to acquire husbands, and we certainly weren't dying to learn how to run a big house. In fact, we soon made a pact: I did her sewing and work in the house, and she would do my gardening (not the flower arranging) and muck out the horse I had to look after. Any spare time we had was spent on the platform of Dawlish station, smoking. It was the only place we could buy cigarettes – keeping one eye out in case Lord and Lady Devon arrived unexpectedly on the London train.

After months of rotations, we completed the course, and

in 1949, I returned to Holkham. My grandfather died that year and I was left feeling very sad that we would no longer sit together listening to the gramophone in the long gallery. His death meant that my father succeeded to his title, becoming the 5th Earl of Leicester.

I was seventeen and Carey was fifteen, and we spent that summer cycling to the cinema in Wells-next-the-Sea twice a week with our mother. My father took me around the tenant farms, treating me like a son, wanting to teach me about the estate. I was really glad and took an interest in getting to know more about the inner workings of Holkham.

In the evenings Carey and I would go off to the local American aerodromes where the big bands would perform, in the skirts we had made from felt, which was just about the only material that wasn't rationed. The American airmen taught us how to jive and we had enormous fun, dancing all night. The only problem was that our father insisted on locking the doors at half past eleven every night, which meant we always got back once the doors had already been locked.

There was always a bit of a palaver getting inside the Park as the gate was locked – we had to break into our own house, which seemed rather odd, but my father never compromised. We came up with a plan: we'd park the car in the village, go through the sidegate, walk across the park with a torch, which would light up all the eyes of the deer, and get to the house. Once there, I would take up the coal grating and hand Carey the mackintosh we kept with us for this very exercise. Carey would put on the coat and I would lower her down the coal chute to the bottom. Then she would go off to fetch an old man called Chris, who was known as 'The Mole', because he spent his life in the cellars, stoking the boilers and cutting up the wood – the house relied on heat from fires in every room, not central heating, which was too expensive. The Mole was extremely obliging and would come up with a key and let us in.

That same summer, the Duke of Edinburgh, who had married Princess Elizabeth in 1947 and often came to Holkham to shoot with my father, rang up my mother one day with an unusual request. He explained he was inventing a new game, inspired by Battleship, and that, as part of the game, he needed photographs of Carey and me dressed up as maids. My mother thought nothing of it and my father, who was totally in love with the Royal Family, would have said yes to anything.

Carey and I were both rather nervous of the very handsome Duke, who was older than us, very confident and rather intimidating. But he came around and was absolutely charming. I dressed up as a maid with a feather duster and Carey donned an apron, taking the role of cook. We made all sorts of funny poses as our mother looked on and the Duke took photos with great enthusiasm. I'm not sure what happened to the finished game: he never mentioned it again.

At the end of the summer, I went to London for a few months to my second finishing school, where I learnt more than I had in my whole time at Downham. It was called the House of Citizenship, run by Dorothy Neville-Rolfe, who happened to be a descendant of Pocahontas. The House of Citizenship was well known and it was Dorothy Neville-Rolfe who coined the phrase, 'The real art of conversation is not only to say the right thing at the right place, but to leave unsaid the wrong thing at the most tempting moment.'

The whole point of this sort of finishing school was to perfect our conversation skills and to allow young ladies to practise the public roles we were one day expected to perform as wives to eligible men. We were taken to law courts, factories, hospitals, schools – everything to do with how the country was run. We also did history of art to boost our knowledge so we could engage in polite conversation. We would all sit in a room and Miss Neville-Rolfe would pick on one of us. 'Anne,' she would say, 'five minutes on one of Isambard Kingdom Brunel's bridges!' and I would have to stand up and speak for five minutes off the top of my head, never knowing what the topic would be beforehand. Having the confidence to be the figurehead of a community, make little speeches and present awards was a skill that girls like me needed, coming in useful a few years later when my mother's time was split between Holkham and London, and I stood in for her.

When I returned to Holkham from the House of Citizenship, I was nearing adulthood. My father's life as earl was in full swing and he was in the middle of the 'Tail Enders' – shooting parties that marked the end of the season, beautifully organised by my mother, but never attended by her as they were male only, all my father's surviving friends from the Scots Guards descending on the state rooms of Holkham.

We girls were left to entertain ourselves – not that we minded because we would take our trays into the drawing room and watch television. It was still a novelty: small, like a postage stamp, black-and-white and only one channel, the BBC, with just a single show each night.

None of us ever questioned the distinct roles of men and women. We just accepted them. I simply understood what was expected of me. I had been prepared for all the things I needed to be able to do in my life as a lady. I didn't compare my role to that of a man, or dwell on it in any detail. I followed my mother's example, and I suppose I thought I would marry someone like my father and have a life like my mother's. How wrong I was.

CHAPTER THREE
The Travelling Salesman

BY THE TIME I was on the cusp of adulthood in 1950, I had hardly seen Princess Margaret for years, our childhood friendship interrupted by the war. Gone were the days of jumping out at the nursery footmen together, and her admiration of my silver shoes. So much had happened since then. A whole life in merely a decade, it seemed. Inevitably we had grown apart: a three-year age difference in those days was big enough to put us on different trajectories.

Our fathers remained close friends, and as the King's Extra Equerry, my father assisted His Majesty in his public duties, as well as looking after foreign nobility and dignitaries when they came to England. In their spare time, they would often be together at Holkham or Sandringham, and when my father was needed in London, he would stay at the Guards Club, which he loved because he was surrounded by his friends from the Scots Guards. When my father wasn't with the King, he would be found in the estate office at Holkham or with the gamekeepers and tenant farmers on the estate.

Meanwhile, my mother had set up a pottery at Holkham, having been inspired by one of the German prisoners who had made his own kiln in the camp in the park. She was determined it would be a success and understood the need to raise money because, like all of the stately homes in England after the war, Holkham was becoming more and more expensive to run.

People were impressed: it was unconventional for a lady to set up a business, let alone of her own accord. As well as being extremely capable and practical, she was rather liberal, in the sense that her headstrong characteristics meant she not only allowed Carey and me to be a part of it, she actively encouraged us, wanting to give us something to do. My father was cynical about the whole enterprise: 'And how are you doing in the potting shed?' he would ask her, infuriatingly condescending.

Carey and I did our best to throw pots but neither of us had the knack. So, Carey started to paint and design instead, with my mother, whose artistic talent, honed at the Slade School of Art, finally found its moment. Between them they designed a marvellous hand-painted dinner and tea set in a beautiful celadon green with snowdrops, and also a very smart blue and white chevron set. We developed a whole range, from mugs to butter dishes, and made quite a few things especially for Sandringham.

I tried to paint, too, but it turned out I wasn't at all artistic. My mother, determined to sustain my interest in the business, asked me what part I would like to play. 'Can I sell?' I asked, instinctively knowing I was much better suited to that side of things. She agreed and, almost straight away, off I set in my mother's Mini Minor, with suitcases in the back containing all the samples wrapped up in newspaper, making my way around England.

If friends lived near to where I was going I would stay with them, but often there was no option but to stay in travelling-salesmen hotels. These were quite a shock. They always smelt of cabbage, and each morning I would stand outside the bathroom clutching my sponge-bag in a line of travelling salesmen. They never invited me to go first – I was made to jolly well wait my turn and they all took ages shaving.

Not only was I the only aristocrat on the road, I was the only woman on the road. All the men looked and acted the same wherever I went: wearing ill-fitting suits, they would congregate in the only heated room of the hotel, known as 'The Lounge'. Inevitably, this room was dimly lit with a single 60-watt bulb and perpetually filled with cigarette smoke. In the evenings I would sit, awkwardly reading a book. In the salesmen would come and start asking me questions, and the more I answered, the more shocked they'd become. Once they found out I was the daughter of an earl, their chins would drop to the floor. I got used to the expression of confused amazement. At nine o'clock a trolley would be wheeled in and sometimes a mini-bar would appear, and the men rather sheepishly would ask, 'Will you be Mother?'

Despite being the odd one out, or perhaps because of the freedom that my stays in those hotels entailed, I really enjoyed it – the independence, the responsibility, the satisfaction of making a deal and, most of all, the feeling of being taken seriously for the first time in my life. The experience taught me the importance of staying down to earth and adapting to any situation. My mother had learnt this trick particularly well – she was as good with tradesmen as she was with the Queen.

My mother would also take Carey and me off to trade fairs in Blackpool, where big companies, like Wedgwood, would set up their goods in prime locations in the foyer of the hotel. We couldn't afford a decent stand and had no choice but to set up in the attic or somewhere equally obscure. Determined to overcome the disadvantage, my mother would encourage Carey and me to bring the buyers up to her. She would say, 'Use your feminine wiles.' Carey was a whizzo at this, and off we'd go, down to the foyer, reappearing with the buyers while the Wedgwood sales force looked on, furious, as we disappeared up the stairs.

Holkham Pottery went from strength to strength, eventually employing a hundred people and becoming the largest light industry in North Norfolk. But in the spring of 1950, my debutante season was upon me, leaving me with little time for the pottery. I would turn eighteen in July, which meant I was old enough to be introduced to society – I had officially reached the age where I was deemed ready to marry.

The pressure was unspoken but evident – my entire life had apparently been gearing up to this moment.

My father wanted me to marry one of his best friends, Lord Stair, who was the same age as him. Lord Stair had represented Great Britain in the four-man bobsleigh team at the 1928 Winter Olympics – four years before I was even born. My father loved him because he was such a great shot, but I wasn't interested. I was a teenager; he was in his forties. 'But, Daddy,' I said, 'there is absolutely no spark between us at all. He's very nice but no.'

'Well, if you don't like him,' responded my father, 'then what about his younger brother, Colin Dalrymple?'

I reluctantly agreed to go out with Colin. My father got us tickets to Henley Royal Regatta, and we spent the day together – but, as with his brother, there was nothing between us. The date was a complete non-event. My father was disappointed and lived in hope that I would change my mind.

Declining all of my father's suggestions, I was thrust into months of socialising. For girls of my background, the point of being a debutante was to be introduced to a generation of eligible men, with the intention of marrying one as soon as possible. Girls didn't have the freedom to shack up with a single boyfriend to test them out, and if we did, we only got as far as the heavy-petting stage. I wouldn't have dared risk getting pregnant, and with no contraceptive pill then, it was safer for girls to keep their distance.

The Season, as it was known, was a deliberate solution to the problem of finding the 'right' man: a series of dances and weekend parties held throughout the year to introduce aristocratic young men and women to one another. During the spring and summer, the dances were in England, and when winter came, everybody would go off to Scotland for the Highland balls.

Each girl would have her own 'coming-out' dance or cocktail party either at home or in a London hotel. In London, two or three dances would be held on the same night so when I was there, I would either pick one, especially if it was a friend's, or I would go to a couple.

The problem with being 'out' in society in the early 1950s was that there weren't any likely husbands around as there weren't many men. My generation had either died in the war or were still away doing National Service. If you weren't married by twenty-one, you were on the shelf. My mother was nineteen when she married my father, so even though I was only eighteen, I felt very conscious that time was running out. Being in the country wasn't helping anything so I was sent to Knightsbridge, London, where I stayed with my maternal grandmother, Ga. I adored Ga. Born Ellen Russell, she came from New Zealand and, like Great-Aunt Bridget, was a commanding Christian Scientist. She and her sisters were all very good-looking and had come to England in search of eligible husbands. Soon she was married to Charlie, 8th Earl of Hardwicke. As Viscount Royston he was interested in sport and in particular in ballooning. He was an explorer in Western Australia and then worked for two years as an ordinary miner in the United States. My grandmother was responsible alongside Sir Thomas MacKenzie, the High Commissioner for New Zealand, for a new hospital to treat New Zealand soldiers wounded in the First World War. The New Zealand General Hospital opened in Walton-on-Thames in 1915 and she received a CBE for all her work in helping the many injured soldiers who arrived there. Sadly their marriage did not last long and my grandmother filed for a divorce.

Ga found me a job in a pottery shop in Sloane Street, owned by a Christian Science man she knew. I dreaded going in, spending most of my time avoiding the shop owner because he would brush past me, making unnecessary contact. When I mentioned this to my mother, she snapped, 'Anne, for heaven's sake, can't you stand up for yourself? Just slap his hand hard!'

In the evenings, I would go off to the dances. Having got used to greasy breakfasts on the road, I had become rather plump and my mother put pressure on me to slim down because the dances were all about first impressions. It was a game of luck, and wallflowers were completely invisible.

All over London different hotel ballrooms would be filled with girls in evening dresses, spinning around the wide breadth of the polished parquet dance-floors. Before the war the dresses would have been made from silks and satins, but with post-war rationing, many were made from curtains and other unlikely fabrics. At my coming-out dance I wore a dyed pale green and pleated parachute, which my mother had managed to get from the American officers who were based at the aerodrome near to Holkham.

At first glance, those dances looked like the stuff of dreams, a moving image of one of Cecil Beaton's fairytale creations. But on closer inspection the scene was full of nervous antici-pation, thick with the anxiety that sprang from the girls and boys, who had lived separate lives away at boarding schools, only to be flung, quite literally, together.

The Season was one huge rush of hormones and expectations binding the aristocracy together. While the aesthetics made it look innocent and romantic, the façade simply disguised the impending necessity to secure an heir for every titled family in England.

The whole idea was that each dance of the evening would be reserved for an array of different suitors, so that by the end of the night and, by extension, of the Season, one man would have danced you off your feet and into married life. A game of probability, the dilemma came when you didn't have a dance partner. During those dances, any spare girls would congregate in the cloakroom under the guise of powdering their noses, striking up long conversations with each other and the cloakroom attendants, half forgetting about the main event. We came to know the cloakroom attendants very well.

I was still shy and, having no brothers and an old-fashioned father, I found it hard to navigate the fine line that every girl had to tread in their relations with the opposite sex. On the one hand you had to attract men; on the other you couldn't attract them too much. Too little flirtation would mean they gave up on you for a more exciting girl, and too much would land you a bad reputation. Promiscuity didn't do girls any favours and that was why there were chaperones. A hem of golden chairs circled the dance-floor. On those chairs would sit a mother, an aunt, an older sister or anybody who was deemed responsible enough to prevent any possibility of scandal. They acted as a stern reminder, a deterrent for young men's (and sometimes young women's) frowned-upon ideas. There was even an acronym, NSIT – not safe in taxis – used of certain young men to remind the girls not to allow their dates to get too carried away.

In the spring of 1950, like all the debutantes, I was presented at court to the King and Queen. My mother had been presented wearing a flowing white evening dress, but times had changed. Tradition was modernised: my presentation at court was held in the afternoon, and we wore short dresses.

Just before my eighteenth birthday, in June 1950, I had my coming-out dance at Holkham. The first of these had been held in June 1740, for Thomas Coke, 1st Earl of Leicester in its second creation, where 130 guests sat in the orangery, lit by thousands of candles hung in lamps. More than two hundred years later, Holkham was lit again, this time by searchlights left over from the war. The whole of the long avenue was covered with criss-cross coloured lights, and the house was floodlit. Even the obelisk and the woods were lit up. It was like a Walt Disney production and the music spilt out of the ballroom into the park.

Tatler had just declared me 'debutante of the year', which I was delighted by, although the status added to the pressure I felt. The season had only begun in May, so having my dance in June meant I hardly knew anyone.

As I was about to change into the parachute dress that my mother was so thrilled by, my father said, 'Well, I hope you don't look like a parachute,' which didn't help settle my nerves. He always said slightly the wrong thing and never exactly filled me with confidence. A few years later on my wedding day, all he could muster was 'I suppose you'll do.'

The guests, who had filled many of the houses in North Norfolk, had dinner parties together before arriving to dance the night away. The dances started at ten or eleven o'clock and went on all night. Although Princess Elizabeth didn't come because she was in Malta, Princess Margaret and the King and Queen arrived at about eleven, my father meeting them at the South Gate and escorting them down the long avenue.

As I came down the marble stairs I stopped to take in the scene: there would have been nothing more romantic than to meet a young man that night, at my own dance. But the odds were low. My father had allowed me to invite only cousins and girlfriends from school because he was very careful about the men. He was in receipt of a list, given by friends, full of the 'right sort of people' for me, so my dance was full of strangers, cousins and my father's friends.

My dance was held in the state rooms, which came alive to the sound of Tommy Kinsman, the most popular band for these parties, known as the 'Debs' Delight'. Tommy Kinsman had played at several of the dances I had been to and would happily play requests, so my school friends and I had made lists of all our favourite songs ready to give him. Queen Elizabeth was a big fan of the band and was equally thrilled they were there, smiling and sparkling throughout the night.

A buffet supper was served between dinner and breakfast, with eggs, venison and vegetables from the estate, and champagne from the cellars. In the days beforehand, I had spent a lot of time visiting the kitchen, watching as the delicious food was being prepared. With rationing still in place, the supper felt luxurious and, all in all, the evening was an amazing spectacle of frivolity and fun.

Magical as it all looked, I found it quite terrifying and I ended up spending a lot of time lingering at the edge of the ballroom and going off into the park, handing out champagne to the people in charge of the lights. I felt shy either not knowing or trying to avoid most of the men there. Instead I watched Princess Margaret dance with Mark Bonham Carter – Helena Bonham Carter's uncle – Billy Wallace, a family friend, whom she later considered marrying, and my cousin David Ogilvy, having a lovely time as she swirled around in her light blue dress.

One thing the evening achieved that made me happy was to reunite me with Princess Margaret. As the sun rose, I stood next to her, chatting, on the front portico at Holkham, watching the geese fly overhead in the dawn. I realised then that, even though we were now both grown-up, when you have been childhood friends with somebody, you can pick up where you left off. A lot had happened to her. A lot had happened to me. And here we were now, both on the threshold of our adult lives.

While the evening unravelled into the most beautiful night I will ever remember, something terrible happened that I didn't find out about for years. Once people started to rise, having gone to sleep at dawn, David Ogilvy passed the fountain, which had been playing all night, and noticed a coat in the water. He couldn't reach it, so he went back to the house and got some help. To their horror they discovered it was a person, a young gardener, who had somehow drowned, while hundreds of people were dancing and laughing, drinking champagne, only feet away from him. The tragedy was kept from me. My father was absolutely devastated, as were the other gardeners, but none of them wanted to upset me, so that summer and for years afterwards, I had no idea and continued to remember my beautiful dance fondly. Now this much darker memory is associated with it.

Although I met no dashing young men at my own dance, the Season led to a few boyfriends. First, there was Nigel Leigh-Pemberton, who was extremely nice – probably a bit too nice. He was a singer and eventually went abroad and sang under the name Nigel Douglas. He was very kind but keener on me than I was on him. And whatever he planned, something always went wrong.

Once he invited me to the opera. When I said yes, he made a point of warning me that I had to be ready at a set time. Unfortunately I was late. Dashing back to Ga's house to get ready, as I rounded the corner I saw, to my horror, a huge hansom cab with a pawing horse. I thought, Oh, goodness, this is Nigel's treat!

Nigel, of course, was very upset because we were too late to travel to Covent Garden in it. We went to the opera in a taxi and the hansom cab collected us afterwards instead. Sitting in it was frightfully embarrassing because everybody stared as we clip-clopped down St James's Street – and suddenly there was the most awful noise, drawing even more attention to us. One of the wheels had got entangled with a taxi bumper and we were completely stuck. All the drivers started honking their car horns as the traffic came to a grinding halt. I was mortified and felt so sad for Nigel because it was meant to be such a lovely surprise.

Another time, he asked me to help him because he was singing in a nightclub. In the middle of the floor there was a golden cage. 'You're to sit in the cage, on the perch, and swing while I sing "A Bird In A Gilded Cage",' Nigel told me, 'and it will be wonderful.' I sat there and it wasn't at all wonderful and very uncomfortable.

Nigel and I drifted apart.

Then there was Roger Manners, a more successful match. Handsome and intelligent, he was a little too highly strung for me. Ironic, considering my future husband would turn out to be the most highly strung individual anybody could ever possibly hope to meet.

And then there was Johnnie Althorp. He had recently returned from Australia, having been ADC to the governor of South Australia. The moment he arrived at Holkham, at my father's invitation, I fell madly in love with him. I thought he was wonderful: funny, handsome and charming. We went out together in London, and one night he took me into the garden and asked me to marry him. A wave of euphoria swept over me and for days after I really did feel as though I was walking on air. We told both sets of parents but kept the news a secret from everybody else.

Everything went by in a daze. If I was dancing with some other (probably perfectly nice) young man, I was wholly uninterested. I had eyes only for Johnnie. By this time, I had left Ga's house in London and become a paying-guest to Lady Fermoy, a friend of Queen Elizabeth, whose family also lived in Norfolk and had a house on the Sandringham estate.

Lady Fermoy was extremely sociable. 'If you have a young man taking you out,' she would say, 'do bring him to the drawing room to have a drink first.'

So I did. And that was my mistake. When I introduced her to Johnnie, her eyes lit up, and the next time I brought him round, not only was she there but so was her daughter, whom she had deliberately called back from school. Her daughter, Frances, was only fifteen at the time, but after she met Johnnie, she sent him a letter with a pair of shooting stockings she had knitted.

Shortly after that he and I were due to meet at Ascot. He was Equerry to the King and I had been invited to stay at Windsor Castle to go to Ascot with the Royal Family. I was, as ever, looking forward to seeing Johnnie and expected the weekend would be marvellous fun.

I had borrowed my mother's lady's maid, and when we arrived at Windsor Castle we climbed up and up to a room in the tower. Out of the window the view was of the Long Walk, with the copper horse in the distance. As we unpacked, we laid out my four dresses for each day at the races. They were beautiful. I should have been excited, but as I hadn't heard from Johnnie, and there was no message from him, I couldn't settle. All through that first night, I lay awake, listening to the soldiers stomping around under my window, going in and out of the pillboxes, presenting arms.

The next morning, as I had breakfast in bed – the tradition for all of the ladies in royal households – I wondered if Johnnie had arrived and not been able to get a message to me. During the tour of the gardens before lunchtime I was thinking up reasons as to why he hadn't made contact. Even at lunch with Princess Margaret and the other guests, Johnnie was still nowhere to be seen.

After lunch we drove to the top of the racecourse and got into carriages. Riding in the carriages was wonderful. It was like being in a huge pram, fastened in with a cover. The crowds cheered as they set eyes on the Royal Family and the buzz of the excited crowd had a great impact on the rest of us. We arrived at the Royal Box and it was then I was told that Johnnie would not be joining us because apparently he was ill. I felt a pang of heartache and my mood flattened. Something was wrong.

I spent the day managing to pretend to be as happy as everybody else until we all went back to Windsor in cars for a rest, before going down for drinks and dinner. Queen Elizabeth was such a sparkly person and she really suited the crinoline evening dresses she always wore, and welcomed us in her usual charming way. If only I'd been able to enjoy it. I talked to the Duke and Duchess of Northumberland, Billy Wallace and my Uncle Joe, all of whom were there that evening. When someone happened to mention that they had recently seen Johnnie, who was apparently quite well, I realised that he must be avoiding me. I felt awful. I had to stop myself looking really glum. I did a lot of hard swallowing in a bid not to cry. It was difficult trying to be polite and jolly and enjoy it. I couldn't. I couldn't understand what I had done wrong and Johnnie never told me why he had broken off our engagement.

Later, however, I found out that his father, Jack, Earl Spencer, had told him not to marry me because I had Trefusis blood. Trefusis blood was labelled 'mad blood' or 'bad blood' because the Bowes-Lyon girls (Princesses Elizabeth and Margaret's cousins), Nerissa and Katherine, had been put in a state asylum and were hardly visited by anyone in the Royal Family to whom they were related through Queen Elizabeth. Although the family connection was extremely convoluted, my maternal grandmother was Marion Trefusis and, however diluted, I suppose no earl or future earl would want to risk their earldom by contaminating it with 'mad blood'.

Not only did Johnnie then marry Frances, but their youngest daughter was Lady Diana Spencer, who later became Diana, Princess of Wales.

Johnnie and Frances would famously divorce and, rather unusually, Lady Fermoy testified against her daughter in favour of Johnnie having custody of Diana. Johnnie went on to marry my friend Raine, Countess of Dartmouth, who before their engagement often rang me up asking for advice on how she could get him to commit. I wasn't sure why she thought I was a good person to ask, considering I had never succeeded myself.

Whether Johnnie and I would have been happy together I don't know, and will never know, but the whole thing really did affect me. I spent the rest of the summer in a very gloomy mood. I tried to distract myself with the pottery, and my father involved me in the running of the estate, taking me around the tenant farms, but Johnnie and our broken engagement lingered in the back of my mind.

As summer turned to autumn, my father's friends descended once more on Holkham for the shooting season. Christmas came and went, and all through January my father and the King shot hare on both estates and were busy planning the last weekends of the season, the Tail Enders, when on 6 February 1952, the King died quite suddenly in his sleep at Sandringham. He had had an operation the year before, to remove part of a lung, which was reported at the time to have been a success, so his death was a shock. My father hadn't realised how ill the King had been and was left devastated. We all were. I was so used to seeing him going off shooting with my father, and he was so young, at fifty-six, which made his death even sadder.

My mother wrote a letter of condolence as soon as she heard the news. Princess Margaret replied, admitting how desperately sad they all were but they took comfort in knowing he had spent the last days of his life doing what he loved best. She ended the letter by describing the February dawn on the day he died, and how she believed the King would have liked it.

Britain descended into mourning: people lined the railway tracks, standing silent and solemn as they watched the funeral train carrying the King's coffin make its way from Sandringham to London. The mood in Norfolk stayed sombre. A distinct silence gathered eerily inside the walls of Holkham. The King had been such a part of Holkham and of Norfolk: there was a feeling that the community had lost one of its own. Our gamekeepers were especially sorrowful.

King George VI lay in state at Westminster Hall. Three hundred thousand people queued to pay their respects to the Sovereign who had picked up the mantle after the abdication of his brother and subsequently led the country through a world war.

My mother, Carey and I entered the hall to pay our own respects through a side door so we could see my father, who was one of the Scots Guards standing guard on the coffin. I vividly remember that moment: he stood there, head down in respect, holding his bearskin and sword.

On 15 February my parents went to the funeral. I watched it on television and was particularly moved by the sound of Big Ben, which tolled fifty-six times through the grey misty morning, once for each year of the King's life.

The Coronation of Queen Elizabeth II was deliberately delayed. Rationing was still in place and Winston Churchill feared that holding such an expensive spectacle in the midst of a low, post-war economy would threaten the popularity of the monarchy.

Life at Holkham slowly went back to normal but I carried on feeling sorry for myself. Several months went past and my mother got so fed up with me she decided to send me off to America to sell some of the pottery, hoping a change of scene would cheer me up. The idea alone made me feel happier and I was very excited, having been abroad only once – to the South of France, which I'd loved. I was longing to go on more adventures.

Off I went over the Atlantic, in November 1952, on the *Queen Mary* with my suitcase of samples. I was travelling steerage because my family didn't have a lot of money, especially after the war. My parents were not extravagant people and both had a practical approach to travel, so I shared the cabin with four other women. Once we had got onto the high seas, the waves hurled themselves against the ship, so all the others were terribly sick. I had a stronger stomach and, in the end, I went and slept outside in the corridor, which happened to have a sofa.

Luckily my godfather, John Marriott, a friend of my father from the Scots Guards, was travelling in first class and invited me to dine with him each evening. He had married someone extremely rich called Momo Kahn, and her Louis Vuitton luggage was stacked all along the corridor, which became her vast wardrobe. Each evening I would leave the poor vomiting girls and spend the evening with John and Momo, dining at the Veranda Grill, which served copious amounts of caviar – in huge silver buckets. And then back I would go, to third class, bunking in the corridor. It was a portent for my whole life – one minute involved in something very glamorous, the next doing something so far removed that I wondered whether I'd just dreamt about the glamorous moments.

Arriving in New York, I was met by Momo's sister, Mrs Ryan, who was friends with my mother and whose daughter Ginny ended up marrying David Airlie, my favourite Ogilvy cousin. Mrs Ryan was the only person I knew in the whole of the United States, and she lived in a beautiful double penthouse in New York's Upper East Side, opposite the River Club, in the same block as Greta Garbo, overlooking the Hudson River.

When I told Mrs Ryan I was taking my samples to Saks, the famous department store, she politely refrained from saying anything. She wasn't surprised when I came back looking defeated: Saks didn't let anyone in without an appointment. Holkham and the pottery might have gained a reputation in England, but suddenly I was a little fish in a big pond and was being told by a stern receptionist that there were no appointments for six months. Mrs Ryan, who was a frequent shopper at Saks, made a quick phone call and straight away I had an appointment for the next day. To my delight, they bought some of the pottery and off I went to more places, helped by more phone calls from Mrs Ryan. The most popular items turned out to be the Toby jugs of the Queen and the Duke of Edinburgh and the piggy banks. There's no accounting for taste.

Mrs Ryan introduced me to her whole circle and soon I was under the wing of her friend Mrs Carlson. Before long I was being whirled up by American society and taken on the Super Chief train where at Albuquerque, Indians got on to sell their turquoise jewellery, and to Los Angeles, where I was met by C. J. Latta, the head of Warner Brothers in London, another Christian Scientist, who introduced me to film stars in Hollywood, including Bob Hope, David Niven, Bette Davis and Danny Kaye. I went on to New Orleans, to Mardi Gras where I danced with the city fathers, enjoying myself. There was a real sense of discovery and adventure. I ended up going all over the States on cheap and efficient Greyhound buses – from Florida to Kentucky and back to New York. The experience made me want to travel more and opened up my naïve outlook on life.

One morning in February 1953, after another late night of dancing, I was sitting at the breakfast table, rather bleary-eyed, with Mrs Ryan and some other guests when the maid came in and handed me a telegram. My first thought was that something bad had happened at home but to my astonishment the telegram read: ANNE YOU MUST COME HOME

STOP YOU'VE BEEN ASKED TO BE A MAID OF HONOUR AT THE QUEEN'S CORONATION STOP.

Everybody was so excited, and the telegram was handed around the table and read eagerly by all. I was delighted, although it soon became clear I would have to deal with the daunting consequence of being the centre of attention. The news travelled fast – Mrs Ryan was thrilled and showed me off. The American press soon got wind of it, triggering another wave of excitement. Suddenly I found everybody was treating *me* like royalty, asking me to show them how to curtsy and wave like the Queen. At one of the last few balls I went to, a makeshift throne was presented to me. It was very embarrassing, as were the articles in the local newspapers, accompanied by photographs of me looking like a deer in headlights – the *Washington Post* wrote an article with the headline 'Girl With Pedigree Can Be Pretty Too.'

It was another irony: one minute I was crammed on to a Greyhound bus, the next I was being summoned home for months of rehearsals in preparation for taking part in Britain's most significant ceremony for a generation.

Although I was sad my trip was being cut short, I was absolutely thrilled to be chosen. So many people in my family had been Equerries and Ladies in Waiting throughout the centuries, and now I had been given a role. I felt immeasurably lucky: there I was being selected, all because I just happened to be just the right height and size, as well as being an unmarried daughter of an earl, a duke or a marquess – the criteria for being chosen. It's funny how in the end I found the silver lining in not marrying Johnnie.

Poor Carey was desperately envious, as were many families

we knew, especially considering my mother and I would both be part of the procession: my mother had been asked by the Queen to become a Lady of the Bedchamber – a high-ranking Lady in Waiting.

One consequence of the news was that suddenly I was selling a huge amount of pottery, especially the Toby jugs. Everyone went mad for them. When my mother met me off the *Queen Mary* at Southampton, I was greeted by a throng of journalists and photographers and there I was, waving my order book, far more excited about my pottery sales than my Maid of Honour status. Stepping off the ship into a frenzy of interviews, I was thrust into the limelight.

CHAPTER FOUR

The Coronation

IN MAY MY mother and I moved to London, staying with Ga, so we could attend the twelve rehearsals during the second half of May, held in Westminster Abbey. While Carey was rather glum, my father was extremely proud and waved us off with great enthusiasm.

I was to be one of six Maids of Honour and I knew a few of the others very well: Rosie Spencer-Churchill was engaged to my mother's first cousin; Mary Baillie-Hamilton's parents, the Earl and Countess of Haddington, were great friends of my parents, and Jane Vane-Tempest-Stewart, I knew best of all: not only was my Aunt Silvia married to her uncle, but Jane's sister, Annabel, was Carey's best friend. They were such good friends that when Jane and Annabel's mother had become ill, my mother organised a joint coming-out dance for Carey and Annabel at Londonderry House in London. Not that Carey and Annabel were there for much of it themselves: when the Duke of Gloucester asked to be introduced to them at the dance, my mother realised to her horror that my wayward sister and her friend had sneaked off to a nightclub. I wouldn't have *dared* even to contemplate doing that, but Carey was always rather naughty.

I had never met the remaining two Maids of Honour, Jane Heathcote-Drummond-Willoughby and Moyra Hamilton, and it took some time to get to know them because the rehearsals, conducted by the Duke of Norfolk – to which we came dressed in black suits, hats and gloves like our mothers – were formal affairs so there wasn't time for chatting.

As hereditary Earl Marshal, the Duke of Norfolk had already been in charge of organising the Coronation of King George VI, and while he was experienced, he left nothing to chance. He had ninety-four diagrams, each depicting different parts of the ceremony in which every minute was worked out, and every movement within each minute prescribed. He even had the foresight to work out that his bald head would need to be powdered a few times on the day itself, due to the aerial shots the television cameras would take. There were so many facets to arrange and get right that a great many people were involved in these rehearsals, including Richard Dimbleby, the BBC commentator who would be broadcasting live to the nation. He was so committed, in the direct run-up, that he moved out of his house and into his boat that he docked at Westminster Pier so he was as near to the Abbey as possible.

Our role as Maids of Honour was to carry the Queen's twenty-one-foot purple velvet, ermine-trimmed train in the procession, during which the six of us would walk directly behind the Queen. The Mistress of the Robes, the Dowager Duchess of Devonshire, would come behind us, followed by the Groom of the Robes, then the two Ladies of the Bedchamber – my mother and the Countess of Euston, and behind them, the four Women in Waiting. My mother's role was largely ceremonial but the Dowager Duchess of Devonshire had an active role because, as Mistress of the Robes, it was her job to assist the 5th Marquess of Cholmondeley, the Lord Great Chamberlain, who helped with the Queen's costume changes.

The Marquess of Cholmondeley was the most handsome man and he seemed very proud of his looks – he always sat bolt upright with his head slightly to one side. The trouble was, he was simply terrible at doing up hooks and eyes, probably never having to dress himself, let alone anybody else. As the Duke of Norfolk repeatedly showed him what to do, the attempts only resulted in yet more fiddling, and the Duke becoming ever more exasperated. In the end, the Duke of Norfolk ordered the hooks and eyes to be changed to poppers.

After the Coronation, I asked the Queen whether he had done up the back of the dress all right, and she said it was tiresome because every time he did up a popper he pushed her rather violently.

It was as though my travelling-salesman days had never happened: instead of unwrapping pottery on the floor of shops all across America, I was being instructed on how to walk, how to stand, how to hold the train and how to move with the Queen and lay it out behind her throughout the ceremony. The Queen took part in dozens of rehearsals but, needing to practise all sorts of different aspects of the day, she took part in only one of the final rehearsals with us. In her absence, we walked behind the Duchess of Norfolk. Prince Charles later told me how he had gone into her study and seen her at her desk, with the crown on her head. When he asked what she was doing, she explained that the crown was very heavy, and she wanted to get used to wearing it.

The one rehearsal we attended with her took place in Buckingham Palace. The Queen, who took everything in her stride, asked a great many pertinent questions of the Duke of Norfolk, always keen for the answers. She wandered up and down the White Drawing Room with all of us following behind, wearing a curtain draped over her as a substitute train.

By now, we had had a rehearsal each day for ten days, always wearing our black suits, so it was terribly exciting when my dress arrived. All six Maids of Honour had the same design by Norman Hartnell, made from ivory silk with gold embroidery. The dresses weren't lined, which meant the underside of the embroidery was uncomfortably scratchy. They had also been made extremely tight. But, despite this, they looked sublime and we were all delighted. The headdresses were also beautiful: gold and pearl, similar to those made for the Queen's bridesmaids at her wedding five years before.

Although I had tried on the dress many times, the first time I wore it for any length of time was for the final rehearsal in Westminster Abbey. The Duke of Norfolk told us all to wear them but to cover them up so the design could stay a secret. Unfortunately, at the end of the rehearsal, I walked down the steps and the breeze blew my shawl, revealing my dress. I didn't realise at the time that photographers were lurking on the steps until the next day when a photograph of me was splashed over the front pages of the newspapers, with headlines such as, 'She Didn't Know It Was A Secret'. I was horrified, instantly convinced the Duke of Norfolk would ring me up and sack me. To my relief, there was no such telephone call and the Duke never mentioned it.

A few days before the Coronation, my sisters came up to London to stay with Ga, who did her best not to let them feel left out. The flat wasn't big enough for us all and, being preoccupied with the rehearsals, my mother left it too late to book a hotel room – every one in London was booked. Instead, we stayed with my Great-great-uncle Jack, in his flat conveniently located off Berkeley Square, not far from Buckingham Palace. Unfortunately, it only had one bedroom, which my mother took. I had to sleep on a mattress on the floor and poor Uncle Jack had to move out altogether. He was used to taking the rough with the smooth: as Lord-in-Waiting to Queen Mary, he had followed her around her country residences, reluctantly hacking down trees and ivy, as she instructed him with great enthusiasm.

While I was sleeping on the floor, at the eleventh hour Moyra Hamilton's mother was frantically painting brown gardening sandals gold for her daughter, having been unable to find gold sandals that fitted Moyra's large feet.

The day before the Coronation, a page from Buckingham Palace delivered a diamond brooch in the shape of the letters ER, designed in the Queen's own handwriting, with a little note from the Queen inviting me to wear it on the day. I felt another rush of excitement, fully aware of how lucky I was to be a part of history.

That night I hardly slept – I was far too excited, nervous, and my sleeping arrangements were no help. I watched the light of dawn peep into the flat and light up my dress, which was hanging in the corner of the room. After hours of lying alone, imagining what the next day would be like, going through all the instructions in my head, worrying about making a mistake, the morning was upon me and a surge of activity began.

By 5 a.m., the small flat was crammed with people, putting ridiculous amounts of make-up on me and my mother to make sure we looked normal under the bright television lights. In daylight, we both looked extraordinary with blusher as red as our lipstick and great dark eyebrows, rather like George Robey, whom we all knew for playing pantomime dames. When the hairdresser arrived, she insisted on curling my hair, which took ages, and when I looked in the mirror I was appalled, thinking, Oh, my heavens, I look like a sheep!

Outside the day was grey. Rain had been falling all night and the temperature was brisk – the weather report saying that, at 12 degrees, it would be the coldest June day in a century. The wireless broadcast quickly turned attention back to the preparations, the commentator John Snagge stirring up excitement by telling us that thousands of people had spent the night on the streets and were already claiming their spots on the procession route.

As my mother and I changed into our dresses, John Snagge reminded all the listeners to stay tuned while also declaring the time that the live BBC television broadcast would start.

The thought of so many millions of people watching was simply terrifying. I was too nervous to eat anything. Meanwhile my mother left for Buckingham Palace to have breakfast there before joining the Countess of Euston in one of the carriages processing to the Abbey.

A few minutes after she had left, a car arrived to take me to Westminster Abbey. The journey was one of the most surreal fifteen minutes of my life. London was an extraordinary sight, the streets full of tremendously cheerful people sitting or standing in the pouring rain. After the doom and gloom of the post-war years, it was an especially incredible sight to behold. The news of Edmund Hillary reaching the summit of Mount Everest earlier that morning made the day all the more remarkable and added to the excitement. 'Hillary's got to the top of Everest!' proclaimed the waiting crowds. When the car pulled up to the Abbey, the crowd cheered and, nervously, I got out and was quickly ushered through the door of the specially built annexe.

The Abbey was relatively empty when I arrived, the blue carpets being brushed, the Duke of Norfolk engrossed in the final preparations, while the thousands of seats all the way up to the ceiling lay empty of occupants for another hour or so.

Richard Dimbleby, the BBC commentator, had been there since dawn, surveying the Abbey from his seat in the triforium, as had the choir boys, who were fidgeting in theirs. I could feel their nervous energy, aware of how close yet how distant the reality of the day ahead seemed.

Rosie Spencer-Churchill and Jane Vane-Tempest-Stewart, who had been deemed the grandest pair of Maids of Honour, had been chosen to go to Buckingham Palace to be part of the Queen's procession. The rather less grand four of us stood together watching as the Abbey filled. Although we were offered seats there were so many very old men all dressed up – some of them more or less in full armour – we felt we had to give our chairs to them.

There were five processions to the Abbey, converging into one after the ceremony, consisting of Commonwealth Prime Ministers, members of the Royal Family, and the Regalia peers, all wearing their uniforms and colourful robes. The Abbey had been beautifully lit, the television lights creating a feeling of sunlight despite the dreary weather outside, so the stained-glass windows shone, and the light danced on all the embroidery and jewellery.

People spoke in hushed tones, and we watched as more and more arrived, the Abbey filling – thousands of people filing through the doors. It was like a scene from a medieval tapestry. There were so many different things going on: people were adjusting their robes or fussing with other people's; coronets were being used as an alternative to a handbag, with everything from sandwiches to small sewing kits appearing and disappearing into them; they were not to be put on until the moment when the Queen was crowned.

Cecil Beaton sat up in the rafters, drawing sketches and taking photographs, while the choir sang the Litany just before 10 a.m. With an hour to go, the atmosphere mounted, the buzz of anticipation tangible.

Then the Dean of Westminster, with his sepulchral face, the canons and other clergy processed from the altar to the Great West Door, delivering the Regalia to the annexe. Each piece was placed on a special table, one after another: the

Chalice, the Sceptre, the Orb, King Edward's Crown, all under the care of the Lord Great Chamberlain with his handsome profile, and his nine-year-old page, Viscount Ullswater, who stared unblinking as the Regalia spread across the table.

By now the State Procession was fully under way. The Queen, in the Gold State Coach, pulled by eight greys, was scheduled to arrive at exactly 11 a.m. having left Buckingham Palace with the Duke of Edinburgh at precisely 10.26 a.m., surrounded by a thousand guardsmen, including the mounted Household Cavalry troops, among them Johnnie Althorp, who was on horseback as Equerry to the Queen.

My mother arrived, as did the Mistress of the Robes, 'Moucher', Dowager Duchess of Devonshire. Her daughter-in-law, 'Debo', Duchess of Devonshire, was wearing an eighteenth-century scarlet velvet robe over an ivory silk dress with a low scoop neckline, which my mother had told me the Duchess had found in a trunk at Chatsworth and had belonged to Georgiana Cavendish, the 5th Duchess, who had been known in her time as the 'Empress of Fashion'. Despite it being two hundred years out of date, it didn't look at all out of place in a setting and on an occasion that felt timeless.

Outside, the crowds in the specially built stands cheered louder and louder every time guests arrived; the higher their profile, the more enthralled the crowds became. When Winston Churchill, dressed as a Knight of the Garter, arrived at the Abbey, the crowd erupted, and a great roar went up when the Queen Mother and Princess Margaret got out of the Irish State Coach. The Queen Mother glided in with Princess Margaret, who wore an embroidered light gold dress, and they both looked as if they'd come straight out of a fairytale. A guard of honour from the Grenadier Guards took up their position in the Vestibule and the Duke of Gloucester strode past with his family, looking as serious as he was rotund.

When Rosie and Jane arrived, all six of us waited together just outside the annexe steps, ready to receive the Queen. We had been given vials of smelling salts, which we each stored in our long white gloves. Unfortunately, when the Archbishop of Canterbury came up to us all, Rosie had shaken his hand rather too hard and somehow broken her vial. Out came this appalling smell.

'Good heavens!' the Archbishop exclaimed. 'What on earth have you done?' at which we were all overcome by a fit of giggles. He didn't think it at all funny, wiped his hands with a hanky and disappeared off.

When the crowd started cheering non-stop, a wall of sound coming from the direction of Victoria Embankment, we realised the Queen was approaching. Although I had known the Royal Family from an early age, seeing the Queen's golden coach appearing from around the corner, I felt as if I was dreaming. The crowd really accentuated this feeling and the cheers reached a crescendo as the coach stopped. In that moment it felt as though the whole nation was bursting with excitement.

The pages came forward to open the coach's doors while the Duke of Edinburgh got out of the other side, rushing around all of us, checking that everything was in order and generally being very fussy. I think he wanted it to be the most perfect day for the Queen and thought he was helping, but we knew exactly what to do and his frantic behaviour only added to the tension.

The Queen looked absolutely ravishing. She had the most wonderful complexion and her eyes were glistening, and finally we, and the nation, set eyes on her Coronation dress under her Parliamentary train of crimson velvet, which, by now, we were very familiar with. The dress was exquisite: designed by Norman Hartnell, of ivory silk, covered with embroidery of the rose, the thistle, and all the different emblems of the British Isles and Commonwealth.

I have often been asked whether the Queen seemed nervous. She didn't: she was as calm as she always is. She knew exactly what to do. She had seen her father being crowned, and although she had been quite young, I am sure she would have remembered everything.

Once the Queen had got out of the carriage, we gathered up her crimson train, using the silk handles as the velvet rippled over our hands. The Duke of Norfolk stood on the steps of the Abbey in his ducal robes, just as he had done in May 1937 at the late King's Coronation. He had greeted the young Princess Elizabeth that day, and now, sixteen years later, he was receiving her as Queen Elizabeth II. After greeting the Queen, the Duke stepped back and the six of us waited behind her while the Duke of Edinburgh went inside and put on the robes of a Royal Duke, and the peers carrying the Regalia got ready. The Duke of Norfolk had worked out it would take the Queen fifty-five seconds to walk from her spot, marked by a single red thread stitched into the blue carpet, to the Gothic Arch, at which point the trumpet fanfares would start.

It was fifteen minutes from when the Queen arrived to when she walked into the Abbey, signalling the beginning of the ceremony. As I stood behind her, I felt so unbelievably lucky. There I was, just happening to be the right person, in the right place, at the right time, quite literally attached to the Queen. Before she set off, a hush fell around the Queen, who stood in front of us, ten yards away from the Great West Door. Then she turned to us and said, 'Ready, girls?'

We nodded and off we went after her, disappearing into the Abbey. This was a very nervous moment because as the Queen set off we realised that she walked slightly slower than the Duchess of Norfolk, whom we had practised with for so many weeks. All of a sudden we were having to adjust our pace, but as we were all so in tune with each other, having walked together through so many rehearsals, we adjusted as one.

Fifty-five seconds later, when the Queen reached the Gothic Arch, the State trumpeters sounded, and the congregation stood up in unison. As we followed the Queen up the aisle, the choir sang Hubert Parry's almost seven-minute-long anthem, 'I Was Glad', the choir boys now focused and resonant, their voices ringing out the glory of the occasion.

Over the years, I have relived this historic day by watching the film footage and I often find myself noticing new things. Inevitably, I find myself holding my breath, hoping that I, or someone else, won't make a mistake. Even though I know there won't be any catastrophic errors, there is still a sense of relief when it comes to an end and I can breathe again, much as I did on the day itself.

There was actually one moment during the ceremony that could have led to disaster. The service had started perfectly,

with the Archbishop presenting the Queen to the congregation in the Recognition – during which the Queen curtsied
to all four sides of the Abbey, a beautiful gesture and a rare
one (though she does bow twice to the peers at the State
Opening of Parliament). From there, the Queen took the oath,
and was presented with the Holy Bible before the most
solemn part of the service began: the anointing. The anointing
is considered the most vital part of any coronation, because,
without this sacred moment, the new King or Queen cannot
be crowned. So significant and so holy is it that, despite the
traditional canopy set up around her, held by four Knights
of the Garter, the cameras were diverted so she was hidden
from view, with only a handful of people, including me, able
to witness it.

Afterwards, the television cameras were allowed back and
the canopy removed. As the choir sang 'Zadok The Priest',
the Queen was de-robed by the Lord Great Chamberlain, with
help from the Mistress of the Robes, and a simple white
dress put on over the Coronation dress. As I and the other
Maids of Honour stood back in two rows near one of the
Abbey pillars, watching the Queen as she walked towards
the altar and the throne, I began to feel dizzy.

Fortunately, I was in the second row, so I was slightly
hidden. Next to me stood the Gentleman Usher of the Black
Rod, who was dressed from head to foot in black velvet and
held a rod that looked like a billiard cue. He and the other
Maids of Honour were looking intently at the Queen as I
tried very hard to ignore the dizzy feeling that was rapidly
clouding my vision.

Just as the sacred consecration was about to start, I began

to sway. Conscious that I risked ruining the ceremony, I broke my vial of smelling salts. To my despair it didn't seem to have much effect. Neither did wiggling my toes, which I was doing frantically. I just had one thought, I must not faint, I must not faint, because I knew there were millions – billions – of people watching. I held on to the thought, I can't faint in front of the entire British Empire.

As I was swaying, Jane Vane-Tempest-Stewart noticed and so, luckily, did Black Rod, who calmly and discreetly put a firm arm around me, encouraging me to use the pillar next to us to steady myself. Goodness knows what was going through the poor man's head. Black Rod was Lieutenant-General Sir Brian Horrocks, a war hero several times over, described by Eisenhower as the most 'outstanding British general under Montgomery', and there he was, hoping against hell he could stop me fainting and causing a scene. Whatever battles he had helped win in the desert in the Second World War, he certainly saved my day. He held me there until I recovered, much to our mutual relief.

Adrenalin must have kicked in because the rest of the ceremony wasn't marred by my wondering whether I would collapse. Time ran away with itself as the Queen was robed in a cloth of gold, then presented with spurs that, as a female Sovereign, she would never wear. We stood in the same place while the different blessings and presentations took place, ending with the Lord Great Chamberlain fastening the poppers on the Queen's robes, then standing bolt upright, showing off his handsome profile once more.

After the Queen had received the Regalia, it was time for the Archbishop to crown her. In one movement, the 8,006 people in the congregation rose to their feet. This was the moment the world had been waiting for. I am certain that every hair stood on end, every person held their breath, as the Archbishop held King Edward's Crown high above the Queen's head, his arms outstretched. As soon as the Archbishop placed the crown on the new Queen's head, the distinct silence that had fallen broke, replaced by 'God Save the Queen!' ringing out in a wave of jubilant cries. There was a flurry of movement as all the peers and peeresses put on their coronets in a sweeping gesture.

Fanfares of trumpets added to the continuous cheers. Outside, the crowds shouted too, and the salutes could be heard, fired by artillery, the low boom of gunfire in the distance.

The rest of the service was a blur. After the enthroning and the homage, a full communion service commenced, and I remember singing 'All People That On Earth Do Dwell' with particular enthusiasm before the recess when we made our way to St Edward's Chapel. Inside the Chapel, the Queen took off St Edward's Crown, which weighed over four and a half pounds. That must have been a relief. There, she changed from the Robe Royal into her train of purple velvet, and the lighter Imperial State Crown – the one she wears at the State Opening of Parliament.

During this recess, the Archbishop of Canterbury got out a small flask of brandy and offered it around. The Queen, along with the other Maids of Honour, declined but I took a sip. Having had no breakfast and still feeling rather peculiar, I hoped it might give me a boost.

With the relief that the ceremony was almost over, a wave

of happiness spread over me. As we followed the Queen down the aisle to Elgar's 'Pomp and Circumstance', the music captured the joyous element of the day perfectly. What was even more exciting than walking down the aisle was the moment we stepped outside the Abbey where we were greeted by the outside world. The sound reached fever pitch, so loud it felt as if the whole nation was entering into one massive long cheer.

Despite the hard work involved in navigating the steps without putting a foot wrong, I can vividly remember how amazing it felt to be part of that moment. The Queen managed with ease, and luckily none of us fell. Off we went into the annexe, where the first servings of Coronation Chicken were ready for the guests, a dish invented specially for the day. I should have been starving by then, but I was still preoccupied with making sure I was in the right place to hold the Queen's train as she moved around.

By now, the rain was pouring down on London, but the crowds stayed put, waiting for the Queen to reappear. They didn't have to wait long, and as we helped her back into the State Coach, the crowds, reunited with their Queen, roared in approval. As the coach rolled away, I watched the ecstatic lines of people waving in the rain.

While the Queen processed through half of London, accompanied in another carriage by Rosie Spencer-Churchill and Jane Vane-Tempest-Stewart, the other three Maids of Honour and I were driven to Buckingham Palace to wait for the Queen's eventual return after the long procession.

When we got to Buckingham Palace, we stood just inside, waiting to receive the Queen, watching as everybody arrived and filed past us. Queen Salote of Tonga, who was wearing a skirt made from *tapa*, red feathers in her hair from the sacred kula bird, was soaking. She had kept the roof of her carriage down so she could be seen – a unique and hugely popular decision. She passed us with a wide smile, as enormous as her large frame.

More and more people walked past until finally the Queen arrived. Shortly after she got out of the coach, she turned to us with her magical smile and thanked us for all we had done, saying we'd done it beautifully. I was extremely relieved – we all were – and any remaining feeling of anxious concentration was instantaneously replaced by elation.

Inside Buckingham Palace there was a similar sense of excitement as there had been in Westminster Abbey, but it was markedly more relaxed. Although it was still formal, there wasn't the feeling of a whole nation holding their breath, and without the television cameras, it was easier to enjoy what was going on. The role of Maid of Honour continued to be one of great privilege because staying at the Queen's side meant we were right there to see everybody.

Prince Charles and Princess Anne were ushered in to see the Queen and, straight away, they dashed under her dress. The Queen didn't mind a bit. She was walking on air, although when she took off her crown and placed it on a table designated for the job, Prince Charles made a beeline for it, diving on to it with great enthusiasm. Somebody – it might well have been my mother – got the crown from the clutches of the Heir Presumptive, and put it back on the table.

Just as in the Abbey, time ran away with itself. Soon I and the other Maids of Honour were following the Queen down one of the long, wide corridors of the Palace, on our way to be photographed. The Queen was so full of excitement that she started running so we all ran with her. Equally spontaneously, she sat down on a red sofa in the gallery, her dress billowing and settling down around her. We sat with her, and when she kicked up her legs for total joy, we did the same. It was the happiest of moments.

But all the while we were having the time of our lives, a private film, commissioned by the Queen, captured Princess Margaret looking forlorn. Years later, I mentioned this to her. 'Of course I looked sad, Anne,' she said. 'I had just lost my beloved father, and, really, I had just lost my sister, because she was going to be so busy and had already moved to Buckingham Palace, so it was just me and the Queen Mother.'

Little did Princess Margaret or anyone else know that less than a fortnight after the Coronation her private hopes would come crashing down when the press decided she was, as it turned out accurately, in love with her late father's Equerry, Group Captain Peter Townsend. Peter Townsend was a dashing war hero, sixteen years older than her, and after she was seen removing a piece of lint from his uniform when she was outside Westminster Abbey earlier that day, the press wouldn't let it go. It fuelled a scandal that would shake the monarchy and divide the nation.

During Coronation Day, though, I was completely oblivious to Princess Margaret's feelings of sadness. I went on with the Queen into the White Drawing Room, preoccupied with getting ready for the official photographs. Cecil Beaton had come straight from the Abbey and had already set up two backdrops so that one group could be posed while he photographed the other. The Queen, reunited with the crown, stood in the middle of us, and we waited to be instructed.

The Duke of Edinburgh had wanted his friend Baron to take the photographs, but the Queen Mother was very fond of Cecil Beaton so she had overridden him. The Duke began to make a great deal of fuss, being frightfully bossy again, telling us where to stand and when to smile. Cecil Beaton was very commanding behind the camera. He was well known for taking a dislike to interfering comments, and the more the Duke of Edinburgh tried to have his say, the tetchier he became.

The Duke persisted, either not realising or not caring that he was disrupting the photographer, and eventually Cecil Beaton snapped. He put down his camera, glared at the Duke of Edinburgh and said, 'Sir, if you would like to take the photographs, please do.' He then gestured to the camera and started to walk away. The Queen looked horrified, as did the Queen Mother, and realising he had gone too far, the Duke of Edinburgh moved off.

When the photographs were finally over, the Queen stepped on to the balcony and we went with her. This felt like one of the most momentous parts of the whole day. The crowd was enormous – there wouldn't have been enough space to put a pin between the people – stretching right down to Admiralty Arch and covering St James's Park. As soon as the Queen walked out, the crowd cheered so loudly I could physically feel the noise hitting us on the balcony.

As I stood there, it struck me that the cheers marked the beginning of a new Elizabethan age. We'd been through the war and we were still suffering from it, but this day was one to celebrate.

I was lucky enough to see a crowd just as big for the sixtieth anniversary of the Coronation. It really brought home to me the difference between that crowd and the crowd that had stood there in 1953. Only then did I realise that the original crowd had had no colour, a direct result of the war: rationing was still in place and many people were still in uniform. For years Carey and I, like everybody else, had made our own skirts from felt because it wasn't rationed and was easy to sew. So standing on the balcony in a Norman Hartnell silk gown, surrounded by regalia, was even more surreal.

The Queen was visibly moved by the reception and her eyes shone as she took in the nation's support. Along with the crowd below, we lifted our eyes heavenward to watch the planes as they flew over the Palace, dipping their wings towards the Queen. The pilots were among those who had survived the war. And not only had they survived but they had saved us all from peril. And, as if we were one, we all knew it. Their actions had enabled the day to take place, so the flypast was a magnificent tribute, simultaneously a look to the future and a reminder that we had escaped, that we were free and at peace. It was confirmation that we could all, as a nation, put the war behind us. I could see and feel the Queen's pride as we all shared a distinct feeling of unity and hope

Once the planes had flown away, the crowd turned their attention back to the Queen: every time she looked as if she might be going inside, the crowd's cheers would pull her back. Even when she finally did disappear into the Palace, they stayed there, cheering after her.

The cheers carried on as we milled about inside Buckingham Palace, the day drawing to a close. It was late afternoon when I left the Palace, but I couldn't help returning. Knowing that the Queen would go out on the balcony to greet the crowd one more time after dinner, I persuaded a friend to come with me and joined them. Only hours before, I had been standing on the balcony next to the Queen and it was strange being one of the crowd, back in my felt skirt, waving and cheering up at her, but the buzz was addictive. The Queen didn't know I was there, of course – I think I told her afterwards – but we stood and shouted for her as she appeared in an evening dress, feeling the cheers go through us.

My day didn't end there but took an even stranger twist. All the people in the Royal Household had been charged to look after the foreign dignitaries: my father looked after Queen Frederica of Greece, whom he immediately thought was wonderful, and my uncle, Major Tom Harvey, who was at the time an Extra Gentleman Usher to the Queen Mother, was allocated Sheikh Salman Bin Hamad Bin Isa Al-Khalifa, the ruler of Bahrain, and Sheikh Abdullah Al-Salim Al-Sabah, the ruler of Kuwait.

Uncle Tom decided to take them to the 400 Club – a smoke-filled and dimly lit nightclub in Leicester Square. Bands played all through the night and breakfast was offered at dawn. The bottles of alcohol bought were each labelled with the guest's name and kept for their next visit, if left unfinished. It was *the* place for the popular crowd, who all went there to cosy up on the velvet seats, drinking until the early hours.

Since it was so popular with the English aristocracy, Uncle

Tom thought the Sheikhs would enjoy it too and asked me to help him entertain them. In the run-up to the Coronation, I had imagined all sorts of glamorous elements of the day, but I hadn't expected to end it in a dark, smoky club with two Sheikhs, feeling out of place and trying to drum up conversation.

It was impossible to tell how they felt, because their expressions gave very little away. They didn't dance or drink, which Uncle Tom had hoped they might do once the evening got under way, so we sat there, rapidly running out of ideas as to how to entertain them. Very generously, they presented us with expensive gold watches. I wasn't used to that sort of present and shyly accepted, feeling increasingly anxious we hadn't exactly repaid them with an appropriate evening's entertainment.

When I went to sleep that night, on the floor at Uncle Jack's flat, it was hard to think any of it had really happened. All I knew was that I would cherish it for the rest of my life.

Still now, all these years later, I am always being asked about that day and have done my best to do it justice, but nothing ever feels adequate. There was so much going on, and when I've reminisced with the other Maids of Honour, we always seem to remember something different. What resonates most of all is the solemn promise the Queen made that day in giving her life to the nation. It's an oath she has kept faithfully. She has never put a foot wrong. She has been the most wonderful Queen and she really *has* given her life to the nation.

CHAPTER FIVE

For Better, For Worse

AFTER THE CORONATION, I was photographed for the covers of magazines and even got a few very peculiar love letters from strangers asking for my hand in marriage, but I remained single, not having found the right man.

With two sisters and no brothers, the opposite sex was inherently a mystery to me. Men seemed old-fashioned, traditional and predictable. They were creatures whose interests lay in country pursuits during the day and military reunion dinners during the evening – to neither of which women, needless to say, were invited. The season had whipped up dozens of brief interactions for me: Nigel Leigh-Pemberton had taught me that there was a sensitive side to men, but

81

Johnnie Spencer had contradicted this with brutal rejection. I was left wondering what would become of me and whether my father would succeed in persuading me to marry one of his ageing friends from the Scots Guards.

In the summer of 1955, when I was twenty-two, I met Colin Tennant for the first time, at a deb party at the Ritz, held by Lord and Lady Northbourne for their daughter, Sarah. I was waiting at the bar with a friend and they must have known Colin, who was with his stepmother Elizabeth Glenconner, whom he adored: she was always brilliant with him and so kind to me. He obviously took a fancy to me because he rang me up and we started to go out. I was relieved and excited. Not only was a man paying me serious attention, but the man in question was like no one I had ever met.

Colin was tall and terribly handsome, and I found him very attractive. The son of the 2nd Baron Glenconner, he had grown up between Glen, his ancestral Scottish estate in the Borders, and London, living in Admiral House, Hampstead, as a boy. He'd gone to Eton, where he rowed, then New College, Oxford, where he became popular on account of the large breakfast parties he gave in his rooms.

After Oxford, he was commissioned into the Irish Guards, then transferred to the Scots Guards, before joining C. Tennant & Sons, the family merchant bank. His family was very rich, which allowed Colin to be very generous, and he found any excuse to hold a party. He often entertained friends at the Gargoyle, his Uncle David's private members' club in Dean Street, Soho, right next to the Mandrake, another popular haunt. Colin was very much part of 'the Princess

Margaret set', composed almost entirely of men, who spent hours and hours at clubs like the 400.

He also had another set of creative friends, including Lucian Freud and Ian Fleming. As it happens, a few years before I met Colin he was staying with Ian in London. After dinner one night, Colin and the other guests read out some of the pages of the book Ian had just drafted, dismissing the story with roars of laughter, having no idea of the iconic fame it would reach. It was Fleming's first James Bond novel, *Casino Royale*.

Although his background might have been similar to others, Colin's combination of intense charm, quick wit and intelligence made him unique. He hardly drank and didn't touch drugs: his energy was completely natural and he was creative and fun in a way that other men I'd come across weren't.

People were drawn to him from the moment he set foot in a room, including Princess Margaret. Their friendship was platonic, but Colin had had several affairs before he met me, with, among others, Ivy Nicholson, a model, who ended up falling for Andy Warhol; Pandora Clifford, Samantha Cameron's grandmother; and the 11th Duke of Argyll's daughter, Jeanne Campbell, who went on to have many famous lovers, including Presidents Kennedy and Castro.

Colin's charm rarely failed him, although there was one occasion, at the 400, where he dug himself into hole while talking to Princess Marina, the widow of the Duke of Kent. Colin exclaimed that one way of finding out whether a sapphire was real or paste was to drop it in water to see if it kept its colour. To prove that genuine sapphires would keep their colour, he invited Princess Marina to drop her colossal sapphire ring into the water glass. She did but, to Colin's horror, the sapphire's colour drained. Colin immediately said he must have got the theory the wrong way around. She was not amused.

Suddenly this charismatic man was with me. All through the summer, he took me out in his Thunderbird, which was impossible to get into because it was so low. It was not a fun experience at all because of Colin's terribly fast, erratic driving. We went down to Bray, Berkshire, for long lunches and spent a lot of time lying about in meadows. In London he took me out to dinners, introducing me to his friends, before returning to his flat, where a lot of heavy petting went on.

My idea of love and romance was based entirely on the black-and-white Hollywood blockbusters, starring the likes of Grace Kelly and Cary Grant, which my mother and Carey had watched at the cinema in Wells-next-the-Sea. Reality was marred: romance didn't come very naturally to Colin. Although incredibly charming, he wasn't very affectionate and was nothing like Heathcliff, the character from Emily Brontë's *Wuthering Heights* on whom I based all my daydreams.

Colin also had a very unfortunate temper, which I did witness occasionally in our early days together. In those moments he always said, 'Oh, Anne, when we get married, I won't need to lose my temper.' Excited that he might propose, and not wanting to dismiss his advances because of what seemed the one bad point about him, I convinced myself he would keep his promise. After all, there were so many brilliant things about him – one of them being that he *wasn't* like my father's rather staid friends.

Colin's good intentions didn't stop him making known his complaints: when we first went to dinner to meet his father, for some reason Colin thought he hadn't paid me enough attention. On the way home, he blew up into a dramatic state, ranting about how his father had let him down and hadn't been nice to me. As far as I was concerned, his father had been perfectly pleasant, but that didn't seem to matter to him.

My mother had also seen Colin lose his cool. They had been in the Bahamas at the same time and she had witnessed an incredible outburst while they were both on a boat. She had also heard about some antics at Balmoral the summer before, and the Royal Household disliking him, labelling him unruly. She warned me about his temper but Colin kept reassuring me with the same promise: that when we were married everything would be all right.

At the end of the summer I took him to Holkham to introduce him to my father, who gazed at him stiffly and with great suspicion. Not long afterwards, for better or for worse, we got engaged. I went home to tell my father, who was expecting the news and was very carefully ignoring it and, therefore, me. We were at Holkham, where I pursued him around the house, through the endless rooms, as he kept saying, 'No, no, no, not now, Anne.' Finally, I cornered him and blurted out the news. He didn't really react, offering me no congratulations. Not only was my father still fixated on the idea of marrying me off to one of his friends but also he saw the Tennant family as worlds below the Cokes. While our family had been established in the fifteenth century, springing from fortunes in law and then land, the Tennant family had made its – albeit vast – fortune through the invention of bleach in the Industrial Revolution. Not only were they tradesmen, as far as my father was concerned, they were also *nouveaux riches*.

This was not the first time a young Coke had brought their betrothed to Holkham only to receive a negative reaction: when my grandfather, the future 4th Earl of Leicester, fell in love with Marion Trefusis, my grandmother – a great beauty and a marvellous lady I remember fondly – he took her to meet *his* grandfather, the 2nd Earl. Pretending he could no longer hear or speak, the 2nd Earl of Leicester had taken to writing messages in his truckle bed. Taking one look at Marion, he scribbled furiously and handed the note to my grandfather. 'Take her away,' it read.

On 16 December 1955, when our engagement was announced in *The Times*, my father promptly wrote a letter to Colin telling him, in no uncertain terms, that he was to continue calling both him and my mother Lord and Lady Leicester. Colin was rather dashed by this. I felt it a shame, especially as my mother would have been perfectly happy for Colin to call her Elizabeth.

Years later, I discovered that before the official announcement Princess Margaret had written to my mother on the subject of Colin, agreeing that she was quite right to be concerned, describing him as a 'fairly decadent fellow', before going on to offer reassurances by saying he had 'shown good taste in loving Anne', which meant she felt 'he must be better already'.

This letter was never mentioned to me, and I only came across it after my mother had died. It is very telling that Princess Margaret described Colin as decadent, and typical of both her and my mother to settle on acceptance rather than to intervene too much. I can see why my mother didn't show it to me at the time, and it is impossible now to say whether it would have made me think twice or not.

With only three months between the engagement and the wedding in April, I set to work busily making lists, arranging everything from the flowers to the music, while Carey designed the bridesmaids' dresses. For my dress, I looked at designs from Norman Hartnell and Victor Stiebel, another top designer of the day – he went on to make Princess Margaret's going-away outfit for her honeymoon – but it was Norman Hartnell's that I fell for: its A-line design, made from embroidered silk, was exquisite.

My father prepared for the wedding as though I was a son, ensuring all the workers and tenant farmers I had got to know through shadowing him were included by setting up three tents in the park with a wedding cake in each, and then the main reception in the state rooms of the house.

In the days before, the surrounding area was taken over by guests, including a coachload of staff and workers from Colin's home, Glen, in Scotland, a lot of whom had never seen the sea before. The long gallery filled with wedding presents, including a silver inkwell from the Queen and the Duke of Edinburgh, and a gold compact mirror from the Queen Mother. Everybody from the surrounding area came to look at them.

On 21 April 1956 we got married in St Withburga's Church

on the Holkham estate. Once again, I stood on the marble stairs, just as I had done for my coming-out dance, but this time in my Norman Hartnell wedding dress, with the very handsome Coke diamond necklace, instead of my debutante dress made from a parachute, and I breathed it all in. This time I wasn't rushing off to offer champagne to the workers, having not been asked to dance. This time I was the bride of Colin Tennant, *the* socialite of our generation, on the verge of being an independent married woman.

My father's Rolls-Royce was polished up, and we had a chauffeur called Smith, who drove us through the park to the church. My father was rather nervous, quietly fussing over tiny things. My mother was already at the church, having made it lovely by arranging the flowers around the hanging lamps.

The service was a blur, but I remember coming out to huge crowds cheering as they saw us. A lot of people from the village and around had come to see us, and especially to catch a glimpse of Princess Margaret and the Queen Mother, who was in her furs, waving and smiling. The Queen wasn't there as she was celebrating her birthday, something my father hadn't realised when he had set the date.

I was pleased Princess Margaret was there even though since my coming-out dance we had seen each other only occasionally. She spent a lot of time in London, going out to nightclubs, and I didn't: I stayed at Holkham, busy with the pottery.

It was Colin who brought us back together, rediscovering a friendship that would last a lifetime. At our wedding, however, Princess Margaret looked quite cross. She was said to hate any of her friends marrying, presumably because it would not only mean she would have fewer male friends to take her out to nightclubs but also remind her that she was still unmarried. She arrived at our wedding looking like a slightly frumpy nurse in a dark blue coat and a blue hat and gloves, oblivious then that she would marry our wedding photographer, Tony Armstrong-Jones, four years later.

Although Tony was an Eton and Cambridge man, my father considered photographers tradesmen, and rather rudely called him 'Tony Snapshot' and didn't invite him to have lunch with the wedding party. While Tony ate on his own downstairs, his future bride was the guest of honour. Tony took the most wonderful photographs, which was why we hired him – he was the very best of the day and people raved about him for good reason. But he also took an instant dislike to Colin, which became more and more apparent in later years. Incidentally, Cecil Beaton had approached my father, wanting to be the official photographer, but when my father said he had already booked Tony, Cecil was disappointed. My father decided to invite Cecil as a guest and he took some wonderful photos, then sent the bill to my father, which didn't go down well.

Colin and I returned to the house for the reception in the Rolls-Royce and, as was the tradition, drove the long way around the park, so that we went through the village, to enable everybody to see us. Smith stalled on the hill in the village. With the car at a standstill, the crowd came looming up, peering in through the windows. I felt very on show and started to feel anxious, saying, 'Smith, please hurry. Can't you get the car going again? It's so embarrassing sitting here.'

He was very flustered but eventually he got the car started and off we went.

The guests were greeted, the cakes were cut, the speeches made in all three tents and then the state rooms. Then the photographs were taken, all with the backdrop of a perfect sunny day. I enjoyed myself, although as the time ticked past, I began to feel distracted. I imagine every bride catches herself in a surreal moment at some point during her wedding day. For me it was the anxious anticipation of the wedding night that played on my mind, especially when it was time for Colin and me to leave Holkham. Most brides of my background, in those days, were virgins. And apart from a broken heart, courtesy of Johnnie Althorp, I was totally inexperienced when it came to love affairs.

My mother had told me about sex. I was eleven and about to leave home to go to boarding school. I hadn't yet started my periods, so my mother covered that too. She began talking about Biscuit, our dog: 'You know how we shut Biscuit up when she has blood coming out of her bottom? Well, that is what will happen to you soon.' And then she said, 'Later on, when you're grown-up and get married, do you remember Daddy's Labrador getting on top of Biscuit? Well, that's what happens when you get married and have sex, except you will probably be lying down in a bed.' I was never told anything else.

As the afternoon turned into early evening, I went up to my mother's bedroom to change out of my wedding dress and into a blue silk coat, hat and gloves. It was at this point that a wave of horror hit me: I realised I was about to leave not only the house but my life as I knew it. My mother wasn't surprised when I broke down. 'I thought this might happen,' she said. 'This is the beginning of a whole new life.' She told me she understood the weight I felt and that she had been in that position herself when she was only nineteen, much younger than my twenty-three years. When I eventually reappeared, Colin saw my red eyes and I think it worried him because the journey from Holkham to the little airfield was strained.

From the airfield, a small private plane took us to Croydon, for our passports to be checked, and then on we went to Paris, the first stop on what was supposed to be a six-month honeymoon. By the time we got to the Hôtel Lotti, right next to the Arc de Triomphe, it was the middle of the night and I was exhausted, ready to go to bed immediately. But not Colin. On seeing that our room contained two single beds, he became absolutely furious.

Off he went to the front desk, where the tiny night porter got quite a shock as this imposing Englishman flailed his arms, his voice raised to the roof, not caring that he was waking up all the guests. The porter soon realised that the only prospect of calming him down was for him and Colin to haul a double mattress from the basement all the way up four or five flights of stairs. Colin shouted all the way as the hotel's other guests came out into the corridors to see what all the commotion was about. Finally, over the top of the twin beds was flopped a dirty, sagging double mattress. And underneath it all, somewhere, lay the exhausted Frenchman.

And there I was, waiting silently, clutching my closed silk handbag with both hands, wondering what would happen next. To my surprise, Colin climbed on to the bed and was snoring within minutes. I lay there bewildered. Colin had already broken his promise – only hours after we had left the church, I had witnessed his first meltdown of our married life.

Although I didn't experience the wedding night, it caught up with me in the morning and our first attempt at sex was not as enjoyable as I had hoped it to be. It was awkward, painful, and certainly not the night of passion I had been hoping for. Colin was obviously dissatisfied, which made me feel terribly awkward. I knew he had been very promiscuous, often visiting Mrs Fetherstonhaugh, who ran one of the 'poshest brothels' in London, where the 'ladies' were quite often vicar's wives, who would work part-time shifts for pocket money, returning to their civilised lives in the evenings.

I suppose he had never been to bed with a virgin before, but rather than teaching me, he was critical and, instead of easing me into the physical side of marriage, he had an alternative plan. 'I'm taking you out tonight for a surprise,' he said, after a slightly uncomfortable day at the Louvre. Imagining he was whisking me off to the Ritz, or maybe the Palace or Le Grand Véfour, I put on my best dress and felt excited, but as we drove through central Paris and out the other side, I began to get nervous.

The day before I had been in my wedding dress, exchanging vows in front of the Queen Mother, Princess Margaret and hundreds of other people, and now I was in a car being driven through the seedy outskirts of Paris, getting further and further away from what I had hoped and expected. What was even more disconcerting was that for the whole journey Colin refused to tell me anything. 'It's a surprise,' was the only thing he said.

The destination was nothing short of appalling – a filthy, run-down hotel, with a funny smell. After climbing some stairs, we entered a room and sat down in a pair of red velvet, winged-back chairs. Then I was presented with Colin's 'surprise': two strangers, naked, in front of us, having sex.

I had been conservatively brought up. I was wearing a demure silk dress. This was the first day of my honeymoon and *this* was the surprise. Why he thought it was a good idea, why he thought I would like it, I can't tell you to this day. We sat next to each other but, thankfully, out of sight because of the wingback chairs. I stuck the back of my head to the chair, sitting bolt upright, wincing and keeping my eyes closed, dreading what Colin might be doing next to me.

The intertwined pasty bodies of the French couple squelching into each other on the bed was the most un-attractive thing you could possibly imagine. I found it perfectly disgusting. Every now and then they asked us if we would like to join in. So, I found myself saying politely, 'That's very kind of you, but no thank you.' They carried on, oblivious, and once they had finished, they got up and left the room. Colin and I were still sitting in the wingback chairs. We hadn't exchanged a word. I thought: This honeymoon is going to continue for six months. *Six months.* How am I going to cope?

From Paris, we boarded the *Queen Mary* to New York. During the first night on board, Colin lost his temper again, shouting and screaming in a way I would become used to but which, at the time, was still a huge shock. This time it was my fault. My father, a stickler for fresh air, had always insisted I slept with the windows open, so as soon as we arrived in our cabin I opened the little round porthole. Later that night, once we were on the high seas, a huge wave crashed against the ship, the water coming through the porthole, completely soaking us and the cabin. Colin was incandescent, accusing me of having done it on purpose. Then he got a cold, which meant he wouldn't let me forget about the wave through the porthole until he was better. With Colin bedbound, I spent the days away from him, which, by this time, was quite a relief, exploring what the *Queen Mary*'s cinema, shops and places to eat had to offer. I could enjoy, too, just sitting and people-watching as dozens of very old ladies dripping with jewels were romanced by gigolos.

By the time we got to New York, Colin had recovered, and we went straight on to Cuba, which was thick with political unrest. Fidel Castro's popularity was rising, but at that time President Batista was still in charge. Even though the hotel we were staying in wasn't fully built, and the island was riddled with mosquitoes, the honeymoon was improving by then. There hadn't been any more nasty surprises, and Colin and I were getting on well together. He seemed to be settling down a bit, but everything changed when he took me to a cock fight.

Apparently cock fights are, or at least were then, a major part of social life in Cuba. We sat among the crowd, huddled round a clear circular area, in a dark room, dimly lit by hanging naked bulbs. In the clearing, there were two cockerels and a few men. I didn't feel very relaxed or excited:

cock fighting was not my idea of fun and the atmosphere was rather shifty. Conscious of the experiences in Paris, I wondered, with imposing dread, whether this would simply add to the budding collection. I watched uncomfortably as the men cruelly set about provoking the cockerels – pulling their feathers, shouting at them, making them puff up their chests in defence. Once they had cajoled them enough, they let the cockerels go, throwing them towards each other, so the fight would commence.

Well, that's what normally happened. However, on this occasion, one of the cockerels, instead of confronting the other, immediately flew up into the air and made a beeline for me. I was the only fair-haired person in the room, and I think it must have mistaken my blonde hair for straw because, before I knew it, I had a cockerel sitting on my head with its spurs digging into my scalp, my blood dripping down the side of my face. Colin's response was to be absolutely furious, shouting at me that I had ruined the cock fight and ruined all the bets that had been placed. Soon, the entire crowd was shouting at me, leaving me feeling as bewildered as the cockerel, which continued to cling to my head.

I was left shell-shocked and things stayed tense, the honeymoon continuing to rack up uncomfortable situations. On the very long train journey to Yellowstone, Wyoming, Colin lost his temper once more, this time over a card game. It wasn't one of those grand trains like the Orient Express so there wasn't a lot to do on it. We spent most of our time in our cabin, which was a squeeze even with Colin on a chair and me on the bunk, which could be pushed up against the wall by a lever to make more room. We both enjoyed playing cards, but there was always a major problem: Colin didn't like losing. This time, I kept getting good cards, all of them better than his. I prayed that I would pick up bad ones, but it wasn't to be. I was winning and could sense Colin's mood changing. Suddenly he exploded, stood up in a rage and deliberately flipped the lever switch. The bed I was on shut like a trap. I was squashed, my arms and legs sticking out, my head bolstered against the wall. Fortunately, and by this time perhaps surprisingly after the number of shocks he'd given me, Colin realised I was hurt. He was apologetic and relatively sympathetic, and rushed off to get help.

Fortunately, Yellowstone marked the end of our honeymoon and the end of my baptism of fire. It was cut short when I began to feel sick because I was pregnant. This was some relief. As far as I was concerned the honeymoon had gone on quite long enough and I was very pleased to be going home. As we left Yellowstone, I experienced the great sinking feeling that I was now going back to face the rest of my married life, almost certainly replete with uncomfortable situations.

It had all started in Paris, a place I have never quite been able to relax in since. The next time Colin and I went, he took me to a stage show of a man making love to a donkey.

CHAPTER SIX

Absolutely Furious

A MAN OF extremes, Colin is hard to explain and was even harder to understand. One thing is for certain, though: he was never boring. He had a great many stories to tell, loved throwing parties and, when it came to clothes, had all sorts of brightly coloured ensembles. A firm favourite was a suit made from different tartans, which he called 'the gathering of the clans'. He'd often change outfits several times in one evening, rather disruptively. On one occasion, when we were having lunch with our friend Patrick Plunket, Colin was dressed head to toe in PVC and, although I could see him getting hotter and hotter, he refused to take off the jacket, and a few minutes later he fainted. This simply added to the theatrics of the outing, as far as he was concerned. He also liked attracting attention, wanting to shock people. On flights, he would change outfits in the aisle, apparently oblivious to the sensibilities of the passengers around him, and he had no qualms about making a scene in public. As with all marriages, I married all of my husband. Colin could be charming, angry, endearing, hilariously funny, manipulative, vulnerable, intelligent, spoilt, insightful and fun. I got to know the good parts and the bad.

Back at the beginning of our marriage, returning home from our honeymoon after three months, when we should have been away for six, meant we had nowhere to live. Since I was expecting our first child, Colin's solution was for us to move in with his mother, Pamela. Although I liked her, I wondered what it would be like to start married life living with my new mother-in-law, who was quite a character.

Pamela loved to dress up, too, told funny stories and also attracted attention. As for her driving, it was even more appalling than Colin's. She would reverse out of the drive extremely quickly and without looking in any of her mirrors. If any pedestrians had a close shave with the car, she would dismiss them entirely, or not even notice them in the first place. Once Colin and I were walking down the road near her house and a car shot past us, taking off all the wing mirrors of the parked cars. 'God, that driver's as bad as my mother!' Colin said, then realised it *was* his mother.

Pamela had set an unruly example for Colin that knew no bounds. It seemed to me that her flamboyant characteristics, and those of other members of the family, had managed to weave themselves into Colin's DNA, alongside the sturdy foundations of an intelligent eye for business formed during the Industrial Revolution. It had been Colin's great-grandfather, Charles Tennant, 1st Baron Glenconner, who had made the Tennant fortune through his discovery of bleaching powder in 1798. Somehow this large fortune had survived, despite the extravagant tendencies of the following generations.

Eccentricity ran in the family: there were stories of bacon rashers being used as bookmarks, of the rooftops at Glen being climbed at night, and of horses being ridden into the house. Colin's paternal grandmother, Pamela Wyndham, was one of the Wyndham sisters immortalised in John Singer Sargent's painting, *The Three Graces*, which now hangs in the Metropolitan Museum of Art in New York. Both Pamelas, despite not being blood-related, had uncanny similarities and, like all of Colin's relations, had a palpable charm and would use it to seduce a room effortlessly. And, like Pamela Wyndham, they all behaved like spoilt children. It was a trait that defied age. Apparently, Pamela Wyndham would turn around from the table in stubborn silence if she felt she wasn't being paid enough attention – Colin used to tell people that she was known to lie down and bite the carpet when lost in a rage. She had dressed her child, Stephen Tennant, Colin's uncle, as a girl throughout his early childhood because she had wanted a daughter instead of a son.

When Colin first took me to see his Uncle Stephen just after we were married, I was in for quite a shock. Arriving at Wilsford Manor, his house in Wiltshire, we were greeted by the housekeepers, Mr and Mrs Scull, who referred to Stephen as though he was a child, even though he was in his sixties. 'Master Stephen is upstairs, *longing* to see you,' they told us.

We climbed the stairs of the very dusty old house, which was covered with fishing nets and shells and collections of feathers and false flowers, and lit by huge chandeliers. As we neared his bedroom, Uncle Stephen called out, 'Come in! Come in, darlings! How lovely to see you!'

And there on the bed lay Uncle Stephen. Although he had been a beauty in his youth, he certainly wasn't by then. Bloated and heavily made-up, he had arranged *himself* so he was surrounded by shells and flowers. Behind us came Mr Scull, who had staggered up the stairs with a tea tray upon which sat a solid silver teapot, a kettle, cups and saucers. Uncle Stephen gazed up forlornly and said to me, 'Oh, darling Anne, I'm not strong any more. Do you think you could be Mother?'

I could hardly lift the teapot either, and as I laboriously poured the tea, he turned his attention to Colin. 'You're looking a bit pale, darling boy. Don't you remember what I told you? You must put on a little eye shadow and a touch of pink on the lips.' Uncle Stephen reached for his make-up and beckoned Colin over. I watched in horror. 'Come here, darling boy!' he said, proceeding to dab the carmine on Colin's lips.

I assumed Uncle Stephen was too poorly to get out of bed but it turned out he was perfectly healthy, he just didn't get out of bed at all, except in June to see his roses. 'Well, there's nothing to see, but I simply can't resist the roses,' he explained. There I was, thinking Colin was rather unusual, but within minutes I had reassessed my new husband.

When we were leaving, Uncle Stephen clutched both my hands and said, 'Anne, you're a pretty little creature. I stay in touch only with the people I really love so I think you will be getting one or two letters from me.'

To my absolute horror, he sent me lots of letters, which smelt appalling – he had clearly gone to great effort, including a silk handkerchief, doused in scent, inside the envelope. I don't know what the postman thought. The letters were filled with obscene drawings of sailors in frightfully tight trousers. Perhaps he thought it would do me good to look at pictures of extended penises. I hid them, not wanting the maid to think I was encouraging vulgar correspondence from one of Colin's elderly relatives.

Uncle Stephen's mother, Pamela, had been part of a close-knit group of aristocrats known as 'the Souls', who were flirtatious and intelligent and carved themselves out of stuffy society. In his youth, Uncle Stephen was described as the 'brightest thing' in the set that became known as the 'Bright Young Things'. Colin had been at the heart of the 'Princess Margaret set' before settling down with me. A pattern had emerged. No wonder Colin was eccentric.

Not surprisingly, living with Colin *and* his mother for the first three months of our marriage was almost as hard as being on honeymoon. I once asked Pamela for advice about how to respond to Colin when he lost his temper. She told me it was easy to calm him: 'All you need to do is give him a lovely cup of cocoa at bedtime.' I could never work out whether she was in total denial, or whether Colin only behaved in his peculiar manner to me. Either way, I knew that cocoa was not going to help.

Thankfully before too long, our friend Patrick Plunket, who was a great favourite of the Queen and was, at the time, her Equerry, later becoming Master of the Household, suggested we move into his brother's house, since he was away in Africa. Leaving Pamela in London, we moved to Kent, and a few months later, in February 1957, Charles, our eldest son, was born.

Colin and I were thrilled. Charlie was much admired and, of course, since he was a boy, I was praised for having managed to produce an heir for Colin immediately. The relief was tangible.

Life subsequently settled into a routine. Every morning Colin commuted from West Malling station into the City to the merchant bank his father owned. He wore a bowler hat and carried an umbrella – the City uniform of the day. I stayed at home looking after Charlie and organised fund-raising events for various charities I had started to become involved with. This was the pattern I expected our lives to follow.

But behind this conventional façade, Colin was a man who was troubled in ways I never fully understood. No one had told me before our wedding that he had had two nervous breakdowns and been taken off by his beloved and equally eccentric Aunt Clare to a clinic in Switzerland. Once, he had run barefooted through London in his pyjamas to hospital, claiming his heart had stopped. The doctors must have wondered how he had got there if that had been the case.

But there were also many great things about Colin: he taught me all sorts of things I knew nothing about, and he was the best conversationalist around, his stories vivid and energetic. When he was in a good mood, there was nobody as much fun as him to be with. The problem was that all the time he was being fun and engaging, I would be wondering at what point his mood would change. From one moment to the next, Colin could change completely, his face becoming mad, like a werewolf's, exploding. Anything in his vicinity became hostage to a cataclysmic bombardment of anger. Once, when in the office of C. Tennant & Sons, he cut an artery in his leg by kicking a plate-glass window through the stress of trying to give up smoking.

It was usually something trivial that set him off, and once he'd flipped, he would insist that I didn't move, not an inch, until he had calmed down. If I moved it would provoke him more so I learnt to stay still, like a rabbit, holding my breath until he had finished. He would then act as though nothing had happened. For gas bombs, people carried gas masks, for rain, umbrellas: solutions, armours, defences. But for Colin, there was nothing.

Not long after we were married, sparked by one of Colin's outbursts, I did run home to my mother, thinking I had made a big mistake in marrying Colin. I don't know what I expected her to do but my thoughts of separation were stamped out immediately, she telling me in no uncertain terms, 'Go straight back. You married him.'

I think she knew that if she had shown even the slightest bit of sympathy, I would have clung to it, and since I had married him, and was pregnant with Charlie at the time, leaving him was not a good option. This was how my mother dealt with things: she just got on with life, whatever it threw at her. Everyone did. My mother led from the front – a true role model, prioritising practicality over sentimentality, favouring denial over confrontation.

So that was that. I went back to Colin straight away, accepting my fate. He used to keep me awake all night, talking and lying on the floor in a foetal position. I wasn't used to this. Not surprisingly, I had no experience in dealing with a grown man who carried on in this odd manner. Colin didn't behave normally at all, objecting to things that seemed perfectly reasonable to everybody else. He hated going to the theatre because he couldn't stand the interval, so he would always leave before the second half And he rarely ate from a plate, preferring to eat out of paper bags – at one point he had a passion for jellied eggs of all things, which I couldn't stand. Then there was the habit of buying houses. I had to learn to accept and deal with this, as much as having to cope with his histrionics – I had no choice. Suddenly, he would announce he had bought a new house and we would move, often almost straight away, sometimes after just having arrived at our current house. He never consulted me, so I just had to get used to it. I've lost count of how many houses in London we lived in.

My father observed this flaky characteristic and suggested I should buy one of the redundant farmhouses from the Holkham estate so that I had my own stable base, thinking it might make my life easier. There were two to choose from. One was right on the marshes with Dutch gabling, but I imagined bleak winters and Magwitch appearing. So I chose the other, further inland, a few miles from Holkham. I had to buy it, but I got it at a discounted rate. Colin, who had been in control of our houses in London, picking and decorating them as he wanted to, was a bit unsure about coming to stay at *my* house but I was desperate to show it to him once I had finished decorating it because I was very house proud.

The bathrooms were brand new and had carpets, and when Colin first came to see the house, I kept the plastic covering on them: whenever Colin had a bath, most of the water was on the floor by the time he had finished. When he went to have a bath, and discovered the plastic, he got very cross. 'How dare you put plastic down because of me?' he fumed. 'Protecting the carpet against me. Typical.'

And with that, he dressed and disappeared. I had no idea where he had gone, and eventually, when I started looking outside, I heard moaning coming from a dilapidated farm building on the opposite side of the road. I followed the noise and, to my horror, I saw Colin crouched right at the back behind two rotting tractors. He refused to come out and I began to panic in case the people in the village heard what was happening.

I rang my mother, who came round with the doctor. He managed to crawl under the tractors to give Colin an injection. The sedative worked and the moaning stopped but then the doctor, who was utterly bemused, had to drag Colin, who was now limp, out from behind the tractors. My mother and I helped lug him inside, put him to bed and thanked the doctor, who left as quickly as he could. The next day Colin acted as though nothing had happened, as did my mother.

Despite their ability to carry on as if nothing had happened, this behaviour had alarmed me and I subsequently persuaded Colin to let me take him to see a doctor, hoping he, and I, might get some support. The doctors explained his condition by describing him as having one less skin than the rest of us. He was too sensitive and too highly strung, they said. This polite explanation didn't help with the reality. So, after months of my suggesting he go to a psychiatrist, he eventually agreed. He went through several very quickly, seeing them once and never returning, but then he found an old man who suited him. When I asked what happened during the sessions he said, 'I do nothing. I just lie there. Very cross. Very cross and silent.'

I didn't think that was much good. The whole point was to talk but he insisted that lying there and being cross did the trick. It sort of did for a while. But then one day the old man died so, once again, I had to deal with Colin, who carried on having tantrums all over the world for the rest of his life.

Once we were in Russia with his cousin, the writer Susanna Johnston, known as Zannah. Colin had been invited to give a speech, live on Russian television, at the unveiling of a plaque dedicated to his grandmother, Lady Muriel Paget, who was being honoured for her war work and specifically for having set up the Red Cross in the Balkans. On the way, Colin had been overflowing with enthusiasm, telling me and Zannah about how his grandmother had once hidden Tomáš Masaryk, the first President of Czechoslovakia, under her skirt while travelling through Russia. 'When the Soviet guard came to inspect the carriages, ordering everybody to stand up, my grandmother refused,' Colin explained, with evident admiration. 'She simply replied, "How dare you ask Lady Paget to stand up?" and waved her umbrella.'

Colin stayed in a high state of excitement as we walked

to the rehearsal. The plaque was to be unveiled at the Dmitry Palace in St Petersburg, which Lady Muriel had turned into an Anglo-Russian hospital for wounded soldiers during the First World War. But we got lost on our way there. Colin quickly blamed me for going in the wrong direction, and before long he had started to shout. A passing group of Japanese tourists looked on bemused.

I carried on over a bridge towards a tourist shop to get directions. From behind me, I heard ghastly screaming and raced back to find Zannah bent over Colin, who was lying in a foetal position on the pavement. The same group of Japanese tourists stood around taking photographs as they watched Colin, curled up on the ground in the middle of St Petersburg, until he suddenly got up and sped off. Zannah and I looked around for him but, realising we would be late, we continued to the palace. When the organisers asked where Colin was, I said, 'He's got a headache,' at the same time as Zannah said, 'He's got a stomach ache.' They looked at us suspiciously. They had never met Colin.

The following day, at the event itself, Colin got awfully cross with the interpreter when it became apparent, because the audience wasn't reacting, that his jokes weren't being translated. Despite being on live television, he stopped his speech, had a go at the interpreter and complained to the organisers that the whole speech was being ruined. By now I wasn't surprised, but naturally I was mortified.

Years later, when Colin and I were in India with our three youngest children and our American friend, who lived in India, Mitch Crites, Colin lost his rag spectacularly. We had ridden tuk-tuks into the middle of Delhi to go shopping, and

Colin and Mitch arrived at the shop first. By the time I got there with the children, I could hear Colin's screaming coming from the shop. I found Colin having an enormous row with the shopkeeper, whom he was grappling with. Within minutes the street was filled with angry Indians. Mitch shouted at me as soon as he saw me, 'Take the children, get back in the tuk-tuk and leave!' So I grabbed the children and made a dash for the hotel on the tuk-tuk, which stalled many times before I got away. By that point, I didn't care whether Colin was torn limb from limb but, luckily for him, Mitch – a calm but imposing man, fluent in Hindi – defused the situation.

'What happened?' I asked Mitch, later that afternoon.

'Colin was really nasty. It's so dangerous. He must learn how to behave,' Mitch said, still not knowing what had sparked the rage.

I approached Colin gingerly, unsure what state he would be in. 'You could have been lynched. You can't behave like this.'

That wasn't the first or the last time he had got into a bad situation and I always wondered whether anybody would one day turn around and retaliate, but Colin never changed. He remained generous and, on his best form, got on with people from all walks of life. He always insisted on throwing parties, he was a complete shopaholic – a magpie of the first degree – and his temper stayed a part of him. I once asked him why he screamed at people, and he replied, 'I like making them squirm. I like making them frightened.'

It was a shocking sentiment that I couldn't begin to relate to, but I concentrated on the good things about him, which

Colin had predicted I would do. I once asked him why he had picked me, when he had millions of sophisticated girl-friends. He could have married any of them. Why was it that he wanted to marry me?

He replied, 'Well, I knew that with you, you would carry on, you would never give up.'

This was quite true because I was married to him for fifty-four years and I didn't give up – although I continued to have many moments when I thought that I might.

CHAPTER SEVEN

The Making of Mustique

IN 1958 COLIN took me with him to Trinidad to see the land that his family owned, leaving Charlie behind in the care of a nanny. I was very excited, having never been somewhere so exotic – the days of grand tours were over and my family had not had the money to travel much. Colin, on the other hand, had travelled extensively and had fallen in love with the West Indies on his many visits. Not all of the Tennants had taken to life in Trinidad: Colin's father, Christopher, had been only once, in the twenties, but didn't like it so never returned. He had, however, shipped back a few caimans and given them to his brother Stephen (the infamous Uncle Stephen), who kept them in his house before reluctantly giving them to a zoo. Although the caimans were put on the hotplates in the dining room to keep warm, they were always escaping and the housekeeper spent a great deal of time going round the house with a broom, discovering them behind doors and under sofas.

I was enchanted by the warm air, turquoise waters and white sand bars. We stayed with John and Janet Lovell in the Maracas Valley in the middle of the rainforest on the Ortinola estate, which C. Tennant & Sons owned. Colin adored the Lovells, who had played a significant role in forming his love of the West Indies when he had stayed with them after he'd left Oxford.

When we were there, Colin heard about an island in the Grenadines that was for sale called Mustique – from the French *moustique*, meaning 'mosquito'. Owned by the Hazells, a Creole family, for almost a hundred years, Mustique, which had a dwindling cotton estate, had become an increasingly expensive burden, and by the time Colin found out about it, it had been on the market for five years. Curious, he made arrangements to go and have a look while I went back to England to be with Charlie. After sailing round the island, Colin bought it for £45,000 without even having set foot on it. It was a risky asset, having no running water and no electricity, and only about a dozen acres were under cultivation growing cotton, while the rest of the island's 1,300 acres or so were frazzled to a crisp.

Anybody else who had considered buying it must have concluded it was a non-starter. Even St Vincent, one of the largest of the Grenadines, was much more advanced, and still communication was terrible: letters took a fortnight to be delivered, if at all, and there weren't any telephone lines. If anybody needed to fly anywhere, there was a little seaplane: although it took off on a runway, it would land on the water, much to the horror of any passengers who hadn't been warned. What was even more of a concern was that Colin knew nothing about cotton or agriculture, tropical or otherwise.

But for Colin, it was as though he had been born to live in that part of the world so Mustique offered him a vibrant existence, his character infinitely suited to life on a Caribbean island, a Panama hat much more his thing than a bowler. He was in a high state of excitement from the moment he bought the island, embracing life on Mustique as though he was the embodiment of it all, longing to show it to me.

I was intrigued to see it, but the first time I went to Mustique, I was in for a shock. To begin with, it was a palaver to get there, and after flying from England to Barbados, from Barbados to St Vincent, I boarded a boat, only to endure a very rough two-hour crossing. Eventually, the boat dropped me ashore, on a huge stretch of white sand with a jungle of manchineel trees coming right down to the beach where, I was relieved to see, Colin was waiting for me. Between us and the only road, feral cows roamed freely. Twice Colin and I had to shin up manchineels, which in fact are the most poisonous trees in the world, but that risk was preferable to being gored by ferocious cattle.

When we eventually got to the road, we climbed onto a tractor, with a trailer that had plastic chairs strapped on it to accommodate more passengers. The tractor was nothing like Colin's Thunderbird, although he drove it equally enthusiastically round the island, excited to show me everything. The road took us up from Macaroni beach to a stone building, the Cotton House, where the cotton was prepared: the ladies on the island picked the cotton and carried it in their aprons to the house, where they laid it all out on the floor before teasing it to get out the seeds and bundling it together. It was then shipped to St Vincent where it was packed before being sent to England to be spun. I found it fascinating to find out about each step. It reminded me of the pottery – so many people were involved in making a pretty mug or plate, which the end buyer probably didn't think about, in the same way it hadn't occurred to me to consider where my cotton clothes or bed linen had come from.

The only other substantial structure was The Great House, a building on a stone base with a wide veranda. Inside there was one huge room with a very long table that could seat about thirty people. Perplexed, I said to Colin, 'Why is there such a big table here? Are we going to entertain?' Colin explained that it was for cotton buyers, who came twice a year and sat round the table to discuss rates and inspect samples before striking a deal.

Apart from the cotton houses, there was a tiny fishing community, the islanders living in a collection of tin huts, and that was it. There was almost nothing familiar to anyone from England, and although seeing the cotton estate was interesting, I walked around feeling increasingly bemused, wondering why this had all appealed so much to Colin.

The views were stunning, like picture-postcards, but the land was barren, and I found it hard to imagine that I would ever want to spend any time there. What made it all much worse was that the island was riddled with mosquitoes – it wasn't called Mustique for nothing. My lily-white skin was not made for the Caribbean, but the mosquitoes were sure it was made for them, even biting me through the gaps of the cane chairs when I sat down for a rest, my skin going red and blotchy, coming up in welts.

When Colin turned to me, and asked what I thought, I didn't hold back. 'Colin,' I said, 'this is sheer madness!'

He looked at me. 'You mark my words, Anne,' he said defiantly. 'I will make Mustique a household name.'

Colin's certainty was convincing, but I was left wondering what our lives would have in store. We had only gone to Trinidad for a short trip and now I found myself realising that our conventional life was going to change completely.

We moved from Kent to London, and from then on, Colin and I went back and forth between Mustique and England, staying on the island for weeks on end, leaving Charlie behind. Both of us had been brought up by nannies and governesses, and in those days, no mothers I knew cooked for their children or ate with them. When I was growing up, mothers were put on pedestals, associated with treats and special occasions, while the monotonous discipline and general looking-after were done mostly by others. Children had their routine and adults had theirs. Being a wife seemed more urgent than being a mother. Colin needed support throughout our marriage: he didn't seem able to cope on his own, always needing me to be there, just in case. I never considered refusing to go out to Mustique and, as with everybody else I knew, wives stayed with their husbands.

Colin spent longer away than I did, which was a relief:

although the sound of having your very own desert island was wonderful, the reality was far less attractive. Growing up in freezing Norfolk, in a house with footmen and maids, didn't prepare me for weeks of eating tinned beans and sweating, rather than sleeping, at night. Without the practical attitude I inherited from my mother, the inner strength I had built up living through the war, and from my experiences as the only female travelling salesman, I doubt that I would have managed to cope. While Colin had a 'vision', I was left wondering whether I would ever adapt to this new Robinson Crusoe life, feeling relieved each time I went back to England.

Slowly, I began to get used to island life, accepting that I just had to jolly well get on with it and not complain. We ate fish for almost every meal so eventually, as a change, we would hunt for lobster: Colin and I would make our way down to the beach, through the thickets, avoiding the cows, to the lagoon. In the shallows we found lobsters in their holes and, putting towels over our hands, we would grab them and drag them out. They were more trouble than they were worth, since the warmer water made them very tough. With no running water, we caught rainwater on the roof and showered using a bucket with holes on it fixed up in the tree at the back of the house. It was rudimentary, but we managed. In fact, Colin seemed not to mind in the least, although I really missed being able to have a bath.

As well as Colin's dream of making Mustique a household name, he wanted to establish better living conditions and an infrastructure to ensure that the island as a whole would prosper. Influenced by the Lovells, who had worked hard to generate a fair and stable environment on the Ortinola estate,

Colin worked tirelessly, finding out what could be improved on the island and what might help the local community

The cotton estate on Mustique was a dying business, threatening the islanders' outlook, but although Colin wasn't knowledgeable about the cotton industry, he did have a good head for business. He set about introducing himself to every single person on the island, engaging with everybody, starting to build relationships with them, and I did the same. Without an official purpose, I learnt about their way of life: I went down to see the boats come in, watched the fishermen work and, although most of them spoke only Patois and very basic English, they became more friendly over time, especially when I bought fish from them. I went to the little school and struck up a rapport with the mistress and noted that they could all do with more books. I organised a shipment, which overjoyed her when they arrived.

Some felt at ease with me more quickly than with Colin, and a steady trickle of people began to approach me, starting conversations with the words, 'We didn't like to bother Mr Tennant but . . .' I always listened carefully, then thought up ways to help solve each problem.

When a young man called John Kiddle got in touch out of the blue, asking for a job, saying he had experience in tropical agriculture, Colin hired him on the spot. All John had come with was a sorry story about his business partner running off with all the money and a reference from his vicar, but Colin was just glad to have someone on board. While Colin and John were busy, I spent a lot of time on my own, and there would be whole days when I would read because I had nothing else to do. I read Jane Austen, Proust, and revisited one of my favourite novels, Emily Brontë's *Wuthering Heights.*

Learning to adjust to the much slower pace of life was a big challenge. It was frustrating that nothing ever seemed urgent, and difficult to accept that time was a vague concept in that part of the world. It wasn't just the pace of everything that was hard, but also the completely different culture, and I often found myself wondering what I was doing, trying to make a life somewhere that was so different from home. If I had married my father's friend, Lord Stair, I would have been running his Scottish estate; if I had married Johnnie, my life would have been firmly in England. Instead, I was navigating an entirely new identity on a run-down desert island.

In 1959, having realised I was pregnant with our second son, Henry, I happily returned home. Going back to English society, to stucco-fronted houses and formal dinner parties in London, was like being catapulted to another world: there was London, beginning to be swept up in the new fads of prawn cocktail, duck *à l'orange* and Crêpes Suzette, busy experiencing a revolution of mini-skirts and beehive hairdos. It was a huge transition to make and I found it almost impossible to comprehend that Mustique existed at the same time as England and everything it entailed.

I continued to split my life between England and Mustique, going from being with Colin to being with our two small children. Colin was in his element, remaining passionately attached to the island, his vision for change slowly coming into sight. I think he felt free to be himself and was never affected by the challenges of bucket showers, or lack of electricity.

It was only the bravest of friends who visited in the early

years. In 1960, two years after Colin had spontaneously bought Mustique, Princess Margaret married Tony Armstrong-Jones, our wedding photographer, who was given the title Earl of Snowdon by the Queen, and was fast becoming what many people now consider one of the most iconic photographers of the day.

When their engagement was announced we were thrilled for Princess Margaret. The whole nation was behind the match because everybody had felt so sorry for her when she couldn't marry the divorced Group Captain Peter Townsend. Following the wedding, they set off on their six-month tour of the Caribbean. They waved to cheering crowds as they left London on the Royal Yacht *Britannia*, passing the Docklands and Tony's 'little white room', his famous photographic studio at number 59 Rotherhithe Street, where Princess Margaret had secretly spent so much time.

When they arrived in the Caribbean, they made their way to Mustique. Colin could hardly contain his excitement, while I felt rather nervous that it would be a disaster. The last time we had entertained them in London, at the next house we had moved to in Rutland Gate Mews, Colin had decided that Princess Margaret liked ox tongue of all things and rushed off to Harrods to get some. He brought back a box filled with curled-up grey tongues. They looked far from appealing. In fact, they looked perfectly disgusting – and, even worse, when we all sat down to dinner, Princess Margaret took one look at the solid grey tongue and went green. So did Tony. The tongues met the plates with a thud. We hid them politely behind our vegetables, and no one said a word. Suffice to say, they never returned to dinner at the Mews.

As we stood with our binoculars, scanning the horizon until *Britannia* came into view, I had mixed emotions. It anchored on Walkers Bay, which was promptly renamed 'Britannia Bay'. A smart little boat came to shore and a man in white naval uniform appeared at the door with an invitation to dine with them on the yacht. I wrote back, saying, 'Ma'am, it is very, very kind. We'd absolutely love to, but we haven't had a bath for about two months and we really, really stink, and so I don't think we'd be very good guests.'

A reply came, saying they quite understood but wished for our company regardless and would have a cabin put at our disposal. I was thrilled and took the opportunity to soak, for quite some time, in the bath. It was bliss. I would have enjoyed any old bath, but there was something rather special about bathing on the royal yacht.

The following day, Princess Margaret and Tony came ashore, and we took them on a tour of the island. I'd half expected them to flatly refuse the ride, but they both got into the trailer, and I noticed Princess Margaret had a big smile on her face, enjoying the relaxed atmosphere. For the rest of their stay, we invited them to use any beach they liked, and reassured them that they would be left alone, undisturbed. So, every day the sailors came and set up a tent for them. On the last day, they came and had a drink with us. We didn't have much to offer, just rum and the most disgusting mixer called sorrel, a bright pink drink, made from slightly sour hibiscus, which the islanders brewed. I could see Princess Margaret wincing as she sipped it. I felt the same.

That was the moment when Colin said, 'Ma'am, we haven't

given you a wedding present. Would you like something in a little box or would you like a piece of land?'

Princess Margaret turned to Tony and made up her mind without waiting for him to respond. 'Oh, I think a piece of land would be just wonderful,' she said.

It was Tony's first and last visit. He never returned, largely because of his dislike of Colin, which went back some way. Colin and Princess Margaret had hit it off in the 1950s when they had met at a drinks party held by Elizabeth Lambart, one of the Queen's bridesmaids. In the summer of 1954, when Colin had been invited as Princess Margaret's only guest at Balmoral, the press decided he had either proposed or was about to. It was a made-up rumour but it meant that when Tony came on the scene he didn't exactly take a shine to Colin. I think he also held a grudge from our wedding when he had overheard my father referring to him as 'Tony Snapshot'. Years later, someone rang Tony to ask him about Colin and he blurted out that he had always detested him, before slamming the phone down. Apparently, he referred to Mustique as 'Mustake'. But for Princess Margaret, Mustique would eventually end up providing her with a whole new life.

With the visit a success (at least for Princess Margaret), Colin was even more enthusiastic and, with John Kiddle's help, the cotton estate seemed to have a more hopeful future – the workforce was motivated by Colin's bonus schemes, and the production rate hit a stable rhythm. Proud of his efforts, Colin came back to England, full of excitement.

After that Christmas of 1960, though, I could see why Colin might prefer the freedom and lightness of being on

My grandmother, Marion Coke, on my father's side. The first of the glamorous, married aristocrats to have an affair with Edward, Prince of Wales, later King Edward VIII.

Ga, my beloved New Zealand grandmother on my mother's side, with my mother, Lady Elizabeth Yorke.

Ga's husband, my grandfather, Charles Hardwicke, the 8th Earl of Hardwicke. Their unhappy marriage ended in divorce.

The greatest disappointment. My christening in 1932, held by my father, surrounded by the 3rd Earl of Leicester, left, and Viscount Coke, right. I had tried so hard to be a boy.

Having fun with my mother and sister Carey, right.

My father, right, as equerry, with the Duke of York, later King George VI, heading for a swim.

My adored Great-aunt Bridget, the redoubtable Christian Scientist.

My Ogilvy cousins David and Angus, left, Princess Elizabeth frowning as Princess Margaret stares enviously at my silver shoes.

Prince Charles holding my son Henry at Holkham. Princess Anne looks on, with my mother in the background.

My mother's photograph of Carey and I dressed up as maids and posing for Prince Philip.

Leaving Westminster Abbey (after a rehearsal for the Coronation) with two of my fellow Maids of Honour. Here I am, centre, dressed exactly like my mother.

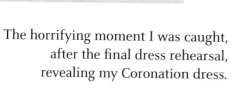

The horrifying moment I was caught, after the final dress rehearsal, revealing my Coronation dress.

DAILY SKETCH

AND DAILY GRAPHIC

Golden Souvenir Number

SHE DIDN'T KNOW IT WAS SECRET

Proud moment as we keep pace with the Queen and move as one in the Coronation procession through the Abbey. I'm the second Maid of Honour on the right.

On my wedding day, 21st April 1956, standing on the marble staircase at Holkham in my Norman Hartnell dress, photographed by Antony Armstrong-Jones.

Queen Elizabeth, the Queen Mother, waving and smiling at my wedding with Princess Margaret and my father. The Queen was away celebrating her birthday, a clash which my father only later realised.

At my youngest sister Sarah's coming out dance at Holkham, June 1962. I'm on the far right next to Sarah. My mother and sister Carey on the left. Only the married women are wearing tiaras.

In the thick under-growth of our early days on Mustique.

Our wedding present to Princess Margaret, the house that meant so much to her, 'Les Jolies Eaux' at the secluded Gellizeau Point.

With Colin at the Great House in 1973. Colin is in the cotton striped pyjamas he boasted he grew himself.

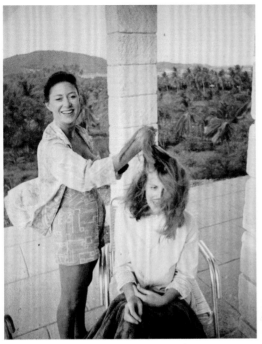

Princess Margaret as my personal stylist. I'm not sure my hairdresser, Simon, would have approved.

My mother and Princess Margaret in the mid 70s.

Roddy Llewellyn, Princess Margaret, me and Charlie.

Enjoying a musical evening at Glen in 1975. Princess Margaret, Henry, Colin and Roddy.

Glen, the magical castle in the Scottish borders that Colin inherited in 1963.

With Princess Margaret at Sandringham. I laughed more with her than anyone else.

Princess Anne at Balmoral keeping the mobile kitchen in the Queen's exact order. Her son Peter, left, looking on.

Mustique. We spent Christmas at Holkham, which was never very relaxing because my father had rigid rules about shooting. The problem for Colin was that there was a long-standing tradition of the guns being placed by rank. Members of the Royal Family were put in the middle of the drive, and that Christmas Eve the Duke of Edinburgh was there. His equerries were placed beside him; next were other dukes, followed by any marquesses, then earls and viscounts. Colin, not being any of those, was right at the bottom of the heap. At the beginning of every shoot, my father would tell him: 'Colin, you're going to walk with the beaters.' Colin wanted to stand in line and shoot and was livid, although somehow managed not to show any outward anger.

On one of the shoots, he did the unforgivable thing of telling my father at lunch, halfway through the day's strict itinerary, that he was 'rather cold' and was 'going to go back in'. My father nearly fainted at the audacity of it. If you were asked to shoot at Holkham it was a tremendous honour, really, and people longed to be invited, so Colin telling my father it was too cold and *leaving* didn't go down at all well. On the other hand my mother, in spite of her reservations about Colin before we'd got married, had become very fond of him, and he of her.

On that Christmas Eve, I was sitting in the smoking room listening to Colin telling everybody all about Mustique, encouraging Carey and Sarah to come out, when he was handed a telegram that read, 'GREAT HOUSE BURNED TO THE GROUND'. We were left completely shocked, especially once we realised that the fire had been started deliberately: John Kiddle had burned it down, making it look like an accident. We later found he had stolen all the money he could find to put in a suitcase and hide in a ditch, started the fire, then returned to the case to run off with what was all the staff's wages, before fleeing the island. Fortunately no one was hurt but so much for the vicar's reference.

After this, Colin lost faith in the whole project and tried to sell Mustique, but when no one was interested, he commissioned a prefabricated house to be built as a replacement for The Great House. When he returned to find it complete, his vision was restored.

A few years later, his rekindled energy was divided when, in 1963, his father handed over Glen, the family estate in the Scottish Borders, deciding he wanted to live on Corfu where he pursued his passion for painting. Glen was a baronial masterpiece built of grey stone that appears round the bend of the long drive like a fairytale castle, sitting in a beautiful valley with Loch Eddy at the top, surrounded by heather. I was thrilled by the idea of living in the Scottish Borders. I had loved my time with Great-aunt Bridget, Uncle Joe and my Ogilvy cousins, and had longed to live in Scotland again. I was as excited about Glen as Colin had been about Mustique.

As the new custodian, Colin darted from Mustique to Glen, modernising one and restoring the other. Glen had been 'Georgianised' by Colin's stepmother: seeking advice from a leading interior designer, Syrie Maugham, she had ripped out the original fireplaces and squared off the rooms, hiding the towers. We set about undoing all the changes, reinstating the William Morris wallpapers, uncovering the original moulded ceilings to reveal the beautiful cornices and plasterwork, and installing the Tennant tartan carpet in the drawing room.

There were a great many rooms – twenty-six bedrooms and sixteen bathrooms – yet even though it was enormous, it felt very relaxed and comfortable. The staff stayed on, including Mrs Walker, the best country-house cook for miles. At the end of each week she would come and find me somewhere in the house and give me a list of menu options for the following week. I would go through them and simply choose. Those were the days. I only wish I had spent more time in the kitchen because now I do all my own cooking and I am sure I would have learnt a lot of useful things from her.

Colin and I had fun transforming Glen together and he was glad I embraced life in Scotland so fully. He admired my resilience on Mustique too. By 1964 life had settled into a routine: after Christmas we would go to Mustique, and we spent the summers at Glen. The rest of the year Colin would come and go, and I would stay in London. Charlie and Henry, who were four and six by then, would come with their nanny up to Glen, and Colin would take them fishing in the 'wee burns' – the little streams that ran from Loch Eddy.

August was always very busy because friends and relations would come and stay on their way up to the Highlands. In fact, so many people came, it was as if I was running a hotel. 'I think I could go down to London and get a job at the Ritz,' I told Colin one summer. 'I'd run it frightfully well.' I was reminded of Great-aunt Bridget, who ran Cortachy Castle and Downie Park with ease. She always wore a neat kilt and a good cashmere twin set; and she would walk quickly around the house giving instructions.

One of the things I looked forward to most was my school friend Sarah Henderson coming up with her son, my godson, Shamus, whom she would take up the glen with my boys to shoot rabbits, which they all loved. She'd help me with the flowers, which took two days to do. Every single dressing room, bedroom and bathroom had Wemyss Ware vases, which Colin collected, full of flowers of one sort or another. All the flowers were picked for us by the gardeners, who were very keen on gladioli – 'glads', they used to call them. I'd take the pale green and the pale pink ones and give the brightly coloured ones back to the gardeners, which delighted them. The hall and the drawing room were so big, rather like those at Holkham, that a small arrangement would have disappeared. Instead Sarah and I would fill huge vases – and the house smelt wonderful.

All the food came from the estate – grouse, pheasant and venison, all kinds of vegetables from the kitchen garden and the huge greenhouses, in which we grew peaches and nectarines. I never went shopping for food because if anything was needed that the estate couldn't provide Mrs Walker ordered it and it would be delivered by the butcher, the baker . . . the candlestick-maker. They all used to come right to the kitchen door and would give Mrs Walker something extra for herself to encourage her to go on ordering from them.

Glen was beautiful all year round: in August the hillside was brushed with the purple of the heather but when Uncle Stephen got out of bed one summer and came to visit, it appeared the heather was not to his liking. 'Oh, darling boy,' he remarked to Colin, 'what a pity the valley is such a vulgar shade of purple.' Not wanting to see Uncle Stephen disappointed, Colin rushed off and somehow managed to buy hundreds and hundreds of blue paper flowers, dashed off over the valley and distributed them among the heather so that, from the house, the view was full of blue. 'Oh, darling! That's much better, isn't it?' said Uncle Stephen, before turning his attention to other things.

In autumn, the light changed to a yellowish tinge, which lit up the house magnificently, and Christmases at Glen were spectacular: outside, the landscape would be covered with thick, glistening snow, while inside, an enormous tree cut from the estate would stand magnificently in the hallway, covered with beautiful pre-First World War decorations I had found tucked away, lit with real candles.

Even in such an isolated place, Colin managed to strike up new friendships and meet new people, often inviting them to have a look round or even stay, so I wasn't surprised when we acquired some unexpected tenants. One afternoon, Colin was walking down the road to the local town when he met a group of people coming up the drive dressed in hippie clothes. Intrigued, he greeted them and asked them what they were doing there. 'Well,' replied one of the girls, heather in her hair, 'we're looking for somewhere to live and we thought you might have something.'

Colin offered them some terraced cottages on the estate called 'The Row', which were in terrible disrepair. The long and the short of it was they said yes and moved in. It turned out they were musicians so, just like that, we had our own resident band, marvellously called the Incredible String Band. In return for their accommodation, whenever people were staying, they would play – at dinners, in the gardens, on picnics – all over the glen.

On another occasion, Colin, who was on his way to Glen from New York, rang up. 'I've met an actress called Brooke Shields and she is on her way to Glen to stay with us for a few days.'

I had never heard of her but when she came she was delightful, staying with us for several days. She was very, very pretty although she had extraordinary bushy eyebrows, which weren't very fashionable in those days. She entered into everything we did – coming on picnics, rowing the boat on the lake and playing with the children.

Some of the other guests were rather more difficult. Colin was not by any means the only demanding person I knew. He would arrange certain things and invite certain people and then leave me to sort them all out, often complaining that I wasn't enthusiastic enough. Once he told me he had invited Raine Dartmouth, who later became Princess Diana's stepmother Countess Spencer, Clarissa Avon and Bianca Jagger at the same time. I said, 'You've asked three of the most demanding women I know. They're lovely by them-selves, but all together? This is going to be a nightmare!'

The evening they all arrived I was going up the passage when I heard this very loud banging coming from Raine Dartmouth's room. I rang for the housekeeper, Mrs Sanderson, who explained what was happening: 'Didn't Lady Dartmouth tell you? She said the cupboard was not suitable for her evening dresses because the rail wasn't high enough up. She asked for the house carpenter.'

While that was going on, Clarissa Avon, former Prime

Minister Anthony Eden's wife, arrived. She was a great friend of Colin's and I suspected had had a fling with him, which seemed to make her more confident when staying with us. I was in my bath, having two minutes of rest, when I heard 'Bang bang bang' on the bedroom door.

'Who is it?' I called out. 'Can it wait a moment?'

'It's Clarissa here,' came a voice. 'You said you would lend me some of your diamonds.'

'Yes, I will,' I replied, 'but I'm in the bath at the moment.'

'Well, get out of the bath,' she commanded.

I didn't really have a choice, so I got out of the bath and, in my towel, handed her the diamonds.

Meanwhile, Bianca Jagger was in her bedroom. All the bedrooms had a bell so that guests could let the maid or housekeeper know they were needed. When in her room, Bianca seemed to spend most of her time ringing the bell, demanding hot coffee. So Mrs Sanderson would traipse up and down the stairs with a constant supply: 'Tring-tring-tring' went Bianca and up and down went the coffee.

It was full on. I had to work out all the place settings for dinner and lunch, which often needed to be considered very carefully, and then, when these three ladies were still there, Princess Margaret arrived. Fortunately, she was by far the easiest: she brought her own maid and was always polite.

So many people came and went that I spent a great deal of time helping Mrs Sanderson change the bedding and get the house in order ready for the next lot of friends or family. When everybody was there, I was always making sure they had what they wanted and trying to make it a success. Sometimes it would all get a bit too much. If I felt I had

had enough I would go for a walk, simply to get away from everybody. In the woods I would pass one of the members of the Incredible String Band, who used to buy and sell gypsy caravans. One day I was on a walk and as I passed by his latest acquisition, on impulse, I asked him, 'Any chance you would like to sell me that caravan? I need somewhere to escape!'

He looked rather puzzled but sold it to me and helpfully moved it so that it was far enough away from the house to give me some undisturbed peace. I loved it: it became my own private space and I did it up with red and white knitted cushions and made red and white curtains. Before I had my bolthole, I would be followed round the house by the guests and the housekeeper alike. Everybody was always asking me questions. The little gypsy caravan made it all so much easier because I would go there to read, knowing no one could bother me because no one knew where I was.

Colin never wanted to get away – he was a ringmaster in Paradise once everybody had arrived. He built a stage in the drawing room and all the guests, including Princess Margaret, who loved Colin's idea of entertainment, would perform, and he would ask people from the village to be the captive audience. I have no idea what they made of it all. It reminded me of when I was a child, performing plays for the Polish soldiers at Cortachy. At Glen we would all change in the library, come out of the French windows and into the drawing room so that we suddenly appeared all at once.

One summer we put on a production of *Swan Lake*. Colin had bought all the swan outfits in America when we were on a family holiday earlier that summer. He had decided to hire a Winnebago and we drove around the States in that ghastly monstrosity. When Colin saw a shop he wanted to go into, he would simply park anywhere and get out. While he was in one such shop, a pair of overweight policemen on motorbikes pulled up, got off their bikes and said, 'Ma'am, you can't park there, it's a violation. You need to move.'

'I don't know how to drive it, Officer,' I replied. 'My husband's just in the shop. He won't be long.'

Sure enough, Colin soon appeared, dressed in a bright pink tutu, wearing plastic boobs, a tiara and carrying a wand. 'So sorry, Officers!' Colin said. 'I won't be a minute.' The policemen's jaws dropped to the ground and, without saying a word, they got back on to their motorbikes and drove away.

Another summer, Princess Margaret dressed up as Mae West and sang 'Come Up And See Me Sometime', and always the Incredible String Band would play late into the night. As long as I could get away when I needed some peace and quiet, I absolutely loved being there. Glen was a constant, somewhere I came to rely on, especially since our London address was always changing.

At last our marriage had got into its stride, and I could turn my focus to trying to adapt to moving between running Glen, with its staff and over fifty rooms, a smart London town house and being marooned on Mustique, showering with a bucket and catching lobster with my bare hands.

CHAPTER EIGHT

A Princess in Pyjamas

WHILE MOST OF our friends stayed put as custodians to a stately home, Colin was always on the lookout for something new and liked nothing better than to try out houses around London, continuing to move us from one to the next. We'd gone from his mother's to Patrick Plunket's brother's house in Kent to Rutland Gate Mews – a house I hated on account of its linoleum floors.

Then, in 1963, Colin declared he had bought another house. This time it was the former home of the famous nineteenth-century American painter James Whistler in Tite Street, Chelsea. Tite Street had been a popular destination for people from the arts, racking up an impressive list of occupants in the past, such as writers including Oscar Wilde, other painters such as John Singer Sargent as well as composers, film critics and novelists.

This creative part of London appealed to Colin and the house was impressive. The problem was that over the years it had sloped so drastically into the mud that it needed to be pulled down and rebuilt. Naturally, Colin threw a demolition party, asking guests to come wielding hammers and wearing hard hats. In return for a donation to one of the charities that we supported, guests were invited to smash the walls down, his mother being one of the last to leave.

After it had been demolished, it was rebuilt and decorated. It took a couple of years to finish, which meant we continued to move in and out of other houses in the meantime. When we finally moved in, we stayed put for several years.

During the sixties, when Colin and I were in England, we had a social engagement almost every night, and every weekend we were invited to stay at friends' houses, all around the country. Often there would be thirty or forty other people invited for big dances, and to allow big guest lists, we would often stay with neighbours, getting to know people by proxy. We went to Boughton, Hatfield, Chatsworth, and once we went to shoot at Wentworth Woodhouse, which happens to be the biggest house in Britain. Built on a coal mine, it smelt dreadfully of coke and the heather was black. We also stayed with Jane, Duchess of Buccleuch, at Drumlanrig Castle with Princess Margaret, although when Jane decided it was time for bed, she announced, 'I'm turning all the lights off – here's a torch.' We were left to grapple through the pitch-black corridors to our bedrooms with a tiny torch in a fit of giggles.

We were invited to Blenheim quite often. The first time we went, I was anxious about the Duke of Marlborough, Bert, who had a reputation for being frightening, with a quick wit and a quicker temper. I excused myself as soon as we had arrived to adjust my wig: at that time all the ladies wore wigs. I only wish we wore wigs now because when we did I never needed to go to the hairdresser. I had a curly wig, which made me look quite like Harpo Marx, who, rather unusually for a man, had a peroxide blond perm.

Reappearing with my wig secure, I prayed I would not have to play bridge with Bert because he had a fearsome reputation for being unpleasant to his bridge partners if they did not play to his exacting standards. But, of course, Bert said, 'I'll play with Anne.'

'I'm terrified of playing with you,' I replied, rather bravely, I felt, 'because you're very, very good and you don't suffer fools gladly.'

Thankfully, we had very good cards and I somehow engineered it so he always played the hand and he was charming – far nicer to me than Colin would have been.

Like everyone else I knew, we left our children in the care of a nanny or governess when we went away for weekends. As well as a nanny, I had a nursery maid and, with the butler, housekeeper and two cleaners, the house was run whether we were there or not. The first nanny Charlie had was Nanny White, who doted on him. Each time she wheeled him out in the pram, if he saw a cake shop he would point, and in Nanny White went to buy a huge iced bun for him. No wonder he liked her so much. When Henry was born, I took him off to Holkham with a maternity nurse. When I arrived back, Colin greeted me with the news that he'd sacked Nanny White over something very small. The truth was, she wasn't very easy to get on with and one remark or scowl from her had pushed Colin over the edge. I hadn't sacked her because Charlie loved her so much.

Charlie was devastated and seemed to blame Henry: from a three-year-old's perspective, Henry had come along, taken Mummy off and somehow, as a result, his beloved nanny had gone away too. Poor Charlie had a mini nervous breakdown and ran away into a cornfield. His hair was blond, like the corn, and the field was so big, and he so small, it took a long time to find him. We went backwards and forwards shouting for him until, in the end, I found him crouched like a rabbit. It broke my heart.

We got a new nanny, but it turned out she wasn't very kind and I didn't find out very quickly, which I bitterly regret. After her, there was another nanny and a few lovely au pairs, including a brilliant Swiss girl called Helen, who stayed until the boys went to boarding school.

I would see Charlie and Henry in the nursery before leaving them to play and be put to bed by the nanny because I normally had an evening engagement. I was always busy with fundraising events, the most memorable being the 500 Ball at Claridge's, in London, for which I organised a headdress competition. Being quietly competitive and not wanting to be accused of not trying, I went to the hairdresser John Olofson, who had created an impressive two-and-a-half-foot headdress of gilded grapes and vine leaves for me. It was so big, I had to sit on the floor of the taxi so it could fit in.

Mostly, these events wouldn't finish until the early hours

of the next morning, so I had a routine with the children: already bathed and dressed, they'd climb onto my bed while I ate breakfast and we would talk. If I was at home during the day, I would take them out to play and in the evenings I would read them books, their favourite being *Where The Wild Things Are*.

While the children's lives were in London, Colin spent most of his time on Mustique, which for many years wasn't a good place for the children to be. They were left behind until they were older. I felt torn, leaving my children, but so much was happening on Mustique and Colin was desperate to have me there in support.

Slowly, Mustique started to become a bit more appealing. In 1965, Colin's friend from Eton, Hugo Money-Coutts, arrived on a small yacht with his second wife, Jinty. They were on their way around the world, but as soon as Jinty came ashore, she told Colin that she was fed up with being stuck on a boat. With that, Colin invited them to stay and Hugo began to help Colin with the running of the island.

Jinty set about making her mark on Mustique by shipping a boatload of horses to the island, and Hugo was intrepid. He taught himself how to fly, using a tiny grass runway to take off and landing on the cricket pitch next to his house. We'd fly to St Vincent for supplies and I was the only passenger who didn't have a contingency plan in case the plane crashed. Jinty always had a bottle of gin and placed herself nearest the window, ready to jump into the sea, and Colin, fearing the same fate, would come equipped with a snorkel and mask. I was just glad we could get about. For one thing it meant we wouldn't be marooned in an emergency – which I worried about far more than Colin ever did.

With friends on the island, life was easier for me: if I got fed up with something, Jinty would understand, and if Colin was full of energy and I wasn't, he would go off with Hugo.

Having a working cotton estate meant that Colin could use a lot of the cotton in clothes and linen. The Sea Island cotton was high quality and very soft, like silk, so Colin was tremendously excited about showing off his new clothes, especially a pyjama-type suit, made in a range of colours. When people admired one, he would smile and say, 'I grew it myself.'

Wearing his cotton pyjamas, he set about modernising the island, employing a local plumber from St Vincent, known as 'Pipeline', to tackle the challenge of running water by making a dam with a collection point, but Pipeline made the awful mistake of putting the filter in wrongly so to start with we got all the silt and none of the water.

One day Colin and Hugo were on St Vincent when they came across a young man lying in a ditch, having been thrown from his motorbike. His name was Basil. They took him to hospital, and a few days later, when Colin visited to check on his progress, they struck up a rapport. When Colin found out Basil didn't have a job, he offered him the position of barman at his soon-to-be-opening bar on Mustique. Basil accepted and, unlike John Kiddle, he was an inspired appointment. The bar was named 'Basil's Bar' and is still there today.

Basil had a way with people, especially with women. Once Mustique was more developed, Colin started to invite widows or divorcees, bringing them over for some 'fun in the sun', and so, of course, Basil charmed them all, ending up living with one of them – the beautiful blonde Viscountess Virginia Royston. But in the mid-sixties, there weren't too many people to charm, and instead it would be normally just me and Colin, with Hugo and Jinty propping up the bar.

As well as Basil's Bar, a new school was built, and the tin village was moved and updated from tin huts to permanent housing. Pensions were distributed to the older people, and jobs were offered to the rest. All the people I had got to know since the beginning told me every time they saw me how glad they were that 'Mr Tennant has come'.

Just before Charlie started school, I brought him and Henry with me to Mustique and the school mistress helped Charlie with his reading, although he was far more interested in exploring the island. Both boys loved being in the sea and played on the beach just like I had done as a little girl at Holkham.

My mother and sisters came out in the early years and continued to visit. My mother especially embraced the life-style, enjoying wearing old cotton trousers and leading a far more relaxed life than the formal one she was used to back in England, but my father never came. 'Abroad?' he would say. 'What for?' Holkham had everything he needed so he stayed put.

One day at the beginning of 1968, out of the blue, Princess Margaret rang Colin to ask, 'Is it true? Did you really mean it about the land?'

'Yes,' replied Colin, thrilled that she was taking an interest. Having given Princess Margaret and Tony a piece of land for their wedding present, we thought they had forgotten about it. For the first years of their marriage Princess Margaret had been immersed in a new circle of bohemian friends, and now that she had two children – David, who was born in 1961, and Sarah in 1964 – her life was centred around her family. We were busy on Mustique so we had not been much in touch.

'And does it come with a house?' Princess Margaret asked.

Colin, not wanting to disappoint, replied he would build her a house. She was delighted, ending the call by saying she would plan to come out to Mustique to see the land.

I got in touch with her to warn her that she probably wouldn't want to do that because the whole island was still far from habitable. Since her first visit in 1960, Mustique had changed substantially but it still wasn't fit for a princess. I explained that there were still only Tilley Lamps, because there was no electricity, that the water had acquired the tinge of a satsuma orange on account of the roof tiles, and that there was certainly no hot water, but she was not deterred and said how much she was looking forward to coming.

When she arrived a few months later, Princess Margaret accepted the limitations straight away and adapted without a fuss. Whenever she wanted a shower, she would use the bucket in the tree, just like we did. The food, too, was really basic. Although we had fresh fish, everything else was tinned, but she didn't seem to mind.

We had no proper furniture, so we sat on plastic or wicker chairs, playing cards when the light wasn't good enough to read. Colin never once lost his temper with Princess Margaret, even if she did have a winning hand.

Mosquito nets covered the beds and during the night we

were inundated with some extraordinary mice. Princess Margaret called them 'flying mice' because they would rush up the net, then jump to the next one in great leaps that seemed to defy the laws of gravity. Perhaps her own experiences had made her surprisingly adaptable – by then she had lived a life of contrasts: riding pillion on Tony's motorbike through the lamp-lit streets of London was a world away from waving in a horse-drawn carriage; Tony's Docklands studio was nothing like an existence within the Royal Household, and his bohemian friends moved in a very different circle from that of the rest of the Royal Family.

She was very excited when we took her to Gellizeau Point, the land where her house would be built. A peninsula at the top end of the island, Colin had suggested it because it was difficult for people to get to and therefore more secure. Of course this meant that it was difficult for us to get to and covered with scrub. I offered her a pair of Colin's cotton pyjamas. There she was, clambering up the hill, wearing Colin's pyjamas, with string tied around her ankles and wrists to stop the brambles scratching and the mosquitoes biting. She wore wide sunglasses, a straw hat and a big smile, not minding at all. She wasn't vain. She just got on with things.

We got to the site and walked around the imaginary house, which Colin had marked out with wooden stakes. When his back was turned, she pulled up the stakes and took them into the undergrowth.

'What are you doing, Ma'am?' asked Colin.

'Well, I think I ought to have a bit more land,' was her reply.

'What do you need more land for?' retorted Colin.

'Gatehouses for my protection officers,' declared Princess Margaret.

And that was what she got.

Although incomparable to a royal palace, Mustique offered Princess Margaret a break from her husband. Like Colin, Tony was unpredictable, sharing similar character traits: he was eccentric and extremely demanding, often rubbing people up the wrong way. But, just like Colin, he could be incredibly charming. Although Princess Margaret and Tony had been madly in love, their relationship had become strained and the press sought stories in every look, every outing, every move the Princess made. There was no press on Mustique and, since Tony had said he hated the place, he wasn't likely to follow her there, though he always made a point of telling her that he *might* come, as though to stop her relaxing.

Princess Margaret was rather like my mother in that she didn't dwell on things. Neither did she spend hours complaining about Tony. She told me enough to allow me to understand her position – including that she no longer looked in her chest of drawers but would get her maid to do it because Tony had developed a habit of writing little notes saying things like 'You look like a Jewish manicurist and I hate you.'

She was used to being treated with the utmost respect – everybody else bowed and curtsied to her and called her 'Ma'am', although she would sign off with 'Margaret' in letters to friends. I never minded: her father had been King Emperor, she *was* royal, so it wasn't surprising she had 'royal moments'. The formalities never interfered with our friendship, but I suspect Tony resented them. Everybody she had ever met had treated her in a certain way and there was Tony, being spiteful in creative ways, bothering to come up with nasty little one-liners to write down and hide in her glove drawer, with her hankies or tucked into books.

I was glad Mustique provided Princess Margaret with sanctuary and I made sure she had everything she needed – she wasn't used to doing things for herself and would often make little requests that it was easier to carry out than to ignore. During the day we swam together, and in the late afternoon we would often go and sit in Basil's Bar, watching the sunset, sceptically waiting for the 'green flash' that is supposed to appear on the horizon just after the sun vanishes. Neither of us believed it, yet we always seemed to be distracted by the thought, pausing our conversation to stare at the view, just in case we saw it. We never did but it became a fun habit.

In the evenings, she and Colin would discuss her house, and it was over dinner one night that Princess Margaret suggested that her friend, her husband's uncle Oliver Messel, the leading stage designer of the twentieth century and a great artist, design her house because she had visited him in Barbados and had loved the house he had built for himself. She also hoped at one point that involving him might encourage Tony to spend more time with her and to like Colin.

Colin thought it was a wonderful idea and got in touch with Oliver, and the following year Princess Margaret came back to Mustique to see the plan of the house that he had created. Colin was pleased to have Oliver involved and, ever resourceful, went one step further than asking him to design just one house. Already a fan of his sets, enchanted by the décor of Truman Capote's musical *House of Flowers* in New York, for which Oliver had been awarded a 'Tony', Colin approached him and commissioned him to design all the houses he planned to build on Mustique.

Colin had turned his attention to building and selling houses because the cotton wasn't making any money. For ten years he had tried different schemes to improve business, but the problem was that the industry as a whole was dying – alternative synthetic materials were being produced much cheaper and in far larger quantities in China, and the traditional crops of the Caribbean couldn't compete.

Conscious of the islanders' livelihood, he knew that the houses would provide more stable employment because each would be set up with domestic staff: the people whose jobs were in jeopardy would have alternative employment options. He was passionate about the new plan for developing the island and it played to his strengths. It also aligned with his visions of making Mustique a household name and creating a thriving community, so he set up the Mustique Company. As well as Oliver, Arne Hasselqvist, a construction engineer from Sweden, came on board with a few investors. The idea was to split up some of the island into plots, design beautiful villas, then sell them to shareholders who would also invest in the rest of the infrastructure.

The plan to use Oliver to attract Tony failed: Tony stayed disinterested, but Oliver was a huge success, although he and Colin did have some frightful rows, which was to be expected since both were so highly strung.

The first plot was sold before any houses had even been designed. Honor Svejdar, née Guinness – the famous Irish brewers – and her second husband, Frankie, had come ashore to visit Basil's Bar. When they met us, Honor complained that she didn't want to stay on the boat any longer, just like Jinty had done earlier. By the end of the conversation she had asked if she could buy a plot and, on the spot, Colin agreed.

Honor and Frankie bought two of the very best plots and a beach, which she named 'Honor Bay'. Frankie drank a lot so he built himself a wooden bar outside the house near the road, where he would entertain the workmen in the evening when they passed by. When my mother visited, she became great friends with Honor, going snorkelling together in bath caps, with bags attached to their waists to collect shells. They would even go out at night with torches to find them. I wasn't quite as fond of shells as they were, once I discovered they would smell terrible if they weren't cleaned properly. Many a time when my mother and I flew home together, her shells would make the plane smell appalling.

Only after Colin had sold the beach to Honor did he realise no more should be sold – that the beaches should be kept for everyone. Nevertheless, the sale spurred him on, convincing him he would achieve his vision for a profitable island, with a thriving community, that he could run as a luxury estate.

CHAPTER NINE

Motherhood

In 1968 we finally moved into the White House in Tite Street, designed by a French architect, and the wait was worth it. The house was a real marvel, described as the most stylish in London. The press were very interested in the interior, and for a few weeks, I appeared in a great many magazines, perched on the edge of a sofa, proudly showing off the house. It was very 'of the time', made from Portland stone, with an iron spiral staircase and a hallway floor of marble that was inspired by the Impressionists, with black, grey and white circles of different sizes. There was an octagonal outer hall, which was bathed in natural light, with branches of coral set against the walls; a bathroom with sunken bath and bronze taps, silk walls in the dining room, and silver door handles everywhere shaped like shells. Downstairs was designed around our favourite paintings – a Turner, a Gainsborough, a Watteau, and a pair of Arcimboldo's fruit portraits.

Colin was delighted that the house was being talked about and praised for its impressive design because he loved to make a statement and the White House was an excellent setting for the many extravagant parties we had.

I found all the parties he got so excited about difficult to enjoy, especially the fancy-dress parties, not only because I didn't like drawing attention to myself but because I always seemed to have to mend an outfit at the last minute. Before the parties, Colin would rush around nervously, making final preparations, and I would be trying to make sure everything was in order so he wouldn't lose his rag at the last minute.

I was far less interested in outrageous ensembles, which was lucky because Colin needed to be admired the most. Probably his most ridiculous fad was wearing paper knickers, which, for a time, he showed off to everybody, drawing attention to them with a new party trick where he would declare, 'I'll eat my knickers,' after which he would put both his hands down his trousers, rip off the knickers and stuff them into his mouth, playing up to the more prudish people he came across, amused by the stir his actions provoked.

Perhaps having such an eccentric and unconventional father affected Charlie and Henry, who by the time we were living in Tite Street were eight and ten, but it is impossible to know for sure. Although Colin was incredibly proud of both his sons, he didn't take an active parenting role with them when they were small. This was completely expected in those days.

Colin was away far more than I was and, like my father, found it difficult to be affectionate or tactile. Instead, he would come home with presents and treats for the boys, who would look up tentatively, with wonder, at their tall, slightly intimidating father. Although he could be fantastic with them – he was so good at telling stories – I did my best to keep the boys away from Colin if he was in a bad mood, on tenterhooks in case they got caught up in it.

When Charlie was about eight, his behaviour started to change, becoming rather strange. For a long time, I couldn't work out whether he was following in his father's attention-seeking footsteps, but there did seem to be a tangible difference. While he was highly strung, like Colin, he didn't have the 'Tennant rages' that ran in the family, but he developed rituals that were nonsensical and took up hours of his time – things like having to wait for somebody to accompany him down the stairs or going around and around in circles in a precise and deliberate way. It was as though he was very superstitious, though in this respect avoiding cracks on the pavements was about the most normal thing he would do.

Gradually the rituals took over, so he was doing a hundred loops of the house before he could go out. At about the same time he developed a dark side. At prep school while the other boys got out books from the library such as Beatrix Potter's *Peter Rabbit*, he picked books on sinister topics. Unsurprisingly he was plagued by terrible nightmares and, concerned for his wellbeing, his form mistress called us in for an emergency meeting. She told us: 'I do see how Charles has a disadvantage. He's very worried about his Nazi grandfather.'

Colin and I looked at each other in astonishment. 'Nazi grandfather?' I replied. 'He hasn't got one.'

'Oh,' she said. 'Come and look at his desk.'

Inside his desk was a collage of Colin's father's head stuck to a Nazi general's body, covered with swastikas. We both left the meeting wondering where on earth Charlie had got these dark ideas from. With no obvious answer, and knowing that all boys seemed to be fascinated by guns and fighting, after a long discussion we dismissed it as a phase.

Unlike the common boyish obsession with blood and gore, Charlie's rituals were harder to dismiss, but children do plenty of nonsensical things and, knowing that making a big deal out of something often exacerbates it, we felt that ignoring his peculiar habits was the best thing to do. With no outward reaction, we hoped Charlie would simply grow out of them. He didn't. In fact, his rituals got more intense, not to mention more time-consuming, so Colin took him to see a psychiatrist, who diagnosed neurosis. These days, he would have been diagnosed with obsessive-compulsive disorder, but then none of us knew what that was, including the doctors. The diagnosis of neurosis didn't exactly solve anything, and the doctors provided no answer as to how to stop it.

When I look back now and think of Charlie as a little boy, my heart sinks because we had no idea of the extent of his torment, or that it would go on troubling him for years to come. He was our pride and joy – a longed-for boy, our first son, the heir to Glen.

Charlie and Henry's relationship was strained, and Charlie

would often be quite mean – moving away when Henry went to sit next to him or refusing to touch something Henry had touched. Henry had a very different character and was easy in comparison, with nothing untoward about him and a calm disposition. Instead of graffitiing his desk with swastikas, Henry went off to Buckingham Palace for weekly dancing lessons with Prince Andrew, which he really enjoyed.

In 1968, after Charlie and Henry, I had a third son, Christopher, who even as a baby had a really lovable character and seemed to bring my two older sons closer together. After a few years, Charlie appeared to be more settled, smiling more, his rituals lessening. Happiest at Glen, he'd go off with the gamekeepers for hours or would ride his mini motorbike round the estate. We thought everything was fine, that his troubled days were behind him. I was so relieved: all I wanted was for my children to be happy – I had desperately wanted to have them. Having grown up in the war, my friends and I had all longed for big families, feeling it was nature's way of replacing a lost generation. But although I had these three wonderful boys, I secretly wanted a girl. I had saved my childhood dolls thinking that one day I would have a daughter to give them to. In 1970, I was thrilled when I ended up having not one daughter but two when our twins, May and Amy, were born. I hadn't been expecting twins. I'd just thought I was having another large boy – Henry had weighed ten pounds nine ounces. When the girls were born, a delighted Colin rushed off to Paris to buy outfits from Baby Dior, as well as coming up with their pretty anagram names.

Life felt complete, but when I think about all five children's childhoods, I see a marked difference in Christopher and the twins' childhoods compared to Charlie and Henry's. Charlie was twelve years older than the twins, Henry ten, so the older boys were already at boarding school by the time Christopher and the girls were born. There was such a big gap between my children's ages, it was almost like having two families.

While Charlie and Henry had had a succession of nannies, who came and went, the younger three had stability, which made all the difference. This came in the form of a nanny called Barbara Barnes, who was from Holkham village, her father working on the estate. The children adored her, and she became an ally to me. She stayed with us for twelve years, until the twins went to boarding school in 1982, when she went on to become Princes William and Harry's nanny but has stayed in our lives ever since.

As well as being adored by the children, Barbara got on well with Colin and dealt with his more difficult behaviour extremely well. Once I heard a terribly loud banging from Colin's study and then I heard him shouting. Unhesitating, Barbara marched into the study, to find Colin standing on the table, stamping his feet and yelling. She said firmly, 'Lord Glenconner, will you get down and be quiet? You'll frighten the children.' And he did. Just like that. Another time, Colin, Barbara, all five children and I were in a tiny plane near Mustique when suddenly the pilot warned us that he might have to make a crash landing in the sea. Having been told to put on our life jackets, we sat very quietly, hoping everything would be all right, except Colin, who panicked. Putting his snorkel and mask on, he started shouting and scrambling around, searching for the inflatable life raft. As soon as he had found it, Henry pulled the rip cord, the raft promptly filling the cabin.

Barbara got out a pair of scissors from her bag and punctured the raft, which deflated, although rather slowly. By this stage, Colin was screaming at the top of his lungs, so she said very loudly to him, 'Will you be quiet, Lord Glenconner! You're scaring us all!' And, once again, he did. He would never have stopped if I had told him to do so. The plane didn't crash but the raft had to be removed before we were able to get out, Colin disembarking rather sheepishly, having taken off his snorkel and mask.

Barbara was always on hand to manage situations and made it easier for me to interact with the children because we worked as a team. With Christopher, I couldn't bear to give up breastfeeding, so for a year Barbara and Christopher came with Colin and me to all the different weekend events, and when the twins were babies, she would give one a bottle, while I fed the other.

It was such a joy to have two little girls, although they mostly seemed to prefer each other's company – they liked sleeping together, tucked up in one cot. Sometimes I felt unwanted because they had each other and didn't need me in the way I'd thought a daughter would. Barbara understood how I felt, which helped. I would never have confided in anyone else, especially not Colin.

I felt relieved I had Barbara because not only did I know that my children were being looked after properly when I wasn't with them but she made it easier for me to interact with them, allowing me a better balance between being a mother and a wife.

When the twins were toddlers Barbara would take them and Christopher to Ranelagh Gardens, part of the grounds at the Royal Hospital, Chelsea. It was a very formal place to go because the nannies would sit on different park benches according to the titles of the family they were employed by – nannies working for earls wouldn't dare sit on the bench full of nannies employed by dukes.

Every morning, I'd take Christopher and on Barbara's day out the twins to the gardens, pushing a huge double pram, which looked like a tank. They loved the gardens because instead of there being a flat lawn, like most of the other London parks, there were hillocks covered with bushes, so they could escape from the watchful eyes of the adults. I was always amazed to see the lengths some people went to – one pram had the family's crest painted on the side, and some children's sleeves were pinned to a piece of white linen that was tucked over the child's lap when they were seated in a pram, maintaining an appearance of perfection as they were wheeled along.

Looking back, Barbara was almost identical in character to my beloved governess Billy Williams, having the same effect on my younger children as Billy had had on me. They were very settled and secure in their routine. But Charlie and Henry lost out, only becoming a bigger part of our lives when Christopher was born. Colin always said he was sure Charlie would have fared better if Barbara had been around when he was small, certain that Charlie's odd behaviour would never have materialised if he had had a decent, permanent nanny like her.

While nannies were a staple part of family life, so was

boarding school, but while the children loved Barbara, they hated being sent away to school, although the twins found it easier because they had each other. It was agonising seeing them all so upset. I would drive them to school and each one would be in tears, which would set me off, making it worse. We tried to make up for this: in the holidays, Colin planned trips for us to take with the children, introducing them to different countries and cultures. At one point he decided to take us all to every capital in Europe. We went to Amsterdam, Madrid, Rome, but, not wanting to go to Berlin, Colin had the wonderful idea of going to King Ludwig's castles in Bavaria. The children loved the castles, on which Disneyland's fantasy designs are based. When I took them to a room that was full of kit-kat portraits of all the women Ludwig had had affairs with, despite him mostly preferring his own sex, they giggled in delight when I pointed out one of my ancestors, Jane Digby, who was staring down at us from the wall, and told them her story. She had fallen for King Ludwig when she was sent away from Holkham after being caught having an affair with the librarian.

The very best holiday we ever went on wasn't until the twins were about fifteen years old. We took Nick Courtney with us, a great friend, who used to work with Colin. Colin organised a camping trip in the Himalayas, which started off predictably shakily because Colin got very cross with me for some obscure reason but then he relaxed. Perhaps it was the mountain air but soon he was interacting with the children and became rather like a child himself, dissolving into hysterics when a cow peed on his tent. The relaxed atmosphere meant we all had a lot of fun, despite the pouring rain, which led to little streams running through our tents. Deciding to abandon camping, Colin managed to sort out an alternative immediately – a Kashmir houseboat, which was painted in bright colours and suited us perfectly. The holiday continued smoothly.

These holidays were a marvellous experience for the children. Colin was like a walking encyclopaedia, knowing a great deal about a great many things, and had moments of being utterly wonderful, getting them to look at things in new ways and igniting their imaginations.

When the twins were young and Mustique was still developing, we spent Christmas and Easter all together at Glen, the house resounding with the children's shrieks of excitement as they opened their stockings on Christmas morning and ran around the garden on Easter Sunday on big Easter-egg hunts. Glen was a brilliant house for children because of the space and size, providing endless opportunities for games. Colin and I used to play a game with them called 'Rescue'. Everybody went to hide, except one of us who was 'the hunter' and would stay on a sofa in the hall, which would be their prison. The hunter had to guard the sofa but also had to leave to find the others, capturing anyone on sight. Colin was brilliant at being the hunter because he would be so theatrical, calling out as he searched, saying things like 'I'm coming to get you . . . I know you're there . . . fee fi fo fum . . .' following the sound of giggles coming from a linen cupboard or from behind a door.

It was one of those games in which people crept along the corridors, then burst out on each other in peals of laughter, going on for hours if someone was particularly sneaky or patient: the sort of game best played in a house like Glen, full of nooks and crannies and different staircases, giving everybody a circuit. We all loved it. It reminded me of 'the Dark Game' that Billy Williams had introduced me and Carey to: she'd turn all the lights out and try to find us as we ran away, bumping into things, giggling in the dark. In life there are some things, often simple things, that can make you incredibly happy and for me playing Rescue with the children and Colin, and the Dark Game with my beloved sister and governess, are some of my happiest memories.

Every August, Princess Margaret would bring her children, David and Sarah, with Nanny Sumner, to Glen on their way down from Balmoral. As Princess Margaret played the piano and sang Glenn Miller's 'Chattanooga Choo Choo', we all joined in. The song became a firm favourite among the children. In the daytime they would go off to the Military Tattoo while the adults went to the Edinburgh Festival.

We had an Italian butler at Glen called Elio. One evening when we came back, Elio rushed up to me and said, 'Lady Anne, something extraordinary happened tonight. You must ask Nanny Barnes and Nanny Sumner about it.'

The next morning, I asked Barbara and she explained. 'Nanny Sumner and I had just put all nine children to bed, when Elio appeared very flustered. He told us to come – "Quick, quick, quick!" And out of the window we saw a hovering cigar-shaped object with green lights. It looked like a UFO. It came down the valley over the birks and slowly went off.'

When I told Princess Margaret she said, 'What had they been drinking?' but when we went up to where they said they had seen it, all the heather was completely flattened. Colin rang up the nearest air-force base, in case they had been doing some sort of exercise that could explain it, but they were none the wiser. Over the following days, other people reported similar sightings in Peebles and the surrounding area, and we were all left wondering what on earth it was. The UFO was never seen again, but each August the same routine was rolled out, and our families intertwined happily.

As well as Glen, we spent time at Holkham with my parents, going to the beach for picnics and for walks in the pine woods, collecting fir cones and shells. Carey and Sarah would come too with their families: Carey lived near Holkham and had married Brian Basset, a friend of the Queen Mother, so she spent a lot of time at Birkhall, the Queen Mother's house in Scotland, to fish. Carey was much better at fishing than a lot of the men, much to their irritation. She would bring her three sons for picnics with us and was a huge hit with my children. She was double-jointed and would do this funny walk with her bottom sticking out and have everyone in hysterics.

Sarah had also got married, to David Walter, and was living in Perthshire with their two sons. Carey's husband, Brian, didn't appreciate Colin's character but David and Colin got on very well so it was always fun when we took the children to stay in their thatched house. All the children would make dens and campfires next to the stream and Sarah would take them red squirrel spotting. When Sarah came down to Holkham in the summer, she would bring her dachshunds and the twins would walk them along the dunes. Then we'd go crabbing, filling our buckets with crabs before turning the buckets on their sides and watching the crabs race back to the water.

I taught all the children to sail in the creeks of Burnham Overy Staithe, just as my mother had taught me. I'm not sure I successfully transferred the passion to my children. Sailing brings out the worst in people and I think I was rather fierce. Suddenly requests are demands – I suppose because of the risk involved there is an unusual priority of clarity over politeness – so there I would be suddenly shouting orders: 'Pull this!' or 'No, not that!'

Although none of them naturally took to sailing, they all loved going to Holkham and enjoyed all the things I had done as a child, like jumping into the fountain on a hot day, and dashing off around the park. I would tell them all about Lord Nelson, how he had grown up in the next village and paced along the banks of the creeks we sailed on, looking out to sea, hoping to be called to battle, which captured their imaginations.

Once the twins were older, we often spent Easter and Christmas on Mustique. There was an Easter-bonnet competition every year, which the twins loved. May was staunchly independent but Amy sought Colin's help and he approached the task with characteristic enthusiasm. One year Amy won with a bonnet Colin dubbed 'Goldilocks' and stuck gold streamers to her hair; the next year he made a hole in a gourd and she wore it like a deep-sea diver's helmet, complete with a snorkel and mask. Everybody entered these competitions, including the adults – I remember Bianca Jagger parading around with the top of a cactus stuck to her head.

But, of course, the better the time the children had at home, the more they would dread going back to school, and nothing I was able to do made saying goodbye any easier for any of us. I don't know if anyone ever enjoyed being carted off to boarding school – Prince Charles used to write long letters to my mother from Gordonstoun, saying how much he longed to come home and complaining of the endless weeks without a holiday: the longest term was fourteen weeks.

When I was at school, parents only visited the school once a year and the conditions were far from ideal. I also had to endure the doodlebugs, which were bombs, flying overhead and the hard stale bread that was put into the oven for a second life. We were all given five boiled sweets a week, which I would hide in my doll's petticoat so they weren't stolen, and we had to endure powdered egg, which was utterly disgusting.

In comparison, my children went to good schools and were made a fuss of when they were at home in the holidays. When we were all in London, a weekly delivery of the freshest food from Glen would be sent down on the overnight train and our butler would fetch it from King's Cross. Schools had changed so much by the time I had children that there were all sorts of exeats and opportunities to visit or take the children away for weekends. Some terms it seemed they spent more time out of school than in.

But, despite my efforts, Charlie, as an adult, described Colin and me as 'remote figures in his childhood'. He was right, but I had never thought about it like that until he said those words. Only through my relationship with Barbara, and her relationship with my children, did it occur to me that there were different ways of approaching motherhood, that maybe the approach I knew, especially with the older boys, was not necessarily the most fulfilling for me as a mother or for the children. Sadly, by the time I had grasped this, the children had grown up.

I look at my daughter May now, and I am in awe of how she works full time, supports her husband *and* brings up her children without a nanny, so much more consistently involved in their everyday life than I ever was. Compared to some friends in my generation, I was quite hands on, but compared to my daughter's generation, I can see how much things have changed.

CHAPTER TEN

Lady in Waiting

ONE DAY IN early 1971, after the twins' christening, at which Princess Margaret had become a godmother to May, she said to me, 'I do hope you're not going to have any more children.'

I replied, 'Absolutely not. Three boys *and* twin girls are quite enough.'

'Well, in that case,' she said, evidently pleased with my answer, 'would you like to be one of my Ladies in Waiting?'

The invitation couldn't have come at a better time because Colin was going through a particularly difficult phase of which Princess Margaret was fully aware. She wasn't daunted by his behaviour, having been used to the King's temper – my father was always retrieving wastepaper baskets that the

King had kicked across the room. It had been Princess Margaret who had been the best person to calm the King down, often being summoned to change his mood, and she was always able to ignore Colin's behaviour, reminding me to do the same.

From time to time, Princess Margaret witnessed Colin's histrionics, the most public of which ended up with him receiving a letter from John King, the head of British Airways, banning Colin for life from using his planes. The three of us were flying back from America, and for some reason, while Princess Margaret and I had first-class tickets, Colin didn't: he was ushered right when we got on to the plane as we went left.

Princess Margaret and I sat down in our seats, oblivious to Colin's plight. He flipped, demanding to be seated near us, and when the cabin crew denied him, he lay on the floor, in the middle of the aisle, having a full-blown tantrum. His wails were loud enough for us to hear and we were absolutely horrified by the scene he was making, I instinctively got up to try to sort it out. Princess Margaret said very firmly, 'Sit down, Anne.'

There was a kerfuffle as security dragged him off the plane. We saw him out of our window being hauled away, still screaming, 'Help me, Anne! Anne! Help me!'

Princess Margaret said, 'Take absolutely no notice, Anne.'

Colin was arrested and the plane took off without him. Just like my mother would have done, Princess Margaret disregarded the incident but knew only too well that I sometimes needed a break. Colin turned up three days later, but nothing more was said.

Given an official purpose and responsibility not only gave me a distraction but also meant I became more independent of Colin. He was utterly in awe of the Royal Family, especially Princess Margaret, so he was very proud that I had been given an official role and very supportive in my acceptance of her offer. I think he felt it somehow cemented his closeness with her, and would mean that we'd spend even more time in her company, assuming he would be able to come along to everything I was invited to. It didn't quite work like that, much to his disappointment, but he did spend more time with her, something he always looked forward to. I think their friendship accentuated his desire to impress – Princess Margaret being on Mustique was the perfect reason to throw parties that he made even more spectacular, which in turn meant that he would be seen as a wonderfully creative genius, which he was.

Princess Margaret was no fool, deliberately choosing friends to be Ladies in Waiting. She appointed quite a lot of us, including her cousin Jean Wills, Janie Stevens, Davina Alexander and Elizabeth Cavendish, who had introduced Princess Margaret to Tony Armstrong-Jones, and Annabel Whitehead, who now holds the office of Lady in Waiting to the Queen.

I was Lady in Waiting to Princess Margaret until her death, spanning three decades, merging friendship and duties: sometimes I would spend my time with Princess Margaret as her official Lady in Waiting; at others, she would be assisted by another and I would be with her as a friend.

My mother was Lady of the Bedchamber to the Queen from 1953 until 1973 so for two years we overlapped, carrying out similar roles. Most of our commitments revolved around accompanying the Queen and Princess Margaret on royal engagements and special occasions, making sure the event went as smoothly as possible. Just as my mother was for the Queen, I was there so Princess Margaret felt she had someone with her she knew and trusted wherever she was, in case she needed something.

Ladies in Waiting are only a small part of the Royal Household and the Queen has a much bigger household than Princess Margaret did. Princess Margaret had a chauffeur, a butler, a chef, a scullery maid and two daily maids, who spent a lot of time replacing her ash trays since she was a chain-smoker. She also had a dresser called Mrs Greenfield, who would organise each outfit, laying the clothes out in advance so Princess Margaret could choose what she wanted to wear. Mrs Greenfield also helped her dress as well as running her bath every evening. The Princess also had a hairdresser who would either come to the Palace before an event or she would go to the salon, where she would also have her nails done, but she always did her own make-up. There were several protection officers, headed by John Harding, who became a friend over the years, staying at his post for decades. These people made up the personal staff, and then there was Nigel Napier, her private secretary, who would be found in the office, along with four secretaries.

Princess Margaret had a good reputation for looking after her household, making sure her dresser and maid had nice rooms if they went away with her and that everybody was being looked after. Every year, Princess Margaret had a Christmas tea for her Ladies in Waiting. Under the huge

Christmas tree there would be lots of parcels and she would hand them out to us. Sometimes she gave us really thoughtful presents, but at others she would give us things she deemed useful: she was rather fond of kitchen gadgets and once she gave Jean Wills a loo brush, saying, 'I noticed you didn't have one of these when I came to stay.' In fact, Jean had hidden the loo brush when Princess Margaret had visited, and was rather upset by the gesture. Sometimes we'd be given handbags that had clearly been given to her and rejected after she had used them a few times. But she could also be generous, giving me several antiques I had admired while out shopping with her.

Most of the royal engagements I went to with Princess Margaret involved visiting hospitals, factories, schools or charities of which she was patron. John Harding and a couple of other protection officers would come on day trips, and if we went away for longer, Nigel Napier would come, as well as the dresser, Mrs Greenfield.

All these engagements might have been boring, but they weren't. It was interesting to meet all sorts of people, and when it came to her charities, Princess Margaret chose only the ones she really wanted to be a part of and, determined to make a difference, would embrace her duties fully. This energetic approach meant we had long discussions about each of her charities and she offered all her Ladies in Waiting the chance to be a part of the organisations we showed an interest in. Because my cousin Angus Ogilvy suffered from arthritis, I became involved in the National Rheumatoid Arthritis Society, and I was president of SOS (now called Scope), and the National Association of Maternal and Child

Welfare, arranging masses of fundraising events, held mostly on Sundays when stars such as Vera Lynn, Roger Moore, Bob Hope and John Mills were free.

Similar to Colin, Princess Margaret was fiercely knowledgeable about a great many things, so when we were on our way to an engagement, she would eagerly tell me an array of facts, anything and everything about the regiments to which she was Colonel-in-Chief, and quotes from the Bible, which she often used, rather naughtily, to put the many clerics she met on the spot.

Being married to Colin had afforded me years of good practice for the role. Always trying to pre-empt issues that could easily arise meant I had become very good at anticipating his needs, and this skill was vital for any Lady in Waiting. If we were at lunch or dinner, I would stay within sight of her so she could always look at me. From her expression, I would know if she needed me. When we arrived somewhere new, I did things like find out where the lavatories were so that she wouldn't have to ask, and would always stand outside the door so no one else came in.

There were dozens of little things that became second nature to me, which helped her to relax and meant the official engagements ran more smoothly. I got to know small but useful things, such as that she drank a gin and tonic at lunch and whisky with water in the evening. It meant I could tell the people at each event, so she wasn't given the wrong thing. Not only did having someone with her who could communicate her needs help everybody relax a little, it also meant that Princess Margaret wasn't constantly faced with having to answer the same, albeit well-meant, questions each time she went to an event, which made it more enjoyable for her too.

If she was going to a cocktail party, or anything that involved a lot of people, I would be given a list of the most distinguished guests and anybody else she particularly wanted to meet so I could find them among the crowd and lead them to her. This was a delicate process of diplomacy because I would have to judge by Princess Margaret's expression whether she wanted to stay in the conversation she was having, or whether she was ready for the next introduction, whereupon I would usher the person forward. There I was, hovering nearby, waiting to swap one person for another, trying to be as seamless and polite as possible.

Once I had successfully set Princess Margaret up with the next guest, I would be studying the list, trying to match names with the faces of people I'd often never met before. I wanted to scurry around and identify them prior to any encounter, but instead I had to be relaxed and glide around alongside her. Sometimes I would lose her – she was so small and would always be surrounded by people, so if I had gone off to find someone in particular, quite often I would then have to search frantically for her but without giving away my panic. I had to be like a swan, looking calm on the surface when actually I was paddling like mad underneath the water.

On days when Princess Margaret didn't have an engagement and was at home in Kensington Palace, she was a creature of habit. She always had lunch at half past one, sitting down for three courses, often eating the same thing, especially prawn cocktail, which she enjoyed, remaining convinced that the Marie-Rose sauce was a far more exotic mix than its staple ingredients of mayonnaise and tomato ketchup. She was rather fond of teatime: at five o'clock she would be found drinking a cup of very weak Earl Grey with a ginger nut or Leibniz chocolate biscuit to accompany it, and at dinner she always had the same pudding: a lemon sorbet served in half a lemon, like the ones found in some Indian restaurants. Cream was offered alongside the sorbet, and she would pour a little bit on at a time, endlessly amazed by what happened to the cream. She'd say, 'Oh, do look, it's so lovely – it's freezing, it's freezing just like that.'

I really enjoyed going to Kensington Palace and especially looked forward to being in the office to help write and sort out the thank-you letters after an event because I was very fond of Nigel Napier. The most diplomatic person I've ever come across, he employed his tact throughout his often challenging role, which involved getting Princess Margaret out of sticky situations with his clever and inventive explanations . . .

Ever protective, he was also very fond of Princess Margaret and we always had a lot of fun together. Getting on with the other people who supported Princess Margaret made everything much more enjoyable and a lot easier, although when she came to Mustique, only John Harding, and occasionally Nigel, would come with her. Instead, when she arrived, Colin would have arranged local security that would team up with John and they would stay with us in our prefabricated house. Colin, accepting that I would be at her beck and call and not his, would rush around in preparation for her arrival, making sure the police were on standby for her and lining up everybody he could muster so she had a grand welcome.

Even though it was basic, and for years there were no celebrities and no grandeur on the island, she had privacy – a bolthole. It was far from formal, partly because Princess Margaret liked feeling relaxed and partly because there wasn't any choice. In the daytime, she would wear one of her many whale-boned swimming costumes with a short skirt. They were patterned with either stripes or flowers and suited her hourglass figure, but I began to notice that whispers circulated whenever she got out of the water. I soon realised it was because her swimming costumes were transparent when wet. Approaching the subject delicately, I said, 'Ma'am, I wonder whether you are aware that your swimming costume is rather see-through. Perhaps I could get it lined for you.'

'Oh, Anne,' she said, somewhat exasperated. 'I don't care. If they want to look, they can look.' And that was that.

The days were spent leisurely, revolving around the late hours Princess Margaret kept. Just before lunch, we'd normally go off to one of the beaches for a picnic, setting up a parasol in the sand. The food left a lot to be desired in the early days, often requiring a large dollop of Hellmann's mayonnaise to hide the blandness.

Princess Margaret didn't like the feeling of sand between her toes, though, which was a bit of a problem. Colin came up with a simple solution she was very happy with. Every time she went on the beach, he made sure there was always a bowl of fresh water and lots of clean towels for her, so she could rinse her feet, ridding them of sand, whenever she felt she needed to.

After lunch, we would all go for a swim, the conversation

never ceasing, Princess Margaret in full flow. As she swam breaststroke, keeping her head above the water, I would swim sideways, treading water, rather erratically, so I could continue the conversation. We would swim out in the bay and around the yachts. Often, we'd be invited up on deck for a drink of water. We'd accept, although wishing we'd been offered a more exciting drink. Everybody was always stunned when they realised Princess Margaret was dripping wet on their deck, a reaction that never failed to quietly amuse me.

In the late afternoons we'd return to the house and, like a big sister, she loved untangling my hair. Standing behind me while she brushed it, she would comment on all the different natural highlights, leaving me with a feeling of contentment, once she'd finished, and my hair beautifully sleek. She enjoyed doing things like that – she always offered to rub on sun lotion or apply ointment to mosquito bites.

In the early evening we'd sit at Basil's Bar, drinking sundowners and watching for the green flash, as we'd done ever since she had come alone for the first time. Then we'd have dinner with anyone who was there at the time, although friends were limited and sometimes it would just be Princess Margaret, Colin and me, drumming up our own entertainment, which Colin was good at, or playing cards late into the night.

By the early seventies, not only was there an electricity generator but the houses on Mustique were being built and the once-barren scrubland full of manchineel trees showed a glimmer of things to come: more and more villas appeared, statuesque, on the hillsides. Between 1960 and 1978, Oliver Messel designed seventeen house plans in his particular style, which was eventually described as 'Caribbean Palladian'. Most of the houses were based on a classic plantation house and he concentrated on creating what he described as 'indoor-outdoor living'. A master of scene-setting, he incorporated arches in all the houses to frame the views, which became like perfect backdrops.

All the houses were slightly different, and had wide verandas or terraces; the interiors were generally white, with accents of bright colours. A lasting legacy that went beyond Mustique was Oliver's use of his favourite colour – a sage green, which he used for the wooden shutters and doors, now known as both 'Messel Green' and 'Mustique Green'. As each house was finished, crates and crates of antiques and soft furnishings were shipped to Mustique and Colin would unpack them, buzzing with excitement, before I helped him set up the houses. Realising people bought them more readily if no imagination was required, we lived in each one until it was sold, then moved to the next. Although moving around was disruptive, I had got used to it and the children, who would come out on their school holidays, enjoyed comparing each house to the next, seeing it as part of the adventure.

Princess Margaret came only once out of high season, in the year before her house was finished in 1971, curious to see how it was developing, but chiefly because she needed a break from Tony, her marriage continuing to go downhill. The trip was not a success because storms rolled in from the Atlantic, changing the atmosphere, a grey descending on the island, coming as an unwelcome surprise. Princess Margaret promptly renamed where she was staying 'Gloomsville' and never returned again before Christmas.

Having been very involved with the designs, discussing little details with Colin and Oliver, she had become increasingly excited about her house's completion. When we were both in London in the months leading up to it being finished, she had rung up several times to ask me to go shopping with her.

I had been delighted at the invitation, looking forward to going to Colefax & Fowler or some other glamorous place, but she always chose Peter Jones. Off we went to Sloane Square, where we were met by the manager and taken around the furniture and fabric sections. It was all very low key, with just John Harding the protection officer following a few steps behind. She chose very simple things, mostly white furniture and Laura Ashley-type curtains. Later, she had one or two things from antiques shops shipped over for the main sitting room, including some glass lamps, which she filled with shells, carrying on collecting things throughout the year.

In February 1972, she came to stay in her newly completed house, naming it Les Jolies Eaux – French for 'pretty waters'. She was delighted with the house, which had panoramic views, framed by the arch in the sitting room, which had a wall of French windows that opened out on to a swimming pool, surrounded by a terrace.

We all came out to Mustique with the children, supported by Barbara, and everybody helped her unpack. The mood was one of excitement as Charlie and Henry opened boxes for her, and they'd peer inside before she would smile broadly, satisfied with the items she got out of each box.

Les Jolies Eaux made Princess Margaret very happy. It was the only house she ever owned and provided her with an independent base from her husband. Not only was he prone to mood swings, like Colin, they were both also having affairs. We complained but without over-indulging, speaking bluntly, then brushing our troubles aside, concentrated on doing the things we enjoyed. She loved collecting shells to make tables decorated with shell tops, so together we would comb the beach, then take them back to the house to clean, lining them up out in the sun. It is surprising how such activities can have a calming effect and divert attention from any difficulties.

In the summer of 1973 Glen, as usual, was full of friends staying for days on end. Towards the middle of August, Princess Margaret was on her way to join us for a long weekend. As we were busy preparing a huge dinner party for the end of the week, a friend called regretfully to cancel, thereby leaving us one short. Because everybody went abroad in August, Colin suggested that I should ring up his 'Aunt Nose', Violet Wyndham (who had a large nose), because she seemed to know everybody and was bound to come up with a suitable suggestion. When I explained the problem to her, she gave me the number of Roddy Llewellyn, whose father Harry had famously won the only gold medal for Great Britain in the 1952 Olympics – in the team jumping equestrian event with his marvellous horse, Foxhunter.

Young and available, although we'd never met him, Roddy fitted the bill. I remember feeling rather awkward ringing him up, even though Violet had rung him to forewarn him about the invitation. I said, 'Hello, you don't know me, but we're having a weekend party at Glen, and I know it's rather rude of me to ask at such short notice, but somebody's dropped out. Would you like to come?'

To my delight and relief, he accepted and was able to catch the train to Edinburgh almost immediately. Colin drove to Edinburgh station to meet him, accompanied by Charlie, who was by then a teenager, and Princess Margaret, who was intrigued because she knew Roddy's father. I stayed behind, busy sorting out all the rooms, getting ready for everybody. They didn't return for hours. Finally I got the call from John Harding warning me that the car would be arriving in ten minutes – something the protection officers always did whenever Princess Margaret was due to arrive somewhere. I stood outside, ready to greet them at the door, wondering what they had all been up to.

When the car pulled up, there were Princess Margaret and Roddy in the back, more or less holding hands. Colin explained that they had met him off the train and gone for lunch at a bistro in Edinburgh. Princess Margaret and Roddy had immediately clicked, even though Roddy was seventeen years younger than her.

Charlie then explained, with a twinkle in his eye, that they had taken so long because Princess Margaret had whisked Roddy off shopping to find him some swimming trunks for the pool. With a big grin on his face, Charlie said that the trunks were so tight they could have been described as 'budgie smugglers'.

I said to Colin, 'Oh, gosh, what have we done?'

When Roddy had been at Glen for about two days, he told me how beautiful he thought Princess Margaret was, and I said, 'Don't tell me, tell her.'

So he did, and from then on, Princess Margaret and Roddy were inseparable, staying up late after dinner, sitting at one of the card tables in the drawing room after an evening of playing bridge or canasta. They remained very close to each other, their heads almost touching.

It soon became clear that they had, quite simply, fallen in love. Roddy bore a striking resemblance physically to Tony but, unlike Tony, he was very kind. He was full of entertaining stories and had a schoolboy humour that appealed instantly to Princess Margaret. After the weekend in Glen, they were together for eight years, and friends for life, making all the difference to Princess Margaret who, by the time they met, had endured several years of unhappiness with Tony.

By the mid-seventies, Princess Margaret's marriage was at breaking point, but with two children and being very religious, she didn't want a divorce. In the end, Tony pushed her to it because in 1978 his mistress, Lucy Lindsay-Hogg, became pregnant with their first child. Day after day there were screaming headlines, with pictures of Princess Margaret caught looking miserable, not helped by the fact that she had the type of face that looked sombre when she wasn't smiling.

During this press-frenzied time, and in an attempt to escape their ghastly intrusion into her private life, over the next several months Princess Margaret would come quite frequently to stay with me in my Norfolk farmhouse or at Glen. She didn't bring a dresser, just John Harding, whom the children adored on account of his ability to tear a telephone directory in half.

Roddy would arrive later in the evening and I would leave them to relax. Going through such a private matter in public, and the scandal of being the first high-profile member of the Royal Family to divorce since King Henry VIII, was enough to make anybody need a friend.

The visits to Glen and Norfolk were completely different from the formal royal engagements. The house in Norfolk is the one I bought from my father at the beginning of my marriage, and where I live now. It is an old flint-stone farmhouse surrounded by fields. There is no glamour – people wear wellington boots and mackintoshes – but I think that appealed to Princess Margaret. There was a sense of her being truly 'off duty' when she spent time there, similar to when she was on Mustique.

She would turn up with her Marigold gloves and, not wanting to be an imposition with the absence of her maid, she brought her own kettle. This was because she was used to having breakfast in bed: she brought it so she could make her own tea in her bedroom each morning. The problem came when she didn't know how to work the kettle. 'Oh, Anne, do you think you could help? I think there's something wrong with my kettle. It doesn't seem to be working properly.' In fact, although she had been considerate in bringing the kettle, it was more trouble than it was worth, and I ended up doing everything anyway.

Over the years, she adopted the same routine: she would insist on cleaning my car – with Roddy when he came too – and she'd lay all the fires, always reminding me, 'You weren't a Girl Guide, but I was, so leave the fires to me.' Our friendship was ordinary, and she relished mundane activities far more than I did. I would find her dusting the bookshelves and, more than once, dismantling my chandelier to clean it in the bath.

She loved being outside, and we would spend whole days pottering about in my garden, kneeling down next to each other weeding. When we went out, she didn't want to meet anybody new: she just wanted to put on her brown lace-ups and mackintosh and explore gardens, churches or country houses with me and Colin, if he was there, and a few select people I would invite. Often our mutual friend Jack Plumb came to stay. He was a history professor at Cambridge and a brilliant conversationalist. Sometimes we would go and have dinner with him in college with a group of undergraduates, and Princess Margaret would be in her element, easily holding her own, despite being acutely aware she had never been to university.

Another friend I invited to Norfolk when Princess Margaret was staying was Christopher Tadgell, a professor at Canterbury. He knew everything there is to know about architecture and churches so we would go off round the county, visiting churches, and Princess Margaret would ask all sorts of questions, absorbing absolutely everything.

In the evenings, we would all sit in my drawing room, she always in the chair to the left of the fireplace, and talk for hours, often about what we had seen and done during the day. 'What about another little drinkie-winkie?' she would say, and Colin would disappear into the drinks cupboard and come out with another round of drinks – whisky for her, vodka tonic for me, while John Harding bumbled around in the kitchen, reading the newspaper until Princess Margaret eventually turned in for the night.

People complained about Princess Margaret being difficult, but I think quite often it was because she was bored or fed up. She would often be invited to meet strangers at lunch or dinner but, not surprisingly, her idea of fun wasn't sitting next to the mayor, the bishop and the chief of police for Sunday lunch. When she was staying with friends, she didn't want to be on show. She also appreciated being asked what she wanted to do and what she wanted to eat but she often wasn't. Great dinners would be arranged, when actually she preferred much simpler food.

I minded very much when people complained about her behaviour. I knew she could be difficult: she was known for her icy stare if she felt someone had overstepped the mark, often accompanied with a curt remark normally with good reason. She had moments of being very grand indeed, but I worked round these 'royal moments', finding her quietly amusing. I didn't like it when people criticised her, especially when she was already being hounded by the press.

Somehow, Tony had got the press on his side and Princess Margaret was vilified. Before they divorced, I went on a few engagements with both of them, which were no fun at all because Tony was so unpredictable. I would go to Kensington Palace to collect Princess Margaret and would instantly know if he was there because there would be an uncomfortable feeling in the air. One time, when Princess Margaret was unwell, Jean Wills and I were asked to sit outside her room to stop Tony going in. It was extremely awkward because Tony was very angry about it and wanted to let Princess Margaret know how he felt. To discomfort her, I suppose, he stormed off down the stairs, slammed the front door, got into his car and, revving his engine, drove round and round the courtyard near her window, honking the horn.

Princess Margaret was devastated that her marriage had failed, feeling very strongly about divorce, as did I. In some situations I can quite see how it is impossible to avoid, as was the case for Princess Margaret. It was the same for my grandmother, Ga, who had divorced her husband, the 8th Earl of Hardwicke, because of 'cruelty'. The details were vague, but I think he had chased her around the house with a knife enough times for her fears to be taken seriously. They got divorced quietly and it was never mentioned again.

We weren't alone in dealing with difficult marriages. My sister Carey had trouble with her husband, who, after a few years, refused to talk directly to her and instead would talk through his Labrador, saying things like 'Tell her to bring the bloody paper over here.'

When I'd discovered Colin was having affairs, I had been incredibly jealous at first and found it very hard to accept. He had also had offers from men, often rather proudly telling me that Field Marshal Montgomery had taken a shine to him when he'd set the record for high jump in the Irish Guards and had stayed keen on him. Over the years, Colin had lots of girlfriends, some I knew of, others I didn't. I tried not to mind. When he died, a lot of them came out of the woodwork, including one African American lady, for whom he had bought a nail bar in America. I only found out about her when she went to the press and I read about how he had broken her wrist. Hopefully her wrist healed well enough for her to carry on doing people's nails.

There was one particular mistress he had for years. I had heard rumours about her to start with, but it was only when Colin and I turned up to a party in Kew Gardens and I saw them together that I could sense immediately the unmistakable chemistry between them. You could absolutely tell, and I minded very much. There was never a flaming row between us, or a confession of any sort. I was too polite, which always irritated Colin. Occasionally, after a drink or two, I would start a screaming match with him, but not often.

I avoided confrontation and didn't want to degrade our marriage to a constant string of arguments. Apart from his infidelity and his temper, we got on so well and we both valued our relationship, which was based on a solid friendship. More to the point, we had five children, so I wanted to maintain unity for their sake. The odd thing was that Colin would complain to me about his girlfriends. He once told me, when he came back from some sand bar off Africa where he had taken this particular long-term mistress, 'I've had the worst holiday ever. And I'm afraid I've behaved rather badly.'

'Colin, that doesn't sound too good,' I replied, not quite sure what he could possibly expect me to say on the subject of his holiday with his mistress.

'I'm fed up with her! She went and broke her leg before the trip and the whole point of going there was to canoe and see wild animals, but when I tried to get her into it, her leg wouldn't fit in because the bloody thing is in plaster so won't bend. And then we had to lie in the boiling hot straw hut all day . . .' He went on and on, not knowing how ridiculous he sounded.

In the end I said, 'I really don't want to hear about your holiday with your mistress. I'm sorry you didn't have a good time, but can we talk about something else?' There was no point in feeling sorry for myself. Almost every single couple I could think of was interlaced with other people's husbands and wives. Rarely, it seemed, were there just the two partners in a marriage. It was an aristocratic curse. Affairs were expected and wives just worked around it. Even married to a princess, Tony wasn't satisfied, going off with a string of women.

Once I knew Colin had changed the playing field, I levelled it. I had a very dear friend for many years who was always wonderful to me: he made me laugh and we got on terribly well. We had lunch every week and spent the occasional weekend together. It made the whole situation bearable. I felt able to cope, happier and more independent. When Colin found out he was very jealous, but his own behaviour was so appalling, he couldn't really object. It had a positive effect on our marriage because I wasn't consumed by jealousy and it allowed our friendship to stay strong. We were always talking together and laughing a great deal without a feeling of bitterness.

Colin's long-term mistress had tried and failed to get him to leave me and marry her. When it came down to it, Colin and I remained loyal to one another. Colin never tried to divorce me. As he always said, 'We were brought up not to throw in the towel but to bite bullets and fold towels neatly.' While it was rather easier for him to say, I did agree with the sentiment.

CHAPTER ELEVEN

The Caribbean Spectaculars

*Mr Colin and Lady Anne Tennant
request the pleasure of the company of*

at a

*Birthday
Party*

*at Mustique
from Monday 22nd to Sunday 28th
November 1976*

OUR HOUSE ON Mustique, named The Great House after the original one that had been burned down, was the last house to be built by Oliver Messell, in 1978. It was perhaps the greatest of all, influenced by a mixture of eastern architecture. With a central circular room, which had a domed roof, inspired by Istanbul's Hagia Sophia, and ornate screens of open tiles from Asia and Indonesia, it was breezy and wonderfully light. Surrounded by a palm grove, which Colin had had the insight to plant when he had first bought the island, his pride and joy was the exquisitely carved temple brought from India. It looked as if it had been made from lace. Unfortunately, it arrived in various pieces, and the five men who assembled it put it

179

together in the wrong order, leaving Colin furious. This wasn't the first or the last time Colin had lost his cool throughout the development of Mustique: he had had several explosive arguments with Oliver, especially when Oliver wanted to use concrete painted like marble and Colin refused, buying a marble quarry to ensure both a good price and the final word.

The Great House was the last house Oliver ever designed and, sadly, he died just before it was completed. Colin and I attended his funeral in Barbados. We were late for the service, and when the taxi driver drove past the church, Colin got so cross that he communicated not only through shouting and screaming but also by biting the driver's arm, fortunately not drawing blood.

By then, having been married to Colin for over twenty years, I knew to expect this sort of behaviour, which I couldn't control and neither, apparently, could Colin. Although Colin was sometimes impossible to manage, it didn't take away from his achievements. When I look back on those years on Mustique, they are bursting with colour and energy, full of adventure, none of which I would have had without Colin. Recently I read in the papers that Mustique is 'unique', and something that could 'never be replicated'. I agree, and that's down to Colin and his vision.

It was Colin's eccentricity that helped put Mustique on the map: he used his flair to entice people to come and look round the island. To start with, most of the people were passing by and came ashore out of curiosity – Nelson Rockefeller, the American billionaire and 41st Vice President of the USA, anchored his yacht off Mustique, and with Bob Dylan's yacht also nearby, the word began to spread.

Janie Stevens, a great friend and another Lady in Waiting to Princess Margaret, was married to Jocelyn Stevens, who was the editor of *Queen* magazine, now *Harper's Bazaar*. After Colin and I mentioned that Mustique needed some publicity, Janie spoke to her husband, who sent the Queen's photographer cousin Patrick Lichfield, who was also a cousin of mine, to photograph us for an article. The result was a great success. In the glossy pages of the magazine there were double-spread photos of Princess Margaret surrounded by Colin, me and anyone else who was there – islanders and expats alike. The photos alluded to a bohemian atmosphere but with a unique twist of royalty, all within a picture-postcard backdrop of coconut palms and turquoise waters. The scene was as inviting as it was intriguing.

By the mid-seventies, a steady trickle of articles was being published about how Mustique was the new 'place to go'. Other than being a destination for Princess Margaret, this was a huge exaggeration, but it was easy to believe when Colin told people it was so – he made such an impression in his own right that *he* became a draw. He understood this and played up to it, even hoping that his own logo, a red capital G for Glenconner, would become famous.

People certainly had memorable tours with Colin, who went further than most to secure buyers: to show how deep the water was he would sometimes walk, fully clothed, out to sea until his hat floated off, even though the water was in fact only waist deep and actually he was walking on his knees.

Mick Jagger was the first proper celebrity to stay on Mustique, although his initial visit wasn't a success. He arrived, out of season, with his wife Bianca and his daughter

Jade in tow. He stayed for a week and left unimpressed, but his presence legitimised the claim that big names visited Mustique, generating more media attention.

Colin decided that if he threw extravagant parties, people would hear about them and want to be invited to these 'Caribbean Spectaculars'. Out of all the parties, his fiftieth birthday Golden Ball, in 1976, was the one that secured Mustique the label of being *the* hedonistic paradise for the rich and famous. And commercially it worked: directly after the party, Mick Jagger bought a villa called L'Ansecoy, which has panoramic views of St Vincent and Bequia. He also invited Princess Margaret and me to a Rolling Stones concert in London. It was so loud that we kept our fingers in our ears the whole time.

The fiftieth-birthday invitation was for almost a week's worth of parties, all-expenses-paid: the airfare, the accommodation and everything in between. Everybody stayed dotted around the island in different houses: Princess Margaret had Oliver Messel, Rupert Loewenstein, the financial manager of the Rolling Stones, his wife, my great friend Princess Josephine Loewenstein, and Carolina Herrera, the fashion designer famous for dressing a string of First Ladies from Jackie Kennedy to Michelle Obama, and her husband Reinaldo. Carolina always showed Princess Margaret and me her collections when we flew home via New York, and very generously would invite us to choose what we liked, her tailors making little changes for Princess Margaret so that what she picked was unique to her.

Once the island was full, the party started. Colin had planned every hour meticulously: a boat trip to see the wreck of

SS *Antilles*, which had come aground on the coral reef a few years before; there were calypso singers who sang among everyone, making up lyrics about many of the guests, and Dana Gillespie, who was famous for singing 'Andy Warhol', written by David Bowie, sang at the Cotton House. There were lunch parties held at different people's houses – at the architect Arne Hasselqvist's, the rum was served from an enormous old copper sugar pan. And then the finale, the Golden Ball, although Colin got so stressed in the run-up that he collapsed and had to be given an injection by the doctor to revive him for the night. It did the trick, and soon enough he was rushing around in his usual high-octane state of excitement.

It did look spectacular. People have often commented that they think Colin wanted Mustique to be where fantasies came true, and it certainly looked more like a dream than reality that night: everything was gold – the trees had been painted, the grass sprayed, and even the beach had been covered with gold glitter. Colin got some of the local lads oiled up, and they wore nothing at all except a gold-painted coconut strategically placed down below.

When people thought Colin had pulled out all the stops, there would be one more. He was always coming up with ideas to impress the guests, as though they were the audience for some great theatrical production – which, really, was what the parties were. Suddenly, more golden boys appeared on the beach carrying a litter, enclosed by gold streamers. They put it down, and out stepped Bianca Jagger.

The photos of the Golden Ball, taken by Robert Mapplethorpe, became iconic, especially those of Mick and Bianca Jagger: Mick looked slightly weird in a sort of pixie straw hat sprayed gold, and Bianca dressed as a character from *Gone With the Wind*, wearing a gold crinoline. The photos were published, and Colin was thrilled because he was also dressed up to the nines, in a skin-tight white satin suit, laced with gold. I was less thrilled because somebody had suggested that I should paint my face gold, but it had the most terrible effect, high-lighting every wrinkle and crease. I spent a lot of the party trying not to smile.

That night made Mustique famous for ever, mainly down to the golden boys dancing around Princess Margaret. Even for the mid-seventies, the scenes were an unusual sight.

The parties continued over the years, and Mustique's repu-tation grew, the most splendid being Colin's sixtieth-birthday party, in 1986, which he spent two years planning.

Several American guests flew in on Atlantic Records' company jet and some famous people were scattered around, like Jerry Hall, who, by the time of Colin's sixtieth birthday, had replaced Bianca.

Most of the guests, though, were relations: my mother and sisters loved coming out, and a great many rum punches and daiquiris were consumed. Old friends Ingrid and Paul Channon came with their children, who were a great hit with ours because they entered into all the games with such energy, lots of the Guinness family, a few of Princess Margaret's other Ladies in Waiting, and friends like Prue Penn, whom I have always loved and laughed a lot with. Patrick Lichfield was there, busily taking photographs, including one of Princess Margaret's bottom as she leant over to have her portrait taken by someone else, and Laura Brand, the rather eccentric sister of Lord Hambleden, who always wore sombreros and was always in the sea. Sadly, a few years later Laura drowned. She and her husband Micky were in Grenada and she went for a swim. Micky was on the beach when all of a sudden, her hat floated past, out to sea. All of our children were at the party, with many of their friends and endless cousins, and just like Colin's fiftieth birthday, the celebrations for his sixtieth went on for a week. It made the headlines – 'Bring your own jewels,' one paper said, and another described Colin as the 'ringmaster of a crazy aristocratic circus'.

Well: Princess Margaret did bring her own jewels to 'The Peacock Ball' and wore them with the dress Carl Toms, an iconic set and costume designer, designed especially for her. She looked ravishing in ivory silk with gold embroidery, which set off her diamond tiara perfectly. Princess Margaret loved her dress, telling me she'd been waiting all her life to wear a dress that made her feel like a princess. Her son David came with his lovely girlfriend Susannah Constantine, who went on to be one half of the television duo Trinny and Susannah presenting the BBC series *What Not to Wear*.

Princess Margaret was thrilled with her son David's outfit – he had a huge white peacock headdress, which was much admired. Thank goodness Colin had a crown or he might have been rather envious, but when Princess Margaret crowned him 'King of Mustique' during the ball, it was clear he was thoroughly enjoying himself and was glad that everybody else had made such an effort with their outfits.

Colin organised the start of the Peacock Ball so that everybody could make a grand entrance. Jerry Hall sashayed in wearing an almost identical dress to mine, remarking, 'You have the same colour as me,' and I wanted to say, 'No, *you* have the same colour as *me*,' but I didn't.

The ball marked the grand finale of the week-long celebrations, in the same way that the Golden Ball had been the last huzzah for Colin's fiftieth. The press described all the parties as 'decadent' and 'louche'. It would be hard to argue against those descriptions – Colin chartered a newly built boat called *Windstar* for a week, complete with masseurs and chefs at the guests' disposal. There was also a huge collection of pornographic films that kept the younger ones rather too busy, and Colin got very ratty with them all for spending so much time in their cabins.

Being on *Windstar* was like being on a moving island. Colin had thought of every detail, even the clothes: we had gone to India *twice* to choose the outfits. There were T-shirts made to mark the occasion and Indian clothes for the parties, which were laid out for guests when they arrived on board so they could pick from a vast selection.

We sailed around the islands, stopping off to have lunch or play games – there were treasure hunts on Bequia, where Colin had gone to great lengths to produce a collection of life-size cardboard cut-outs of various people, including one of the Queen. He had gone off beforehand, lugging the cardboard cuts-outs around the island, hiding them in all sorts of places. There were shrieks when a group of guests found the Queen in a restaurant bar, and giggles when someone exclaimed, 'Princess Margaret's in the jungle!'

The real Princess Margaret was on Mustique preparing the party she gave – a picnic on Macaroni beach. She had sent an invitation to all the guests beforehand, but that was where the formality stopped. It was like an extravagant summer fête, with coconut shies, a roll-top bath full of champagne and rum punch galore. People rushed or staggered around all afternoon playing games, with great peals of laughter, until the early hours.

As soon as one party finished, another would begin. All sense of time and responsibility was put on pause as we floated around from one island to the next. Raquel Welch, the American actress, threw a party with her husband, André, on their boat, which was decked out in red velvet and chandeliers, looking rather like a brothel. Princess Margaret was always mildly irritated by Raquel, because royal etiquette dictates that members of the Royal Family should always be the last to arrive, but Raquel made that impossible for Princess Margaret because she was always late.

Everybody was so relaxed and had so much fun, as though Mustique was just one private estate. That was one of its obvious attractions, especially for anyone famous – it felt private. It is still known for its privacy today. Colin was very clever in insisting that nobody could be on the island unless they had a house or a room at the hotel. This meant that the press couldn't get on because, even if they arrived at the jetty, they were turned away. The Cotton House has only twelve rooms and the houses rent for huge sums of money, so the exclusivity and privacy has always been maintained.

The Queen's visits cemented the idea that Mustique was also a playground for the aristocracy, which was probably, on balance, nearer to the truth, simply because most of the party guests were members of my or Colin's family, far outweighing the rock stars. The Queen's first visit was in

1977 with the Duke of Edinburgh, who always made me nervous – he made everybody nervous and knew it. When Princess Margaret had told us that the Queen was planning on visiting, we knew we should spruce up Mustique to make it look as good as possible for her. The village people didn't have any smart clothes and there was nothing to buy, even on St Vincent, so Colin rang up his mother, Pamela, and asked her to organise clothes for the villagers – shirts for the men and dresses for the women.

The boat arrived with Pamela, who brought all the parcels of clothes with her. Lugging them up to the house, we opened them and discovered, to our horror, that Pamela had bought a job lot of Victorian garments.

'What have you done?' Colin asked his mother.

'I thought it would be more fun for everybody.' She was delighted with the idea.

We gave the clothes to the villagers without admitting they were vastly out of date. They assumed they were the proper dress for the Queen of England's visit. I suppose they were, just not that Queen! I helped the women into their crinolines and the men put on their striped trousers and top hats and, despite being very hot, they loved wearing them.

I taught the ladies how to curtsy, and the men how to bow, and they all brought chairs down to the quay to wait for *Britannia* to come into view. They had been told to stand up once the Queen and the Duke of Edinburgh came to shore, but they didn't move. I'm not sure how impressed they were – I think they were expecting the Queen of England to arrive in her robes and the crown.

The first thing the Queen said to Princess Margaret was 'I had no idea Mustique was in a Victorian time-warp.'

The first thing the Duke of Edinburgh said to Colin when he came ashore from *Britannia* was 'I can see you've ruined the island.' Colin was dashed by the remark, especially because he had gone to such lengths to plan the itinerary with the Duke in mind.

Fortunately the planning paid off because the Duke of Edinburgh really enjoyed snorkelling among the sharks who were giving birth at Black Sand Bay, while Princess Margaret delighted in showing the Queen around Les Jolies Eaux, proud of the life she'd made on Mustique. She then had a picnic with the Queen, who took to the water afterwards. This was extraordinary as she very rarely swims anywhere, presumably because she doesn't want to be photographed. With no press on the island, she swam in Macaroni Bay.

The Duke of Edinburgh changed his mind about the island. When he was leaving, he turned to Colin, saying, 'I really like your island. I really loved my time here.'

The following week Nick Courtney, the general manager of the Mustique Company, the island's management company initially set up to sell houses, was showing people around the island, and when he got to Macaroni Bay, he said, 'The Queen swam here last week, and we haven't changed the water since.'

It was certainly a radically different visit from that when Princess Margaret had come ashore from *Britannia* during her honeymoon in 1960, seventeen years before. The Queen didn't deal with flying mice or plastic chairs strapped to a trailer pulled by a tractor. Nor did she have to sip sorrel cordial or be clad in striped pyjamas tied up with string to protect her from the mosquitoes. The island had been transformed to the Paradise Colin had known it could become.

Mustique seemed to be a hit with everybody, but I quietly resented the parties that Colin continued to throw because of the expense – some of them cost hundreds of thousands of pounds. There was nothing I could do to stem that extravagance, nothing I could do to rein Colin in. The money was haemorrhaging out. We didn't have an endless supply, yet Colin spent it as though we did.

Glen was also a drain on money, especially during and after the 1979 oil crisis, by which Colin's family bank was affected, and the bills went through the roof. When we needed more money, Colin would simply sell a painting or two. He always said that once he had walked past a painting enough times he didn't mind selling it, always being able to shut his eyes and see it if he wanted to or go to the Tate if he really missed it. Constable's *The Opening of Waterloo Bridge* was a rather wonderful painting he sold, just like that, when he needed to pay off a debt. Some of the paintings I wasn't too attached to, but I was really upset when he decided to sell *Girl in Bed*, which was a portrait of my school friend Caroline Blackwood, painted by her husband at the time Lucian Freud. Lucian was also upset: he took offence at Colin selling his whole collection of Freud paintings, marking the end of their friendship.

By the time that the Peacock Ball was being organised in the mid-eighties, Colin had sold anything hugely valuable and was running out of options. But he said it was all worth it because the parties made Mustique famous and therefore more profitable. I think from that point of view he was proved right: it attracted the top rock stars, from David Bowie, who bought Mandalay Villa, to Bryan Ferry, the lead singer of the band Roxy Music – Jerry Hall's boyfriend before she left him for Mick Jagger – and Bryan Adams, as well as multitudes of celebrities from all over the world. Not only did the celebrities come, but they made it more than just a place where they sunbathed in private, some especially so: ever since Mick Jagger bought his house, now thirty years ago, he has made an effort to be part of the local community, giving money for a new school and joining in with village life by playing cricket, which Patrick Lichfield also loved doing.

I'd quite often go into Basil's Bar and find Mick joining in with a live singer performing an acoustic set. One New Year we organised a skit in which Mick was the doctor and we told everybody he was looking for people to play patients. Of course the whole community turned up, wanting to be cast for the part, longing for him to examine them. David Bowie, too, was a very charming man, immediately sitting my twins on his lap the first Easter he was there, completely at ease with everybody as though we were all old friends.

For a place so small, it certainly has exceeded the expectations I had when I first set foot on the island. Amazing, really, because it still hasn't got all the mod-cons that other places have – there is a small supermarket but nothing major, and there is no golf-course or marina and not a single nightclub. I think the reason it's so popular is that it has kept Colin's distinctive bohemian spirit and adopted it as its own.

Still today it attracts the same sort of people as it did all those years ago, from the Royal Family to the social elite.

The Duke and Duchess of Cambridge take their children, the newest generation of Jaggers have grown up there, and people from the fashion world are still drawn to it: model sisters, the socialite granddaughters of Janie Stevens, Poppy and Cara Delevingne; Tom Ford, who named one of his pink lipsticks 'Mustique'; and Tommy Hilfiger, who based a fashion campaign on Basil's Bar, flying Basil to New York to make his signature rum punch for the launch.

I am rather relieved there are no more fancy-dress parties to organise or go to, and I will never again cover myself with gold paint. My favourite thing about Mustique now was my favourite thing about it then: swimming. Colin rarely came with me because he had had a fear of being out of his depth ever since one of his Oxford friends had drowned. When he did appear, he would often get very anxious and start yelling for me or the children to come back, worried we were going out too far. He preferred to stay in the shallows, eating mangoes with the children, satisfied that all the sticky juice could be washed off.

But while most people came to Mustique for the flamboyant parties, I liked waking up in the morning and walking down to the beach on my own. It's hard to beat those beaches: there are no big concrete hotels or car parks or anything to detract from the beauty. The waves come over the coral making the water frothy in the shallows, so it feels like swimming in champagne. I've always loved the sea and for the twelve years Colin and I ran Mustique as a cotton estate, I had the glorious beaches to myself. Just me – no fancy dress, no theatrics, no rum punch. Just me and the sea – absolute bliss.

CHAPTER TWELVE

A Royal Tour

IN THE HEYDAY of Mustique, Princess Margaret and I would go from dressing up in extravagant costumes to going all over the world on royal engagements. During the three decades I was the Princess's Lady in Waiting, I accompanied her on several royal tours abroad, from Canada, where we dressed up in Victorian clothes and went to a rodeo, to Cairo, where we watched the Royal Ballet with Madame Mubarak, the wife of the Egyptian President, who, at seeing the ballet dancers falling over, clapped enthusiastically, not realising they were actually collapsing because the floor was too slippery, causing disaster.

All the tours were memorable, some especially so. The

first tour I went on was to Australia. I had never been there before so I was thrilled when Princess Margaret asked me to accompany her, in October 1975, for a ten-day trip full of different engagements around the country. It was around this time that stories about Princess Margaret's marriage were appearing in the British press although they were, at this point at least, restrained. The Australian press, however, were far less polite and the barrage of questions and comments started as soon as we disembarked from the plane. The reporters were brash and rude, haranguing Princess Margaret, shouting, 'Why haven't you brought Tony, Ma'am?' and 'Where *is* Tony?'

I could see she was upset and unsettled by this onslaught, so Nigel Napier and I came up with a plan we hoped would appease the press. We knew Princess Margaret had a knack with men of all ages so we held a cocktail party on the train, inviting a whole lot of the press to come. By the end of the twelve-hour train journey from Canberra to Melbourne, Princess Margaret had charmed them all and the result was a succession of much nicer headlines.

When we arrived in Melbourne we went straight to the races, where it was sheeting down with rain. Princess Margaret's shoes got terribly wet, so when we sat down for lunch, I took them to see if they could be dried, giving them to the lady in the cloakroom, who, some time later, gave me an almost unrecognisable pair of shoes back. They were horribly misshapen and completely stiff. When I asked what she had done, she proudly said, 'I put them in the microwave.' Princess Margaret, who had no choice but to put them back on, hobbled around glaring at me for the rest of the day.

From Melbourne we travelled to Sydney, where we stayed at Government House with Sir Roden Cutler VC, an Australian diplomat who was Governor of New South Wales, and his wife Lady Cutler. They were frightfully grand. Somehow, as the Queen's representative, Sir Roden behaved with such exacting manners that nothing was at all straightforward and even the smallest details become nonsensical. To distinguish Princess Margaret from me, I was told I couldn't use the main stairs unless I was with her. Instead, if I was alone, I was told that I should use the servants' stairs at the back of the house. When I accompanied Princess Margaret down the stairs we were met with an absurdly formal ritual. Sir Roden and Lady Cutler would stand at the bottom of the staircase facing each other, expressionless, waiting for Princess Margaret to start her descent. As soon as Princess Margaret's foot touched the first step, like clockwork soldiers, they would turn away from each other to face us. Lady Cutler would then curtsy, and Sir Roden would bow. This extraordinary habit provoked Princess Margaret and me into hysterics as soon as we were in private.

Over the course of our stay, it became clear that Sir Roden felt he knew everything there was to know about the Royal Family, especially the Queen. At lunch one day, I was sitting next to him and I mentioned Princess Margaret wanted to go shopping to buy Aboriginal crafts. 'Shopping?' he said, surprised. 'I didn't think the Royal Family went shopping. I represent the Queen and I have never heard of her going shopping.'

So I replied, 'Actually, the Queen goes shopping. She recently went to Harrods to choose some Christmas presents.'

Sir Roden looked at me, astonished. 'On what authority do you have this information?' he asked me incredulously.

'My mother is a Lady of the Bedchamber and she went with her,' I replied. Sir Roden appeared amazed at this exchange of information and seemed after that to see me in a whole new light. At any rate, he was slightly less formal towards me for the rest of our stay, although I was never invited to use the main stairs without Princess Margaret.

One of the things on the itinerary for Sydney was a visit to Bondi Beach, which included a photo call on the sand with the lifeguards. On discovering this, Princess Margaret wasn't happy. The idea of sinking into the sand during a formal engagement was not something she was interested in. Knowing it would be inappropriate to show her discomfort and take time to rid her shoes and feet of sand, she flatly refused, using the excuse that her high heels were too impractical, agreeing to go to Bondi but not on the beach.

When I told the organisers, they were very disappointed and asked me to try to persuade her to change her mind. I promised to see what I could do and put a pair of her flat shoes into my bag before we set off for the morning's engagements around the city. I had been in this situation before: every now and then Princess Margaret simply didn't want to do something. Having to read the situation and weigh up everybody's wishes, I would try to create more of a balance so that everybody got what they wanted. This wasn't easy – a certain diplomacy was necessary and, over the years, I honed that rather delicate skill.

Later that day, when we were driving through Sydney, nearing Bondi, I said to her, 'Ma'am, you know, they really would like you to go on the beach. It's like kissing the Blarney Stone for them.'

'Anne,' she said, her irritation obvious, 'look at my shoes. They simply won't do. I'll just have to stand on the concrete and look from afar.'

'Actually, Ma'am, I have a suitable pair,' I said, showing her the shoes in my bag.

She looked at me, then at the shoes and then back at me. 'Okay, Anne,' she said, somewhat tersely. 'You win this time.'

She put on the flat shoes and walked on to Bondi beach and, as ever, Princess Margaret was the epitome of charm, never giving away her discomfort. When we got back into the car, she turned to me as she was shaking the sand out of her shoes and said, 'Well, I hope you're pleased.' Before I could answer, she added: 'But weren't those lifeguards disappointing?'

This was typical of Princess Margaret, who always took an interest in young men, and I couldn't help but agree. Instead of the bronzed gods we were expecting, they were all so frightfully pale because it was the beginning of the season.

'Yes, they were, especially with those awful rubber bathing caps,' I replied.

'They didn't do anything for them,' Princess Margaret remarked decisively.

While I might have 'won' that time, she got me back on the next engagement, which was to Sydney Zoo. On arrival, Princess Margaret was offered a koala bear to hold and, without missing a beat, she replied, 'No, thank you, but I'm sure my Lady in Waiting would like to hold it.'

There was no time to decline. She knew I was not entirely at ease with animals, but within moments I found myself holding the koala bear, which apparently was even more uncomfortable than I was, promptly weeing down my best dress.

'Thank you very much, Ma'am,' I said, in the car on the way back, 'for the opportunity to hold the koala bear.'

She laughed uproariously, apologised and looked utterly satisfied that she had got me back for the walking-on-sand incident.

The rest of our time in Sydney passed smoothly, and just before we returned to England, Lady Cutler came to me and said, 'Would Princess Margaret accept a present? It's rather special.'

'I'm sure the Princess would be delighted,' I replied. 'Will you tell me what it is?'

'A boomerang cover,' she replied.

Off I went to relay the news of this peculiar-sounding present to Princess Margaret. I couldn't help but smile broadly when I told her, 'Ma'am, you'll never guess what Lady Cutler is intending to give you as a present. A boomerang cover.'

Princess Margaret laughed. 'How on earth does she know how big my boomerang is?' she asked.

Of course it wasn't anything like we imagined. It turned out to be a quilt that had gone around the country to be stitched by members of different branches of the Women's Institute, which was how it had got its name – because it had gone back and forth – but we dissolved into hysterics and Lady Cutler never really understood why we were laughing.

I think I laughed with Princess Margaret more than with anybody else. She had a quite naughty sense of humour and never lost the sense of mischief we'd shared in childhood, jumping out at the footmen at Holkham. Sometimes she would try to make me laugh when we both knew I shouldn't because when I laugh I cry, and she thought that was very entertaining. In fact, she would make me laugh in front of people and then say in a completely deadpan tone, 'I don't know why my Lady in Waiting is in tears.'

Spending so much time with Princess Margaret gave me purpose but also distracted me. I appreciated the fun we had together especially when other parts of my life weren't so easy. Throughout the mid-seventies, family life was fraught.

Finding the right school for Charlie had been impossible – he had desperately wanted to go to Eton and Colin made a big fuss about getting a tutor for him before the exam, but he failed. He tried again and failed again. Instead, Charlie went to Clifton College, a strict boys' boarding school outside Bristol.

Where Charlie had failed, Henry succeeded, sailing through the entrance exams of Eton and doing well in all subjects, making lots of friends. Although we were delighted that Henry was thriving, it was hard for Charlie to see his younger brother do everything he had tried so hard to do, making him feel even more of a failure.

Charlie was fourteen and still at Clifton College when I became a Lady in Waiting in 1971. We were clueless about him smoking cannabis and taking acid in his early teenage years because being away at boarding school meant it was easy for him to hide this shocking development. It simply didn't occur to us that any of our children would ever get involved with drugs until years later. All we knew was that Charlie wasn't finding school easy and would come home in the holidays very glum, not wanting to go back. For a few years, Colin reassured me that Charlie would settle in and I tried not to worry, hoping he was right. Meanwhile Henry, Christopher and the twins were happily living through their childhood, and were, like Colin and me, unaware of Charlie's decline into drugs.

Maybe Charlie would have been better off staying at Clifton, but in 1973, when he was sixteen, he was still desperately unhappy, having been relentlessly bullied by older boys. Colin moved him to Frensham Heights, a co-educational school in Surrey, which was more liberal.

We had no idea how liberal. The freedom went straight to Charlie's head and he spiralled downwards from there, although we didn't know he was going off the rails to start with. For a while, we thought the new school had been the right decision because Charlie seemed a lot happier. We only realised how bad things had got when he came home only two terms after starting with a suspension letter, having been caught stealing with a gang of friends. The letter made Colin furious. What really alarmed me was that Charlie looked dreadful and smelt atrocious. When Colin pressed him for reasons as to why he was so unkempt, Charlie admitted that he had not had a bath for the whole of the second term. We were appalled, never having come across a school with such lax rules, and decided not to send him back. Instead we kept him at home, getting tutors for him so he was home-schooled, hoping it wouldn't be too difficult to straighten him out.

Charlie and kitten,
aged four.

A cold day on the
beach at Holkham with
Henry and Charlie.

Our wonderful nanny
Barbara Barnes with the
twins May and Amy.

With Colin and Bianca Jagger in my uncomfortable gold make-up for the Golden Ball in 1976. I didn't dare smile.

Princess Margaret with dancer and his strategically placed gold-plated coconut at the Golden Ball.

Centre of attention with Mick Jagger and Rupert Everett on Mustique in the mid 80s.

At the Peacock Ball in 1986 just after I'm told by Colin that Henry has AIDS. Charlie looking at me anxiously. I'm not sure how I got through the evening.

With a happy Prince Philip on Mustique in 1977.

The Queen finally putting us on the map when she arrives on Mustique in 1977 greeted by Princess Margaret. The Royal Yacht Britannia docked just outside.

As Lady in Waiting in 1975, far right, at Government House in Sydney with Princess Margaret and the absurdly formal Sir Roden Cutler VC, second right, and Lady Cutler, second left. Nigel Napier is on the top step on right.

With Madame Marcos in the Philippines in 1978.

King Sobhuza II of Swaziland, centre left, arriving in his traditional dress in 1978 to receive an order from the Queen – and posing a problem for Princess Margaret as to where to pin it.

All our children together at Hill Lodge in 1986. Left to right: Henry, May, Charlie, Christopher, and Amy.

Henry and Tessa's wedding on Mustique in 1984 with Amy and May as bridesmaids.

Henry with Euan.

Charlie and Sheilagh's wedding in London in 1993.

Christopher, back to life, and with the amazing coma kit.

On the beach in Madras, supported by my great friend Margaret Vyner in 1988.

With Prince Charles at my home in Norfolk.

May's wedding to Anton Creasy in 2009, at the same church where I was married in 1956 – St Withburga's, Holkham.

The 200th anniversary of Trafalgar at Burnham Overy Staithe in Norfolk in 2005 – after Nelson's Blood cocktails.

Only years later did he admit that the reason for his poor hygiene was all to do with the undiagnosed OCD – his own mind had convinced him that if he washed or changed his clothes the 'evil spirits' would take control of him. Given this secret reality he faced, I imagine, from his point of view, being suspended was the least of his worries.

With Charlie at home, we began to realise he hadn't grown out of his compulsive rituals at all, but because of his laidback and happy nature, it was hard to know what they were or how much they were affecting him. He would dismiss them and insist everything was fine and, with no useful advice on hand, we didn't know how seriously we should take it.

Colin never offered reasons or excuses to any of our friends about Charlie when they witnessed his strange compulsions; nor did he hide him away or label him mad, although I did worry that Charlie was disturbed. Colin had uncharacteristic patience, sympathising but not knowing how to help.

Princess Margaret never remarked on Charlie's behaviour and always took time to talk to him. When Charlie started hopping in and out of the doorway, she didn't blink an eyelid, accepting it was just part of Charlie.

The other children became used to their eldest brother's ways. If we were all about to go out, they would stand patiently in the hall while Charlie tried to leave. Quite often he would have been trying to leave for ages but every time he left his room and walked down the hallway and out of the house, he would turn around and go back because something wasn't quite right. So, there he would be, turning off and on the light switch, tapping the floor, turning around ten times and then a sudden rush out of the bedroom door only to stop at the front door, turn around and do it again. Once May was in the way and he crashed into her on his umpteenth attempt and was furious because, supposedly, that had been the one. Back into his room he went, and spent another half an hour getting it right. It was all part and parcel of our family life. Going down the King's Road with him, once we had eventually left the house, was at times rather testing, waiting for him as he touched a lamppost ten, twenty times, or the side of the pavement, or while he twirled around on the spot.

In contrast, Henry was a very easy teenager. Despite having inherited a temper, he rarely showed it and was mellow, good-natured, intelligent and completely normal in comparison to Charlie – and Colin, for that matter. As for the other children, Christopher and the twins were happy and secure, thanks to Barbara's stable routine. Barbara looked after them so well that they were completely fine when I went away. I would bring them presents when I returned and tell them all the stories, which they loved.

Christopher had developed a passion for cars and Colin was thrilled by this. When Colin had arrived at Glen during the holidays with a brand new Jaguar, he delighted in Christopher's excitement, and drove him all the way back to London at 140 m.p.h. Christopher was bowled over by the thrill, which bonded him to his father further.

The twins were still very young and lived in a bit of a bubble, coming up with their very own language that no one else understood. It turned out they never did like the dolls I had dreamt any daughters of mine would, and instead would play with Christopher's Action Men.

Daily life continued, although London had become increasingly tense due to bombing attacks by the IRA. In 1974, about half an hour after Christopher had posted a letter for me in the post-box at the end of Tite Street, as he always loved to do, the box blew up. I was in the house with him, the twins and Barbara when we heard the explosion. Twenty-one minutes later, a bigger bomb in a hedge close to the post-box was detonated, injuring more than twenty people, who had come to the scene in response to the first bomb. The threat of these small, neighbourhood bombs was extremely frightening: I was always on the alert every time I walked anywhere, knowing there was a risk of danger even on a quiet street, always crossing the road at the sight of a post-box.

Security was heightened around the Royal Palaces, and every time I drove to Kensington Palace, my car would be inspected with one of those mirrors at the end of a long pole that checked for bombs.

Princess Margaret kept the attitude she had always had, dismissing fear because there was no point in being frightened. I remember once we were on a plane flying over the Atlantic in the middle of a thunderstorm. The lightning was whipping the wings of the plane and I became increasingly afraid. Princess Margaret took my hand firmly and said, 'Anne, there's no point worrying. We will either be all right or we won't, and there is absolutely nothing to be done about it.'

Not long after the bombs, we moved from Tite Street to Colin's mother's house, Hill Lodge, in Campden Hill. Pamela had moved into a cottage in the garden. After she died, it was perfect for the children as they got older: it gave them a bit more independence.

By this time my father was really ill. In the war he had got malaria and had been given huge doses of quinine, which had damaged the valves in his heart, stopping the blood pumping to his brain properly. Poor Dad had become more and more unwell in his last years, thinking my mother and younger sister Sarah were Vera Lynn and Gracie Fields. At his insistence they sang songs like 'The Biggest Aspidistra In The World'. My mother had many, many attributes but singing was not one of them.

This was not the only bizarre request she graciously accepted. My father had got into a habit of chatting up women on the train to London and inviting them back to Holkham, where he would take them off on the fire engine, encouraging them to ring the bell. This was not what my mother minded. It was their husbands, whom they invariably brought with them and who would be left with her in the house. She was obliged to make polite conversation with them until their wives returned.

Sporadically ill, one day my father would be terribly confused, the next he would be fairly okay, and the next he would be absolutely fine. The trouble was that every time the doctor came my father managed to pull himself together for just as long as he was there. Eventually the doctor witnessed him being unwell and he was taken to St Andrew's in Northampton, a famous psychiatric hospital. Over the years St Andrew's has housed many notable people, including Gladys, 9th Duchess of Marlborough, who spent the last fifteen years of her life there; Lucia, the daughter of the Irish novelist James Joyce; and Violet Gibson, the woman who shot Mussolini.

I went with him to St Andrew's, masking my own fear when I was locked into a ward with him, trying to comfort him as all the patients swarmed towards us, curious to see who the new arrival was. Confused as to what was going on, he clung to me, crying, devastated that he was separated from his beloved Holkham. To see my father in such a state was horrendous: he had been so capable, so relied upon by the King and then the Queen, and so popular among his friends in the Scots Guards. He was only in his sixties, and his friends were still going off shooting together, having dinner in the Guards Club, while he was being kept some-where against his will, having no real grasp on reality. In the end we arranged for him to come home with two or three nurses, who looked after him, knowing he would feel comforted by being back at Holkham.

It wasn't easy for my mother and, as his condition declined further, developing episodes in which he was quite violent towards her, she decided to move out into a dower house a few miles away. She returned every day to have lunch with my father, who never realised she was no longer living with him. He was only sixty-eight when he died on 3 September 1976.

When I look back, my father was very, very sweet. I think he realised how fussy he was, but he just couldn't help it. He represented everything I had known. Without him, my childhood home was no longer accessible to me, and with it, the foundation of my identity. He had lived his life in such a comfortingly predictable manner, with shooting parties, and the running of the estate, and it was hard to imagine Norfolk without him. The gamekeepers were terribly sad, and a silence descended on Holkham only matched when the King had died twenty-four years earlier.

Princess Margaret continued being a support, knowing all too well how sad it was to lose one's father, understanding in the way that only people who have lost a parent can be. Time went on and Eddy, my second cousin, took over Holkham. Eddy had grown up in Africa until my father had brought him over to England so he could teach him about the running of the estate. He was very kind to me, my mother and my sisters, including us all, and we were thrilled when his second wife Sarah took over the pottery. Although it was the end of an era, Holkham was in good hands so I focused on my duties as Lady in Waiting and supported Colin in Mustique.

Since Colin had successfully set up the Mustique Company, the island was being run by various people, which meant Colin had time to pursue other things, including a short-lived political career: the Tennant family had long been established as a big liberal family, so unexpectedly, in 1976, Colin tried to get selected as the Scottish National Party's candidate for the constituency of Roxburgh, Selkirk and Peebles.

For a while, Glen became the hub of endless parties for the SNP and Colin quickly became popular, building a reputation for delivering brilliant speeches without notes. But the party decided to select an Edinburgh lawyer, who, they thought, stood a better chance against the opposition. Instead Colin became chairman of the constituency, and Glen continued to hold Burns Night dinners for the SNP.

Colin turned his attention to new business ventures, buying a company that produced stamps. 'The smaller the island, the bigger the stamp!' he would say, as his new passion developed. It just so happened that one of the places he was producing stamps for was the small islands of Tuvalu in the South Pacific.

In 1978, Princess Margaret was to go there, on behalf of the Queen, to give the islands their independence. These tiny atolls are not much more than a sand bar so it was an obscure coincidence that Colin happened to have an office there. Excited, he contacted Princess Margaret and said, 'I thought you might want to use my office on Tuvalu because it's the only air-conditioned place on the islands.'

'Thank you very much,' replied Princess Margaret. 'And seeing as you know the place, I think perhaps you had better come too.'

Colin was thrilled. I, on the other hand, was somewhat nervous at the prospect of him coming with us although, ironically, he was known for his impeccable manners when in formal situations. Davina Alexander came as the official Lady in Waiting on that occasion, and I went along with Colin to help, more as a friend than anything else.

We arrived to a welcoming party of swaying ladies, dressed in golden grass skirts and not much else. Over our heads went the leis: garlands that are signs of love and affection. Although they were very pretty, they were also soaking wet, much to Princess Margret's irritation: 'It will ruin my dress,' she muttered, taking hers off as quickly as she could.

At the welcoming dinner we all had to sit on the floor with our legs crossed. Princess Margaret refused, saying she couldn't sit like that, and sat sideways. Colin was good in these situations, charming everybody and taking to the exotic customs with ease, embracing the green-leaf service. The still-swaying ladies approached from behind us, slapping down a mound of grey matter on to our leaves. Princess Margaret and I were used to eating things that didn't necessarily appeal to us through our experience on royal tours and Mustique. The heat was also something we were used to, although the air-conditioning in Colin's office was welcome and we used to congregate there. The cool on the frigate where Princess Margaret was staying, supplied by the Royal New Zealand Navy, was also a huge relief.

Unfortunately, the going backwards and forwards between the extreme temperature of the climate and the air-conditioning led to Princess Margaret falling ill, and on the final day, when the independence celebration was due to take place, she was very ill, finding it difficult to breathe. This was alarming because she had gone to bed fine and suddenly there we were, looking after her on a tiny island in the middle of the Pacific, wondering which hospital to get her to. Nigel Napier sprang into action, not only giving Tuvalu its independence, but also contacting the Royal Australian Air Force, who provided a troop-carrier aircraft to collect the Princess, bolting down a bed in the empty transport plane, which took us all to Australia.

Once we arrived, Princess Margaret went to stay at Government House in Sydney where she was seen by doctors, who confirmed she had pneumonia.

Princess Margaret was supposed to go the Philippines and then on to Hong Kong. Instead of cancelling them, she asked me to go on her behalf so I could explain the reason for her absence face to face in the hope that my presence would show respect and concern over the efforts that had been made for her. I was to pass on a letter of apology written by her to the First Lady, Madame Marcos, and her dictator husband, Ferdinand Marcos, before adopting the same strategy in Hong Kong. This wasn't official protocol but Princess Margaret was aware that Madame Marcos was especially sensitive and might think that the cancellation was a snub.

I had never been asked to go anywhere on Princess Margaret's behalf, let alone two different countries, so I was apprehensive but excited, intrigued by Madame Marcos.

I embarked on the journey with only Colin, who Princess Margaret thought might be a help, especially since the maids and dressers were staying behind with her. We flew first class to the Philippines, not quite sure what to expect. We were met by the British Ambassador, who had been warned that Princess Margaret wouldn't be there, as had Madame Marcos, and were whisked off to one of the houses they had in the complex of Malacañang Palace. It was slightly eerie as there was no one in sight. The neighbourhood had been made private for fear of protesters after martial law had been declared a few years before.

We were told that Madame Marcos got up very early so we were to be ready to leave at eight o'clock the following morning to start the tour of Manila. And, sure enough, at eight o'clock she came to collect us in a huge bus. She was extremely smiley and friendly, although very disappointed Princess Margaret hadn't come. She undoubtedly thought that having a member of the British Royal Family to stay in the Philippines would cement her and her husband's status further.

She welcomed us on to her bus like a very glamorous tour guide, and took us to lots of different places in Manila – to a shell museum, which Princess Margaret would have loved, and a hospital she proudly showed off, which seemed to be just for her and the family. There were a few token patients but the rest of it was pristine, full of state-of-the-art equipment and doctors, but mostly empty, just ready in case of emergency.

As we drove through the city, Colin and I had the impression we were being shown exactly what she wanted us to see – there were glimpses of the slums, but we only went to the smart neighbourhoods. Madame Marcos seemed very popular: the traffic wardens and street cleaners, who were all women, known as 'meter maids', wore blue dresses with yellow sashes and waved their brooms frantically when the bus drove past, and her equivalent to Ladies in Waiting, known as 'blue ladies' because they wore blue dresses, were extremely attentive, quizzing me about my role, eager to pick up tips.

After a frantic day we were given half an hour to change for the evening. Then Madame Marcos reappeared to take us off to what felt, to both of us, like every hotel in the city. Colin and I would follow Madame Marcos into the ballroom of each hotel, where a band would be playing to the guests. The minute people saw her, everyone was waving, whereupon she walked up to the stage and started singing. When she did this for the first time, Colin and I were astonished. I couldn't imagine other First Ladies behaving like that. She actually had quite a good voice and I have to say I admired her audacity. We wondered if this was something she did for our benefit, although it did seem more for her own enjoyment.

The singing sprees carried on until 3 a.m., when she would drop us off at the house, only to arrive again at eight the next day. Colin continued to be an asset, although after enduring a few days of Madame Marcos's intense entertainment, he declared, 'I simply can't stand this any more. This is the most exhausting thing I've ever done. I'm going home.'

Bound by my duties to Princess Margaret, I didn't have the option of leaving so was left with Madame Marcos, keeping to her hectic schedule for a further four days, during which she took me to several golf clubs. I had sat next to her husband at a somewhat uncomfortable dinner, challenging for me because the conversation didn't flow at all.

Although I came to like Madame Marcos, who was very friendly and so full of energy, it was clear her life revolved around spending vast amounts of money. Her *pièce-de-résistance* was her shoe collection, which she proudly showed me around. It was so big that a whole house was dedicated to it. I walked around, amazed by the thousands of pounds' worth of high heels, a lot of which had clearly never been worn.

It didn't come as a surprise to me when, years later, she was convicted on corruption charges for the greatest robbery of any government, totalling billions of dollars of ill-gotten wealth, after her husband was overthrown in the 1986 People Power Revolution, fleeing to Hawaii.

From the Philippines, I went to Hong Kong, delivering the same message of explanation and apology on behalf of Princess Margaret. This trip was almost as surreal as my time with Madame Marcos had been, because the army took me out at night, complete with night-vision binoculars, to see scores of people desperately trying to get over the border of mainland China into Hong Kong. I watched as the Gurkhas, who were guarding the border, stopped anyone getting across. The Gurkhas were terrifying, but the people never gave up trying to make it across, and I was left wondering whether any of them would be successful and what would happen to them all.

As if things couldn't get more bizarre, I was also taken to Macau to see the famous casinos, which were full of very old ladies, dripping with jewels and with the longest fingernails I've ever seen. It was the sort of place perfect for a James Bond film: it had a slightly sinister air about it.

Fortunately, Hong Kong was the last destination on the trip, and I was pleased to be returning home. By this time Princess Margaret had recovered and was back in London and I was looking forward to debriefing her about Madame Marcos's karaoke sessions and the James Bond casinos of Macau.

I like to think that after that tour I was as good as Princess Margaret at adapting to every unique country and culture, getting on with it all unfazed. Even when faced with challenging circumstances, she had to grin and bear it: to complain would have been rude and ungrateful, and she taught me how to take strange customs and manners in my stride. This attitude was going to be necessary for many tours abroad. The tour to Swaziland, now eSwatini, in southern Africa was no exception.

There, Princess Margaret was to present King Sobhuza II with an order from the Queen in celebration of his eightieth birthday. In return for this honour, he had promised to build Princess Margaret a straw village for her stay. We did wonder how a straw village would be equipped with bathrooms, and imagined how funny Princess Margaret would look coming out of a straw hut wearing a tiara.

When we arrived, the straw village hadn't been finished so we were shown to a house reassuringly made from bricks. I was unpacking when there was a knock on the door from Princess Margaret. 'Anne,' she said, 'could you come and have a look at my room? There's something strange about it.' I was getting used to the oddities on these tours but there was something particularly strange about this place. Apart from the butler, who appeared to be listening outside the door at all times, the bedside tables were very far apart as though there had been a gigantic bed there before. We peered around the room suspiciously and at the same time we discovered a two-way mirror.

Later, we found out that, in those days, brothels were not allowed in South Africa, so people would come to Swaziland to fulfil their desires. We were horrified but it would have gone against protocol to undermine the arrangements that had been made for us so we did nothing about it.

There we were, as though we were part of the strangest of films, going from a brothel to greet King Sobhuza II, looking very English in buttoned-up coats and hats. The King was wearing his national dress, which didn't leave much to the imagination. He wore no shirt at all, a sort of leather apron and had long feathers in his hair. We went to several engagements during the few days before the main event – to ambassadors' houses for lunches and dinners when King

Sobhuza II would either wear his traditional dress or a military uniform.

We began to wonder what he would be wearing for the celebration, and Princess Margaret expressed to me her concern as to where she would be able to pin the order from the Queen, which took the form of a ribbon, that she was to bestow on him during the celebrations. 'If he doesn't wear a top of any sort, I don't know where I will put it!' she exclaimed, somewhat bemused. 'And if he wears feathers, how am I supposed to get the ribbon over his head?'

At the dinner the night before the celebrations, I raised Princess Margaret's concerns directly with the King. 'Your Majesty, Princess Margaret does hope that you will be wearing your uniform tomorrow.' The King smiled, nodded and said nothing. With no straight answer, both Princess Margaret and I were left wondering what to expect the next day.

We had to wait hours at the Mbabane Arena before the King appeared. The stadium was full of people, some of whom had walked for up to three weeks from their rural communities to catch a glimpse of him. The atmosphere was electric, the crowds bursting with anticipation.

Prince Kabani sat next to me so I asked him what his father would be wearing, but he was noncommittal. There was no choice: we just had to wait until the King appeared to find out.

Princess Margaret and I sat there, stifling in our English clothes, watching the different things happening in front of us. There were many dance troupes, who moved in perfect unison, and I admired the clothes they wore, knowing how much Colin would have liked to wear feathers in his hair and parade around to a loud drumbeat.

Meanwhile, the King continued to keep his own time so we waited and waited, while Princess Margaret became more and more tetchy. She kept looking at me, pointing at her watch.

Finally, a shining black stretch limo came to a halt in front of us. Out got King Sobhuza II. He was wearing a similar outfit to the previous day: huge feathers in his hair and nothing on except his leather apron. I could see Princess Margaret's mood sinking further, a look of despair in her eyes.

The King's daughters followed their father out of the limo. They, too, wore nothing on their torsos and were rather large, emerging from the car with their big bare bosoms and wide smiles. The crowd were delighted to see them and erupted into cheers. At this point, Princess Margaret beckoned to me, mouthing, 'Can you ask Prince Kabani to do something about the King's feathers? Otherwise I won't be able to get the ribbon over his head.'

I passed the message on and the Prince nodded, but nothing happened. We continued to stand for hours, as more people danced past us, and Swaziland's army put on an extensive display. Eventually the moment came where Princess Margaret was to present the King with the ribbon and the order and, luckily, moments before, Prince Kabani took quite a few of the feathers out of the headdress to make it easier for Princess Margaret. However, while the ribbon went over his head all right, she then had to fumble around his groin, working out where best to place the order. When we finally left the stadium, she turned to me, looking completely fed up, and said, 'I'm going to tell the Queen that I shall never again give any of her orders to anybody who isn't properly dressed.'

Before we left Swaziland, as is British royal custom when visiting all countries, she gave various presents to the King. As was usual, she then waited to receive presents from him. Nothing happened. Nigel Napier went to investigate and was told that the boy with the key to the safe had gone missing. But Princess Margaret didn't believe this story, convinced that she wasn't being given any presents because the King hadn't liked the presents she had given to him. However, as we were leaving, the King's ceremonial mother, whose official title was 'The Great She-Elephant', gave Princess Margaret a clay vase. It felt very much like an afterthought but Princess Margaret accepted it graciously and I was in charge of its safe-keeping. Since it was delicate and hadn't been wrapped up, I kept it on my lap on the plane back to London, making every effort to ensure nothing awful happened to it. Had I known what would become of it, I wouldn't have worried as much as I did about keeping it safe from harm.

About six weeks after we got back to England, I was having lunch with Princess Margaret in her apartment. There, on the windowsill, was the Great She-Elephant's pot.

Princess Margaret saw me glance at it and said, 'Now, Anne, I think this pot is going to have a little accident soon.' Sure enough, that was the last time I saw it. I felt rather sad, having looked after it so carefully, all the way back from Swaziland.

CHAPTER THIRTEEN

A Year at Kensington Palace

WHILE I ACCOMPANIED Princess Margaret on royal engagements, and provided sanctuary for her in Norfolk, Glen and
Mustique, she would invite Colin and me to spend weekends
with her at Balmoral and Royal Lodge, the Queen Mother's
house in Windsor.

The Royal Family are very fond of picnics, although their
idea of a picnic goes over and above most people's. According
to Princess Margaret, 'You can't possibly have a picnic without
your butler.' As for the Queen, she has her own meticulous
way of doing things. One summer we were staying at
Balmoral for Princess Margaret's birthday. Every evening
during our visit, the Royal Family – the Queen, the Duke of

Edinburgh and their children, Princess Margaret and the Queen Mother – took us and the other guests to a shooting lodge on the estate. The dinner would arrive in a specially made mobile kitchen – a picnic on wheels, which looked like a small caravan and was towed behind a Land Rover. Inside this wonderful contraption, everything had a set place. The Queen supervised the whole thing, getting everything out of the mobile kitchen and laying the table, and after dinner she put on her Marigold gloves to clean up.

The first time we went to one of these grand picnics, Colin and I started to carry things back to the mobile kitchen, helping to clear up. Suddenly from behind we heard Princess Anne bellowing at us: 'What are you doing?'

'We're just putting things away. We do hope we're putting them in the right place,' we said, as we stopped and turned around. It was dawning on us that perhaps that was why she was looking rather fiercely at us.

'Well, I hope you are, because if you're not the Queen will be bloody angry with you.' Colin and I almost fainted with horror. The thought of the Queen being 'bloody angry' with us was enough to stop us helping at once, realising that the Queen took great care and that keeping everything in exact order was her first rule.

As well as Balmoral, throughout the seventies and eighties the Queen Mother and Princess Margaret would invite Colin and me to stay at Royal Lodge. Apart from the drawing room, which had an exquisite mural painted by Rex Whistler, the house was relatively modest. The bathroom had a cracked lino floor and a lot of the other rooms were a little tired, but the Queen Mother didn't want to change anything: it was where she and the King had lived as the Duke and Duchess of York, before the abdication, and she was happy with how it was.

The weekends were always a lot of fun and varied. In the summer, we spent afternoons lolling about in the gardens, having lunch outside and going for a swim in the pool. In the winter, we were asked to the shooting parties. The men went off to the shoot and the ladies would join the guns at about half past eleven, taking bull shots, made from the traditional mix of beef consommé and vodka, to help warm up the men after a cold morning standing in the fields. Princess Margaret loved pouring the bull shots into little silver cups and handing them round to those shooting, who were always very grateful. She would then take me and any other ladies for a walk around the beautiful Savill Garden in Windsor Great Park before returning to Royal Lodge to meet the men to enjoy a very long lunch.

Those shooting days were much more relaxed than the ones at Holkham, where the men would pack a sandwich at breakfast, eating it under a hedgerow somewhere around lunchtime, before being bellowed at to continue the drive by my grandfather and then my father.

Whatever the season, every evening we had drinks in the Whistler drawing room, where we'd often find the Queen Mother standing in front of the television in the corner, transfixed by *Dad's Army*. One of the protocols of being in the company of a member of the Royal Family is that if they are standing, you have to stand – you can't sit down until they do. They seem to do an awful lot of standing so we'd just stand with the Queen Mother as she watched her favourite TV programme, being a big fan of Captain Mainwaring, sipping a dry martini, laughing until the credits ran.

Once *Dad's Army* had finished, we would all go to the dining room for dinner. The Queen Mother loved very rich food, such as eggs Drumkilbo – hard-boiled eggs with lobster and prawns – and there would always be a lot of puddings, cold soufflés filled with cream and chocolate. Wine was always served with each course, which meant there were several different glasses on the table: little ones for port and liqueurs, next to longer-stemmed glasses for red wine and longer still for white, then delicate water glasses.

The highlight of every dinner with the Queen Mother was when she started her ritual of toasts. She would say the name of anybody whom she liked and raise her glass above her head. And we would all follow suit. For anybody she didn't like, she would lower her glass under the table and say their name, and we would do the same. These toasts went on for ages, often carrying on throughout a whole course, accompanied by roars of laughter and copious amounts of alcohol.

After dinner, we would go back to the drawing room where Princess Margaret would play the piano and we would all sing. She was very good at 'singalongs', as she called them, and they were her favourite after-dinner pastime. After we had exhausted our voices, we sometimes played charades. If the mood was less energetic, there was always a jigsaw puzzle on the go in the corner of the room, although I preferred to sit and listen to the gramophone. If we were feeling particularly merry, we'd dance to the music on the carpet.

Princess Margaret loved organising a treat for us. She was

extremely thoughtful and utilised what was accessible to her in interesting and creative ways. Once she flew us to the Isle of Wight to have lunch at Osborne House and walk in the grounds. On another occasion we had dinner at the Tower of London and had a look at the Crown Jewels. We also went to Kew Palace, and the Queen's House, built for Anne of Denmark, James I's wife, in Greenwich to look at the paintings by Lowry, Turner and Canaletto, as well as the iconic Armada Portrait of Queen Elizabeth I. When in Windsor we stayed at Royal Lodge, and she would take us to the library in Windsor Castle, where she would arrange for a librarian to show us something special – like Queen Victoria's letters to Prince Albert, or documents dating back to Henry VIII – or we would go and look at the beautiful china or the dolls' houses.

These weekends at Royal Lodge were always fun, despite the bouts of bickering between the Queen Mother and Princess Margaret, who at times had a slightly strained relationship. One would do things like open all the windows, only for the other to go around shutting them. Or one would suggest an idea, and the other would dismiss it immediately. Perhaps they were too similar – I don't think it is an unusual predicament for a mother and daughter. And while they had been part of a foursome originally, they were left as the spare pair, to a certain extent.

Colin and I had lots of friends who made every effort to entertain their guests, but I was always especially grateful to Princess Margaret, who was meticulous about her weekends in the same way Colin was about his parties. Princess Margaret's generosity extended to me living with her at Kensington Palace for a time in 1990, when Colin declared he had sold Hill Lodge, our London house, and not only that, we had just a fortnight to get out; he admitted to me that he had already packed up a whole lot of my things. When I was upset and asked him why he couldn't have waited for me to return, he lost his temper. 'No! No! No!' he yelled, even though it was me who had been put out.

I had nowhere to go, so Princess Margaret suggested I stayed with her. I said, 'It won't be for long as I've found a flat I like, but I have to do it up. Could I come for about three weeks?' She said that would be fine and I moved in with her.

Princess Margaret had the stone hall – Apartment 1A, in the north side of the Palace, next to the Duke and Duchess of Gloucester, and she had an ongoing battle with Prince and Princess Michael of Kent's cats, encouraging her chauffeur to drive at them and turning the hose on them in the garden. If I was there, she would give it to me and shout, 'Go, Anne, get them!' as I dutifully ran all the way around the garden, making sure I didn't spray her by mistake. I never got any of the cats, who were far too quick and would sit on the wall, just out of reach of the hose, looking slightly smug.

Princess Margaret had moved there in 1960 when she had married Tony. Their redecoration of the house had been met with criticism by the press, who tried to make out that they were over-extravagant, assuming that the property was in a perfect condition already, being part of Kensington Palace. In truth, it had been a crumbling shell when she and Tony had moved in and hadn't been redecorated since 1891. Used to the press vilifying or praising them, they had shrugged it off.

Princess Margaret's marriage to Tony had ended over a decade before, but it was still clear that when they had tackled the redecoration, Tony's creative flair and Princess Margaret's exceptional taste had made them a brilliant team. Together, they had succeeded in creating a charming, distinctive house, which, despite being within the walls of Kensington Palace, felt very comfortable and relaxed.

There were double doors from the drawing room into the dining room with a long table big enough to seat twenty people, and just off the hall, her shell room, full of cabinets containing her collection. I knew this collection well as, once a year, I would help her wash the shells, plunging them into the bath, filled with water and Fairy Liquid, then drying and polishing each one.

Throughout the apartment, the windows were always kept open, the doors ajar, because Princess Margaret always seemed to need more air, maybe because of her heavy smoking. As the apartment was in the Palace complex, it was completely guarded and safe, and for me it was bliss not having to worry about security, leaving windows and doors unlocked and the keys in the car. A luxury I don't imagine Princess Margaret had any awareness of, but something I really valued.

Upstairs, she had the most beautiful bedroom and a stunning bathroom that Carl Toms and Tony had designed, with Gothic panelling and pink walls and a great big roll-top bath. My room was wonderfully done up in blue silk and I slept in a four-poster bed, with views across the garden. It had a door that went into a museum, which was open to the public, and often I could hear people go around it. I was always worried in case I had forgotten to lock the door, and visitors came in and viewed *me* lying in bed.

When I moved in, Princess Margaret said, 'We'll see each other now and again.' But in fact we spent a lot of time together. If we were both in the house, we would eat together. When I got back from an evening out, I would be tired and would want to go to bed, but Princess Margaret always stayed up late and loved to hold conversations that would last for hours. I would creep through the door and along the corridor as quietly as I could, and then I would hear her call out, 'Anne, is that you?'

'Yes, Ma'am,' I would reply.

'Hello. Come and see me – come and have a nightcap.'

So there I would be for another few hours. I was used to this, having spent so much time with her at Glen and on Mustique, but normally everybody would take turns to sit up with her. Sometimes I would stay only briefly, before saying, 'Do you mind? I must go to bed now.'

One day she came and found me in the house and asked whether I would like to go with her to Washington DC to see the Royal Ballet perform. The ballet was her greatest passion although, secretly, I'd always wished she had loved the opera, which was mine, but I was still thrilled and accepted at once. Over the years we went to Washington to watch the ballet three times and each time we also visited the White House: twice when Ronald Reagan was in office, and once when George Bush Senior was President.

My experiences of the two Presidents and their First Ladies were mixed. Unlike Nancy Reagan, Barbara Bush was absolutely lovely and completely welcoming, taking a genuine interest and including me in whatever was going on. She was relaxed and rather fun, holding good conversations and making everybody feel at ease.

Nancy Reagan was the opposite. When we arrived at the White House we all made our way to the lift that goes to the private apartments. Before I'd even got my foot in the door, Nancy Reagan said, 'Oh, no, Lady Glenconner, not you. Miss Brown will take you down to see the Present Room.'

Princess Margaret looked rather worried, not wanting me to go. The whole point of her having a Lady in Waiting was that she had someone from her own household with her at all times and she mouthed, 'Help!' as the lift's doors closed, but there was nothing either of us could do.

I had been looking forward to seeing the Oval Office and was conscious that Princess Margaret wanted me to be with her, but soon enough I was disappearing into a huge basement room to see all the presents to the President instead. Eventually Miss Brown reunited me with Princess Margaret, who looked very glad when I reappeared.

Returning to the White House some months later, I dreaded being sent off to the Present Room once more, but this time, before I'd even stepped inside, I had to deal with an unexpected case of mistaken identity. As I got out of the car, President Reagan, who was expecting Princess Margaret to get out of that side, mistook me for her and, taking hold of my arm, said, 'Hello, little lady.'

As Princess Margaret and I looked nothing alike, I was very surprised and immediately tried to correct him, but he wasn't having it. As he walked me off, I could see Princess Margaret and Nancy Reagan looking livid, although I'm not sure who they were cross with – me or him. I managed to untangle myself, ushering Princess Margaret forward.

I bore the President and his First Lady no ill will, of course, and when we visited them years later, at their house in California, Ronald Reagan was very unwell and didn't come for lunch. By then he was suffering from Alzheimer's, and it was distressing to hear him moaning in the background – he had been such an upstanding and significant presence on the world stage, and it was very sad to know his health was in a steep decline. I did wonder whether perhaps he was already suffering from dementia when he had so vehemently decided that I was Princess Margaret.

Not all the time was spent doing extraordinary things. While I lived with her, we did very ordinary things together, like listen to the wireless or go on trips to Peter Jones. Sometimes we would go out for lunch: her favourite place was the Ritz and she was always saying she thought it was 'the prettiest dining room in London'. We would go with friends – Carolina and Reinaldo Herrera when they were visiting from New York, or Rupert Loewenstein, and Colin, if he was in London, and the hotel manager would meet us in the lobby and walk us to our table. People would notice Princess Margaret but, with no entourage except John Harding, the fuss and attention were minimal and generally people gave her space and were very polite. After lunch, especially if Colin was there, Princess Margaret would suggest having a look down Bond Street, where he would invariably buy her something, especially if she came across some blue glass, which she collected, or a piece of jewellery that caught her eye.

Most of the time we would have lunch in Kensington Palace, then go for a walk in the gardens afterwards, which she liked, although she hated grey squirrels – she had a vendetta against them. Once we were out walking and she suddenly clapped eyes on a woman who was sitting on a park bench, happily feeding the squirrels. She marched straight up to her and started whacking them with her umbrella. John Harding had to intervene, politely suggesting to Princess Margaret that she move on and leave the squirrels alone, while the woman was left looking utterly bemused.

The three weeks I was supposed to stay went on and on. The flat I had bought in Holland Park took ages to finish, but Princess Margaret didn't mind. In the end I stayed for the whole of 1990, finally moving out early in 1991. I couldn't have enjoyed it more. She was so easy to live with – I think we both felt that about one another, especially compared to living with Tony or Colin.

CHAPTER FOURTEEN
The Lost Ones

ALTHOUGH DURING THE years as Lady in Waiting I got to do many exciting things, by the time Charlie was in his late teens, Colin and I had gone to Hell and back with him. As well as his strange rituals, Charlie was too charismatic for his own good. He was good-looking, with boundless energy and a twinkling, mischievous nature, and he found the world of drugs too irresistible to ignore. There was nothing he wouldn't experiment with and soon he was on every drug you could think of, having his first fix of heroin in 1973, when he was only sixteen.

We noticed a change in his behaviour before we realised what was happening, by which time it was too late – he was addicted. When Colin found out he started yelling and yelling: 'Charlie, you're a disgrace, an absolute disgrace!' Cannabis was one thing, but heroin was terrifying. Colin's patient approach had clearly fallen on deaf ears. His solution of home-schooling Charlie had obviously failed, and what was left was anger born from fear. But by that point words were irrelevant. Charlie later told me that during the six years he was on heroin it was like being in an 'iron grip'.

For me and the family, it was nothing short of a disaster. I was ill-equipped to deal with a heroin-addict son. I had never touched drugs and didn't have the first idea how to handle Charlie, who was moody, gaunt and often high as a kite. He was also untrustworthy and over the years stole vast amounts of money from us to buy drugs. He was increasingly erratic, and I grew worried that his behaviour would affect the other children.

It was such a surreal time. There I was, immersed in royal life, while my eldest son was running wild. Knowing that Colin was better at dealing with Charlie, I gave up trying to help, concentrating on the other children while Colin tried to sort him out.

The twins were only five when Charlie first got on to heroin, and I was worried they would stumble across needles or be frightened by Charlie when he was high. Together, Barbara and I kept a close eye on them and tried to keep life as normal as possible for them. Our two other sons were so innocent in comparison: Henry was flourishing at Eton, taking everything in his stride, and Christopher was at prep school, dreaming about cars. The worst thing he ever did was smash the window of his headmaster's study with an overzealous throw of a cricket ball.

Throughout the second half of the seventies, Charlie went off to various rehab clinics, which were invariably filled with other members of high society, such as Andrew Cavendish, 11th Duke of Devonshire, and Jamie Blandford, the current Duke of Marlborough. When rehab didn't work, Colin sent Charlie to distant places in the hope that the combination of remoteness and hard labour would make a difference, but Charlie seemed determined not to be straightened out. There was a sheep farm in Australia, which he never even got to because he was denied entry, and an estate in the Scottish Highlands, but somehow, he managed to find drugs, defeating the point entirely.

Soon enough he was back in London shooting up, and then he went to New York, which in the late seventies was probably the very worst place an addict could have gone. He was lionised, becoming an instant hit with the pop artist Andy Warhol and up-and-coming photographer Robert Mapplethorpe, immersing himself in the scene of the iconic drug-fuelled nightclub Studio 54 to his detriment. I remember him ringing me up from a hotel, saying, 'Mum, the only thing I ever want in life is room service.' He told people he wanted to be a 'professional heroin addict' – that he wanted to be known for being able to survive the biggest doses.

When he came back to England, he was in a very bad way and we sent him back to rehab but the doctors kept saying the same thing: that he wouldn't give up unless he wanted to. They advised us to stop supporting him, in the hope that, if he didn't have money or home comforts, he would reach such a desperate state he would hit rock bottom and decide to get off drugs.

This is extremely difficult for any parents to hear and act upon, and for years we couldn't bring ourselves to do it. With hindsight, perhaps our love for him assisted his downfall. Although nowadays he might be slapped with the label of 'archetypal rich kid junkie', he was our little boy, known as 'sweet Charlie', who had somehow spiralled out of control. He could quite easily have been like many other rebellious teenagers and experimented with drugs without becoming a full-blown addict. That would have been far from ideal, but significantly better than the reality we were all faced with.

Instead of abandoning him, Colin kept him on Mustique, which seemed to be the only place in the world Charlie couldn't get his hands on heroin. That might be surprising since Mustique was known for its hedonistic parties, but although other drugs, such as cannabis, could be found, heroin did not feature. Charlie described it as a 'Paradise prison', getting very depressed there, feeling trapped and suffering from cold turkey

Of course, as soon as Colin let him go, which he had to from time to time, Charlie would find a dealer, even before he'd got to London. Both Colin and I lived in waves of anxious dread – one minute we hoped Charlie might be rising above everything, the next we would realise he was even deeper into the addiction. When he was on Mustique, I was able to relax a bit, knowing Colin had a firm grip on him and feeling reassured that at least Charlie couldn't access heroin.

I compartmentalised my worries, distracted myself and

focused on other parts of my life. It was the only way I could cope, and since nothing seemed permanently to get Charlie away from drugs, I got used to the feeling of unease. When Colin and I were together, we discussed endless options, hatching several plans, until he became convinced that Charlie had got into drugs to shirk responsibility. Colin had threatened Charlie with the prospect of disinheriting him so many times, but Charlie continued down the same path, either not taking the threat seriously, not caring, or unable to stop. I didn't know what to think but could quite see where Colin was coming from.

Becoming convinced that Charlie didn't want the responsibility of looking after the vast family estate, Colin began to think that the pressure was adding to his problems. We were also dreadfully worried Charlie would simply sell Glen if anything were to happen to Colin and he had the chance.

Reluctantly, in 1977, when Charlie was nineteen and had already been on heroin for three years, Colin made the difficult decision to disinherit him from Glen. This would mean he would still inherit the Caribbean assets, which were, at the time, substantial, but that the family estate would stay protected. I supported the decision, knowing that Charlie wasn't in a position to take over and had to accept that he might never be.

When Colin handed Charlie the contract, Charlie signed it on two conditions: to be given a bigger monthly allowance and for Colin to cover his future medical bills. The conditions didn't make us feel he had realised his pitfalls. On the contrary, they sounded like ways to support his addiction, only making us believe we had taken the right decision. With

Colin's agreement, Charlie signed on the dotted line. It was official: Glen would be Henry's when Colin died. Although other young heirs were dabbling in the world of drugs, it was unusual to disinherit and the decision was a big blow to our family. It was an official failure, marginally compensated through having a second son to hand the legacy down to. But put in perspective, having to disinherit a son was nothing compared to the reason why he was disinherited, and our concern was centred around how on earth we could get him off heroin.

After Charlie was disinherited, Colin let him leave Mustique and packed him off to a clinic in the States, but the cycle continued. For the next three years, Charlie was high half the time and marooned on Mustique for the rest. A real low point came in late 1978, after a summer at Glen where Colin had organised a variety show for fun. The line-up was impressive. Bianca Jagger started it off with some ballet, then Charlie mimed to Elvis Presley's 'Blue Suede Shoes'. Then out came Princess Margaret dressed as Brünnhilde, in a horned helmet and wig, miming to Wagner's 'Ride of the Valkyries' with the twins, who were about eight years old, either side of her as mini Valkyries, loving every minute of it, grinning from ear to ear. They were followed by Roddy Llewellyn, who, dressed as a wizard, rattled off a song that he sang to a skull held in his hand.

Colin and I were left thinking it was one of the best weekends we'd ever had at Glen. But not long after the party, photos of Princess Margaret were splashed across the newspapers. Horrified, I recognised the photos as mine and when I opened my photo album, I saw that they had been ripped

from the pages. Joining the dots, I guessed that Charlie must
be at the bottom of it. When I confronted him, he admitted
that he had sold the pictures to a friend, dubiously called
Muddy Waters, who had then sold them to the *Daily Mail*.
I was furious.

In the beginning, he had stolen money from me, and as
the years passed, he had stolen belongings, including a pair
of ornaments that had huge sentimental, let alone financial,
value, encouraged by Colin's sister Emma, who sympathised
with him when he complained to her he didn't have enough
money. But this was something different. I was not only
worried for him but it threatened my integrity and position
as Lady in Waiting. Princess Margaret was hugely understanding and dismissed the incident, drawing a line under
it and forgiving Charlie.

I was exasperated and tried to reason with him. When I
told him I would rather he just asked for money than deceive
and undermine me like that, I could see he felt terrible. He
wasn't naturally nasty, but his addiction had split his personality, making him manipulative and untrustworthy. When I
saw his reaction, I felt a glimmer of hope that he was still
in there somewhere behind the awful shroud of addiction,
and I started to engage with him more, trying to make him
understand he had to get his act together and stop all this
nonsense. I think he began to see the hurt he had caused
everybody, and it looked like he was beginning to realise he
no longer wanted to deceive everybody around him.

Although he seemed to try, he was unable to make the
necessary changes and once more Colin and I found ourselves
in the same position. When he was arrested for being in

possession of drugs at Heathrow, Colin refused to pay his bail, hoping that a small stint in jail would be enough to shock Charlie into giving up once and for all. Even though he begged and promised, as soon as he was out, he shot up.

It had been six years since he had started taking heroin and only when *we* had got to breaking point did we decide finally to cut him off, using all the courage we possessed to take the advice of the doctors and turn him out. It was the hardest thing to do, far harder than disinheriting him, but it was this decision that finally broke the dreadful cycle.

Colin and I watched him as he sat on the London pavement outside our house. Colin immediately wanted to bring him back in, and it was almost impossible to go against our instincts, but I stuck to my guns, thinking that this might be our very last chance to save him.

What was worse than seeing him looking helpless and bewildered outside was when he eventually moved off and we had no idea where he had gone. There was a constant sinking feeling in the back of my mind, wondering whether we would get a phone call to hear something dreadful had happened.

Several weeks later, after hearing nothing from Charlie, he reappeared, declaring he wanted to quit. We listened and quietly rejoiced. Never before had he said he wanted to quit. He'd promised he would, but he'd never said he actually wanted to. It was pivotal that this came from him, because only with the desire to quit would he stand a chance in succeeding.

Colin bought him a small house in Fulham that was near enough to us that we could check up on him but allowed him independence, cautious that overcrowding him might deter him from his goal, and knowing that if he was going to stay clean, he needed to be determined enough to make his own choices.

When he started going to a drug rehab centre of his own accord, we didn't have high hopes, no longer trusting him or his word, but were tentatively happy when he went on to methadone and there was a marked change in him, as he seemed to really try. He went up to Glen to stay there for a bit and that was the start of the beginning of the rest of his life. On the estate, there was a couple called Mr and Mrs Parsons who were renting one of the farmhouses, making a living by creating rose-scented candles. Mrs Parsons was also a counsellor and was instantly supportive of Charlie. Soon he was making his own candles, which were rather different from theirs. I was on the receiving end of Charlie's psychedelic candles, getting black skulls and huge purple creations in the post, not really knowing what to do with them, but I was glad he was at least doing something. The prospect of Charlie managing to get clean was by then as surreal as finding out he had ever become addicted in the first place.

Meanwhile the other children were blossoming. Christopher was in his mid-teens and in the throes of school, very popular and enjoying life. When he came home in the holidays, he would sneak off to nightclubs with friends and come back late, sleeping in the summerhouse, but having seen what heroin had done to Charlie, he wasn't tempted to follow him.

As the twins got older, they connected more with their brothers. They really looked up to Christopher, and when Charlie was in a more level period, we would all listen to his reggae records in the sitting room at Glen. Henry taught the twins how to play chess and they admired his skill for card games – he was especially good at gin rummy. I was still involved in my charities and would take the twins with me to the events, where they would help out with the tombola at fairs and were very popular with the guests.

As May was goddaughter to Princess Margaret, she was asked to the Royal Variety Performance and was excited to meet all the acts from Orville to Tom Jones.

In 1979, aged nineteen, Henry fell in love while on his gap year in Machu Picchu. He met a young woman named Tessa Cormack, who had pulled him out of a hole he'd managed to fall into. Although a chance meeting, far away from home, it turned out they had a lot in common. Tessa had also grown up in Scotland – she was the granddaughter of Liberal peer Lord Davies, and they shared strong values and a similar sense of humour, so we were all thrilled for them when, a few years later, they got engaged.

Their wedding on Mustique in 1983 was brilliant fun, both families joining in to decorate the jeep and boat with palm fronds and flowers. It was a beautiful day and we were all together celebrating a happy occasion. There were no histrionics, no bad moods. It was perfect.

Sadly, it was the last time my mother came to Mustique. Suffering from emphysema, having chain-smoked all her life, her health declined rapidly. It was a terrible illness, and it was agonising to watch her breathing become more and more strained, until she died in 1985. Everybody was tremendously sad. She had been such a positive force in all our lives and Colin had become very fond of her. She was popular with everyone, including the Queen, who wrote me an exceptionally touching letter to say how much my mother had meant to her. Prince Charles, having spent so much time with her when he was a boy, was also terribly upset and has stayed a loyal and incredibly kind friend, always checking up on me.

My mother taught me many things, above all that I should stay strong for my family, reminding me always to give an air of absolute resolve, just as she had done. So far life had thrown me challenges – from navigating an often tumultuous marriage to dealing with a drug-addict son – but what came next tested me in the extreme.

For a while it seemed as if Henry and Tessa would live happily ever after. In 1984 they had their son, Euan, and there was no reason to doubt their compatibility whatsoever. Henry was busy with his business ventures – first importing fruit from Trinidad and then delving into the stationery industry. He also started up a business called 'Henry's Help' where people would call up if they were looking for a plumber, electrician or a handyman and he would find them one – he was ahead of his time. By then, he had found Buddhism and had become an increasingly positive part of May and Amy's life as they had grown older: he was a calm and loving brother whenever they needed someone to talk to. May described him as her 'guru', holding on to every word he said. He would do little things for them, like making compilation tapes, when they were at school, and taught Christopher and the girls how to chant.

Tessa became close to us all, and we were very impressed with her career: deeply intelligent and a passionate activist, she was a pioneer, going on to co-found one of the first green investment funds in the UK. Because of her full-on schedule, it was Henry who spent a lot of time with Euan when he was a baby, and I was able to see them regularly as they lived in the basement of Hill Lodge.

One day in 1985 Henry asked Colin and me down to their flat. There was a strange tone to his voice and when we came down, there was an equally strange feeling in the flat. I knew at once that something was wrong, but I was not prepared for what came next. As we sat down with Tessa and Henry, he blurted, 'I've moved out because I'm gay.'

I couldn't believe it. He wasn't camp, like Colin's Uncle Stephen, or even as flamboyant as Colin or Charlie for that matter. To me, he gave no outward hint of being gay, so the news came as a massive shock, especially given his apparent happiness with his wife and child.

Although I didn't mind that he was gay, and only wanted him to be happy, I was exasperated that he had married such a lovely girl, then gone on to have Euan, only to turn around and shun the life he had made, in favour of a completely new one. Tessa was calm, and somehow managed to deal with everything with grace and empathy. She never divorced him, even though he moved in with his friend Kelvin O'Mard, an actor at the RSC. It became clear Henry just wanted to stop living a lie and embrace his sexuality, so separating from Tessa was his way of doing that. Surprisingly, Tessa became very close with Kelvin.

Colin, too, seemed more understanding and took the news far better than I did. He was patient and accepting of Henry's choice, and was glad that Henry had felt comfortable enough to tell him. Not only was being gay a taboo

– it had only become legal in the UK in 1967 and was still met with huge prejudice – but it was made far worse because of the risks.

In the 1980s it was dangerous to be gay. AIDS had become an epidemic. Having been a little-known disease, starting in the Democratic Republic of Congo, by the mid-seventies it had spread to five continents. At that stage, no one knew how it was caught. The only certainty was that it was killing thousands of people a year and that it was heavily linked to gay men.

My concern swapped from his broken family to his welfare. I warned him so many times, saying, 'If you are promiscuous, you need to wear protection and be careful.'

By 1986, the British government had released major advertising campaigns on television and newspapers, warning people that one in five people would contract HIV with the tag-line, 'Don't die of ignorance.'

Tragically, Henry wasn't careful enough. As soon as he came out, he went wild, presumably feeling finally liberated. In December 1986, moments before Colin's famous birthday party, the Peacock Ball on Mustique, was about to begin, Colin told me that Henry had been diagnosed with HIV. Why Colin picked that moment to tell me, I will never know. The party was already surreal enough, with Princess Margaret in a turban, crowning Colin as 'the King of Mustique'. To be handed my son's death sentence while standing in a glittering dress welcoming lots of guests felt like some sort of obscure nightmare.

Suddenly I had a son with the most feared virus in the world, as well as a son who was addicted to heroin. I despaired, thinking I had hit rock bottom. But only a few months after Henry had been diagnosed with HIV and had started endless amounts of medication to try to keep it from progressing to AIDS, Christopher had a near fatal accident while on his gap year in 1987.

Christopher was very handsome, resembling Elvis Presley, and had left school as one of the most popular boys in his year. Full of affection, funny, and with a very sunny disposition, he was instantly likeable. Just before he set off, I went to the travel agent to collect his tickets and the man behind the counter said, 'Have you insured him?'

'No,' I replied.

I hadn't thought about it, but after listening to him explain why it might be a good idea – in his experience young travellers often lost key items or needed medical treatment while abroad – I bought a policy, although £150 seemed like a lot of money for insurance. It made me more aware of the possibility of danger, especially through reckless behaviour, so when I gave Christopher the tickets, I said, 'Please, no motorbikes. Whatever you do, no motorbikes.'

Well, of course he and his friends took no notice. They were nineteen-year-old boys with their first taste of freedom, hiring motorbikes just as soon as they arrived. The dog-eared postcards that Christopher sent from time to time made clear he was having a terrific time as they made their way across Mexico and Guatemala. His scribbled messages politely wished I was there, which I'm sure he didn't.

On the final stretch of their adventure, Christopher and his friends arrived at the Guatemala–Belize border at nightfall, only to be told they couldn't cross into Belize without giving a large deposit for the entry of their motorbikes. When they didn't have the money, one of the motorbikes and a helmet were taken in lieu of payment. So, Christopher rode pillion, without a helmet. When two of their friends arrived at the next hostel, they waited and waited, wondering what had happened to Christopher and their other friend.

By dawn they were so worried, they got back on their bikes and retraced their journey from the night before. What they found was a scene from a nightmare. Having got tired, and with the roads winding, unevenly surfaced and unlit, the boy driving the motorbike had crashed into an unlit barrier. Christopher was thrown off and had hit his head on a rock; the other boy had a broken shoulder. It transpired that after the accident, although people had passed, no one had stopped, fearing the boys were bandits and were only pretending to be hurt.

The friends called for help and Christopher and the other injured boy were taken to a local hospital, where the doctors wrote Christopher off. He was given no medical attention or treatment and left in a hammock in a back room to die.

Meanwhile, Colin was packing his suitcase in London, about to leave for Mustique, ready to welcome Christopher and his friends, who had planned to end their gap year there. Just before Colin left, the telephone rang. I picked it up and listened as Christopher's friend told me about the accident. I stopped Colin as he walked out of the door. He could tell by my voice that something was terribly wrong.

Immediately we tried to work out how we could get to Belize. We couldn't think straight, unable to focus on how to get there as fast as possible. So, I rang the switchboard at Buckingham Palace and asked to be put through to Kensington Palace because I needed to speak to Princess Margaret urgently. I just hoped that, because she was such a friend, and with her connections, she might know what to do. On hearing the news, Princess Margaret told me to ring Nigel Napier straight away. He sprang into action, contacting the Foreign Office, who then contacted the British Garrison in Belize. This wasn't special treatment as such, but the process was speeded up significantly because Nigel knew exactly who to contact and did so immediately. Without a doubt, these actions saved Christopher's life.

Through the phone calls from Kensington Palace, the British Army was called into action and sent a helicopter to collect Christopher, flying him directly to the Garrison, where he was operated on straight away in one of the tents. By a huge stroke of luck, a surgeon visiting that day was able to stabilise Christopher's head injury, leaving his head wound open to limit the risk of more blood clots. The army then flew him to a major hospital in Miami.

During his flight there, Colin and I had some more extraordinary luck on discovering Concorde flew to Miami once a week on Saturdays and it just so happened it was a Saturday. We flung some essential items into a suitcase and raced to the airport just in time to catch it.

The journey was terrible. I was shell-shocked and, much to Colin's irritation, I just couldn't stop crying. I have never cried so much. Gone was my British stiff upper lip: my son was fighting for his life. Unlike Henry's diagnosis, this was an emergency that had come out of nowhere and Christopher's life hung in the balance, making it even more traumatic – we couldn't know whether our son would still be alive by the time we arrived.

The whole terrifying experience was made worse by knowing that until the hospital was paid they wouldn't operate. As soon as we arrived, Colin had no choice but to prioritise the payment ahead of seeing his son, frantically trying to make sure there were no delays, very conscious that time would make all the difference to Christopher.

Meanwhile, I was walking down the corridor of this very smart, rather futuristic hospital. It was an intimidating place to be. When the nurse stopped at the bed of a young man, motionless, unconscious, covered with blood and hooked up to several machines, I looked at him and said, 'No, no, that's not my son.' But she remained where she was and I looked again. I simply didn't recognise him, and for several minutes more, I stayed convinced it wasn't him, although I later realised my mind was refusing to accept the reality. He simply bore no resemblance to the Christopher I'd waved off on his gap year only a few months before. More than that, it meant acknowledging that my son was gravely injured, an idea so surreal and horrific, my mind did everything to deny it.

The doctors explained that Christopher was in a deep coma and there was no way of telling whether he would live or die. If he lived, he might lie dormant for the rest of his life, in a vegetative state. Although that sounded terrible, it was more bearable than the thought of him dying. I so desperately wanted him to live. I struggled to process the information, walking around in a daze of excruciating anxiety and exhaustion from the period of limbo we were now in.

On hearing the news, my sister Carey got hold of Amy

and May's school to tell them. As it happens, the twins had just been in their dorm, talking with their friends about how good-looking and cool Christopher was. Carey played down the news, not wanting to scare the girls, who were upset enough by the censored version of events given to them. When Carey ended the conversation by asking them to pray for him to pull through, they realised just how dire the situation was but had to stay at school because they were in the middle of their O levels. Carey meanwhile flew out to Miami with Henry, who, despite being ill himself, wanted to show his support for his younger brother. Their arrival was a godsend because both of them were optimistic, calm and a good influence on me and Colin – we were struggling to hold it together.

Christopher was moved to a circular ward with a nurses' station in the middle and hooked up to monitors, like the other patients. The only sounds were the mechanical beeping of the machines and the squeaky footsteps of the nurses while the patients lay eerily silent and unmoving. The set-up wasn't comforting: the nurses seemed to nurse from afar and hardly spoke, and it was very difficult to get near Christopher because of the machines. Although I understood they were keeping him alive, all I wanted to do was hug him and I couldn't. Only once was I allowed to touch his hand.

Then it was a case of waiting. For a fortnight we stayed in Miami and every minute seemed to drag. At least Carey was a great comfort and did her best to distract me from the horror of the situation.

After two weeks, though still in a coma, Christopher was deemed stable enough to be flown back to London in a private aeroplane. It was so heavy and full, with specialist equipment and two teams of doctors and nurses, that we couldn't go with him. Not knowing whether he would go downhill at any point, we had to travel back across the Atlantic after him, which was almost as bad as the journey in the other direction had been.

When Christopher arrived in London, it was still too early to tell what would happen, but at least he was back on British soil. And thank God the man at the ticket office had persuaded me to buy the travel insurance. That £150 was the equivalent of winning the lottery: in the end the insurance company paid out over a million pounds.

At this point, I knew that Henry would most likely die and that Charlie's future was uncertain. Now Christopher was teetering on the edge of life. How could this happen to us? I might have been powerless to save Henry and Charlie, but I was determined to keep Christopher alive by any means I could.

CHAPTER FIFTEEN

A Nightmare and a Miracle

EVERYTHING CHANGED AFTER Christopher's accident. My whole life became bound up in trying to save his. I was utterly determined that he would recover and convinced that if I gave him all of my attention he just might be all right. I temporarily stepped down from my duties as a Lady in Waiting, staying by Christopher's bedside.

To start with he lay unconscious in intensive care, still on a ventilator and attached to all sorts of machines, at the Wellington, a private hospital right next to Lord's cricket ground in north London. Colin and I sat next to him day in day out, still not sure what the future held.

Although Colin had been distant with all the children

when they were young, their relationships had grown over time and Christopher was the only one of our children with whom Colin never ever lost his temper. Instead I'd often hear them roaring with laughter. Christopher would constantly be telling us how much he loved us, which only made it more painful to see him lying silent in intensive care.

The twins adored him, and it was incredibly difficult for them, made worse because they were stuck doing their exams. When they could finally see him, they were shocked into silence at the sight of the tube coming out of his neck. It was hard to comfort them. All I could do was encourage them to engage with their brother. 'Give him a kiss so he knows you're here,' I said, hoping it might be true.

Both Charlie and Henry visited Christopher, willing him to wake up, but nothing worked. Henry, who was gradually getting more ill, remained a very strong and calm presence, insisting I focus on Christopher, who needed me more, rather than looking after him. I felt torn, but it was true that while Henry was walking and talking, Christopher was lying motionless.

A few weeks later, the doctors told us that Christopher wouldn't die but that it was impossible to know whether he would stay in the coma for weeks or months. He was considered to be stable, so with great reluctance Colin returned to Mustique to deal with all the pressing commitments that had piled up since Christopher's accident.

I spent all my time with Christopher, but he stayed unresponsive, stuck in his limp, damaged body. I kept thinking about how lively and active he had been and now he was getting bed sores, surrounded by beeping machines.

Meanwhile all his friends, as supportive as they were, had gone to university and he was being left behind.

A variety of specialist doctors came and saw him, none of them offering the reassurance I craved. Everything was so uncertain and exhausting. After several weeks without change, the stress began to take its toll and I could feel myself beginning to give up. I started to doubt whether anything would ever make a difference. While I already had quite a strong Christian faith, going to church every Sunday, I hadn't ever felt I had engaged with God, but now I started to pray hard. I prayed and prayed, and just when I was about to give up hope, help came my way.

I had heard of a Christian healer called Mrs Black, who lived up in Scotland and, after curing horses to great effect, had realised she had healing hands. Normally I would have been sceptical, but I was a desperate mother, trying to save my son, so I contacted her. She agreed to try to help and said she could work on him by telephone. Even now, this really does sound ridiculous, but somehow it seemed to work. After every healing session, in which Mrs Black channelled all her energy into Christopher's recovery, praying for Christ to heal him, he would appear to make an improvement – a slight twitch or apparently responding to something. It was minute and would have been unnoticeable to the untrained eye, but by then I had been observing him for over a month. I took hope from these sessions and the tiny improvements they seemed to provoke.

Mrs Black came down once a month to do more intense healing on Christopher. During one of those sessions I felt her hands, which were boiling hot – it was as though the power was coming out of them into his body. In between the sessions, Mrs Black would ring me up to ask how he was doing. One day I was so tired I could hardly speak. She said, 'Anne, I can help you. Tomorrow morning sit in a comfortable chair at ten a.m. and drain your mind of everything. I will sit and concentrate on you and you will feel a difference.'

I agreed, but I was very much a doubting Thomas. At 10 a.m., I sat in a chair, hundreds of miles from Mrs Black, wondering whether I was going mad. But suddenly, to my amazement, I felt as if champagne was flowing through my veins. I felt invigorated. It's the only time in my life when anything like that has happened to me. The only explanation I can come up with is that it felt like Christ was visiting me, laying His hands on me, making it possible for me to carry on, literally filling me with energy and hope and strength – His strength, I suppose.

This miraculous experience came in the nick of time because, shortly afterwards, I met with one of the doctors. Our surreal conversation took place in an empty operating theatre as I anxiously perched on the edge of one of the counters. He said: 'I've got great experience of treating patients in comas and I can tell you now that Christopher will be a vegetable all his life. There is no hope of recovery for him.' He paused, looked at me and continued, in his matter-of-fact tone, as though unaware of the gravity of what he was saying, or perhaps because he had delivered those lines many times before: 'If I were you,' he said, 'I would forget about him improving and get on with your life.'

For some people, perhaps, those words would have come as some sort of relief – permission to give up, an excuse to get out of the agonising and exhausting state of limbo. If I hadn't had the extraordinary healing experience, I think I might have been one of those people, but my outlook had changed. I thought, I am not going to believe this. With God's help, and all the other people willing to get Christopher back, this is not the outcome I am going to accept.

I was left feeling more determined than ever, while also knowing that I had to work out and stick to a plan to stay focused and determined and see Christopher through to his recovery. Somewhat miraculously, Barbara Barnes rang me up. 'I'll clear the next six months and do everything I can to help,' she said. Having left us when the twins went away to boarding school, she had just left her position as nanny to the Princes William and Harry and wanted to help Christopher. He was the first baby she had ever looked after and she adored him as unconditionally as a mother. I was delighted and relieved to hear from her and together we started this incredible journey.

From that moment on, I had a plan to try to revive him out of the coma. I found a doctor whose own son had been in a coma and he stressed the importance of the family doing things with the patient. He explained that sitting there feeling helpless would do nothing except make the family feel miserable. 'You have to engage on all levels,' he told me, 'stimulate all five senses.' He gave me a 'coma kit', which he had invented to help his own son recover. Inside, it had lots of different things to help stimulate a coma patient's senses, such as a coarse brush, a soft piece of material and things that had different smells. He explained that for fifteen minutes in every hour every day for weeks, Christopher needed to be stimulated. Only then would he stand a chance. He warned

me that it wouldn't be easy: unless I was completely dedicated and set up a routine it wouldn't work.

His advice and support made all the difference. Not only
was it full of hope, it gave me something to do. Waiting
around with a feeling of total helplessness had been one of
the hardest parts of it all, and now I had a purpose.

Barbara and I went for it: we used the coma kit every hour
for fifteen minutes, wafting a pair of Christopher's smelly
trainers near his nose, then swapping them for perfume or
cut grass or a bacon sandwich – any strong smell, good and
bad, familiar and exotic. We sang, we talked, we laughed. We
played music softly and then loudly, from rap to Mozart. We
stroked his skin with velvet, then sandpaper or a brush – soft
and hard sensations, hoping that the different textures would
stimulate automatic reactions. We dabbed him with a hot
towel, then a cold towel, in case the different temperatures
triggered a reaction. We read all his favourite children's books,
and his former housemaster at school recorded a tape of all
his friends for us to play to him.

Seeing how exhausting the process was, friends began to
help us. I set up a rota where my close friends Margaret
Vyner, Sarah Henderson, Ingrid Channon and Zannah
Johnston would come in and take turns to stimulate or talk
to Christopher. We'd lighten the atmosphere, joking that
Christopher had a whole host of women trying to coax him
back into the world of the living. It became a team effort,
creating more energy, more motivation and also providing
opportunities to pool ideas. Barbara and I came up with a
crazy one: to re-enact his birth in the hope that some sort
of deep instinct might kick start his brain.

We eventually persuaded the nurses to let us take Christopher out of bed and nurse him on the floor so I could cradle him: I was sure that if he could feel my heartbeat, it would have a positive effect on him. He was still wired up to many machines and I knew it was an unconventional idea, but the more they said no, the more I felt I was right. So there I was, down on the floor with Christopher slumped on top of me, treating this incredibly tall grown man of nineteen like a baby just in case something deep within him was triggered. Nothing happened immediately but we didn't give up.

Princess Margaret kept in regular touch, asking after Christopher's progress, which was still almost non-existent. But as she continued to ask, I was able to describe tiny changes and she helped motivate me to keep trying.

A big change came when, although Christopher was still in a coma, the doctors finally took him off the ventilator and he started to breathe for himself. However, he still wasn't able to swallow. One day Barbara arrived with a baby's bottle. The nurse on duty was somewhat taken aback and asked Barbara what she was doing with it.

'Well,' Barbara replied, 'I thought I might try using it on Christopher. He loved his bottle. Can I just put it in his mouth and see? I think it might trigger him to swallow.'

The nurse raised her eyebrows but gave her permission, while simultaneously dismissing the possibility that it had any hope of working. But it did. Christopher started to suck, and the sucking motion caused him to swallow. His automatic reflex had kicked in. The nurse didn't believe it, so Barbara showed her. It was a massive breakthrough.

In the end, Christopher was in a coma for four months –

the longest four months of my life. I will never forget the day he finally woke up. He had just been moved to the Royal Free, the NHS hospital in Hampstead, for special treatment, and when I visited for the first time, I found him crying. I can only assume that he must have been aware he was somewhere new and felt uncertain of his surroundings. Normally people are upset to see somebody they love in tears, but I was ecstatic. It meant he was feeling something. It meant he was in there somewhere.

I cradled him, comforting him, and started talking about cars because he loved them so much, and although I felt rather silly, I said to him, 'Come on, stop crying. You must get out of here. I promise you I will get you a car as soon as you do. What would you like?'

Of course I wasn't expecting him to answer. But he did. His first word since the accident was 'Lamborghini.'

I could not believe my ears. Having been speaking to him with no response for months, there he was requesting a sports car. I have never felt so relieved in all my life because in that moment I knew Christopher was going to be all right.

From that moment on, he slowly came back to life. Although conscious, he was still trapped in a body that had forgotten how to work. Everything was exhausting and slow – words were hard to form, his muscles were weak, as though his body and mind were only just connected. He would have to learn to walk again but, in the immediate aftermath, that challenge was long into the future. None of that seemed to matter right then – it was just a miracle that his eyes were open and he was aware of his surroundings.

The children were overjoyed, as was Colin, who was deeply

proud of my efforts and sincerely grateful to Barbara and all the loyal friends who had helped, from Princess Margaret and Nigel Napier, who undoubtedly saved his life, to the army surgeon who had operated on him, and all the doctors, nurses, friends who helped week after week.

Once it was clear that Christopher was strong enough, Diane Lomax, a brilliant physiotherapist, set to work, teaching him how to use his body all over again. A big team helped Christopher strengthen his muscles, but walking was still a far-off aim. Instead of feeling frustrated or depressed, he stayed enthusiastic and never lost his sense of humour. Everybody came to adore him.

He went to a rehabilitation centre in Barnes for months and was then moved to Headley Court, an army rehabilitation centre, because the surgeon who had operated on him in Belize wanted to show his support. Other people offered help, including Helena Bonham Carter's parents, Raymond and Elena, because in 1979 Raymond had had surgery to remove a brain tumour, which had left him paralysed. Their support was hugely useful since I didn't know anyone who had been in similar circumstances.

After almost a year, once his basic coordination was deemed good enough, he came home to Hill Lodge, our house in London. He still couldn't walk – his balance was terrible. The doctors warned me that he would 'grow up all over again', behaving like a toddler, then a small child, then a teenager. They also warned me that a lot of coma patients' personalities changed: they were often moody and rude, and there was a high risk of depression. Bracing myself, I hired nurses and au pairs, and reminded myself of how far he had come.

People assumed I would prepare the house by setting up a bedroom on the ground floor and installing rails, hoists and a stair lift, but something inside me was convinced that Christopher should not have any aids. I was certain he would come to rely on them, and they would hinder his progress. He was only twenty and an athletic young man with an incredibly positive outlook on life. I believed my attitude was the right one for him.

Christopher's bedroom was upstairs, so he would have to manage two flights of stairs every morning and evening. While the house doesn't compare to the size of Holkham, it's still large when you think of it from the perspective of a young man who is having to crawl everywhere. But crawl he did. His attitude never wavered, and he accepted it would take him literally hours to get from downstairs to his room. Coming down was a bit quicker – he would slide down the stairs on his bottom.

I doubted my decision many times. Seeing him on the floor struggling, inching his way from one place to the next, felt cruel and I had to override every instinct I had to offer support. Sometimes I did, but mostly I offered words of encouragement. It was agony but I really believed it was the best way. What was a comfort was that he never complained and I could also see how motivated he was to move from place to place – if he had given up, he simply wouldn't have done it. I know this approach wouldn't work for everyone, but we had a relationship built on trust and love, and he stayed optimistic and determined throughout.

Once he advanced from crawling, he fell over a great deal, but he didn't seem to mind. Whenever he fell, he would just wait to be helped or somehow manage to get up.

After many months, there was a difference that motivated him further, and because he had succeeded himself, he took ownership of his actions and built on them. He was so courageous, so strong, and kept every bit of his lovable character and wasn't in the least bit depressed.

As Christopher was recovering, I wanted to share my experience with others: Barbara and I wrote an article for the prestigious weekly medical journal the *Lancet*, and I also raised enough money to put 'coma kits' in various hospitals. Because of the coma kits and my experience, I was contacted by a Saudi Arabian family who asked me to help their son who had fallen off his polo pony and was in a coma. I visited the hospital to find the young man lying in the bed unresponsive, just as Christopher had been. He was surrounded by women in burqas sitting in silence. Not knowing what to do, they had made no attempt at contact and the room had a familiar feeling of mute despair.

I told them to take their head coverings off and their gloves and hold his hand. I told them to talk to him, and showed them all the things in the 'coma kit', doing little demonstrations by wafting perfume under the patient's nose and rubbing different materials over his skin. They followed suit and a few months later contacted me, thanking me profusely, when the young man recovered.

I find it hard to think about this time in my life. It was so agonising, so desperate, and I am so grateful there was a happy ending. What is astonishing is that Christopher doesn't live his life feeling resentful of the accident and in fact he wouldn't change it. To this day, I find his attitude remarkable.

CHAPTER SIXTEEN

Forever Young

BY 1988, A year and a half after Christopher's accident, he still had a long journey of recovery ahead of him. So many people rallied round to help him – the support really poured in. But for Charlie and Henry, the opposite happened.

Nowadays mental health, drug addiction and HIV/AIDS are talked about more openly, albeit still being among the biggest taboos in any society. But in the 1980s, there was no such openness when it came to mental health or addiction and therefore no such acceptance. AIDS was still the most feared disease in the world because it was so poorly understood. After doctors had first linked it to gay men, they realised it could be passed to babies by infected mothers. Links had then been made with needles and blood. The more connections were made, the more people panicked, worrying that it could be passed to another person as easily as a common cold.

Fear born mainly out of lack of information resulted in many young men with AIDS being abandoned by frightened families, leaving them to die alone. Henry bravely decided to speak out when his HIV virus turned to AIDS, hoping he could help break the stigma. I warned him, knowing that he would be ostracised, but his mind was made up. He told the press, conscious that it would be up to young men like him who actually had the disease to bare all. The press lapped up his willingness because he was one of the first aristocrats to contract AIDS and the first who was willing to speak out, so they saw it as a big story.

Not surprisingly, Henry's very open admission led some of our friends to distance themselves from us, just too afraid to socialise with us. Although it made everything more diffi-cult for us as a family, I can quite understand where they were coming from: people do what they think they need to do in order to protect themselves and their children.

I was conscious of the possible risk too, worried for our other children, but not wanting to shun Henry. Nothing was certain like it is today, and as the doctors were discovering things all the time, I compromised. I bought him a new set of towels that were a different colour from everybody else's so I could distinguish them, washing them separately. I also served him food with his own plates, knives and forks, but I never distanced myself from him. Now I know that doing this was unnecessary, but I didn't at the time and it felt like the safest thing to do.

Princess Margaret was one of the few people whose behaviour didn't change at all. Not only did she continue to see Colin and me, bringing her children to Glen as she always had, but she also visited Henry when he was in hospital, and kept a watchful eye open in case there was anything she could do to help. I was incredibly grateful for her loyalty and attitude. It made me feel stronger, and without my mother there, Princess Margaret offered a similar strength that helped me cope.

The more ill Henry got, the more difficult it became, because he had to keep going to hospital, but only certain hospitals would take AIDS patients. Not only that, but because he was six foot eight, none of the beds were long enough, so I'd put a table at the bottom of his bed to make it longer. Once, when he was very ill, and was waiting at St Mary's, Paddington, for a bed, poor Henry was too ill to sit, so I sat on the floor in A and E as the previously full room emptied at the sight of him. It was as though we were lepers but the public's reaction only made me more determined to support my son. I sat there, cradling him, with his head on my lap for hours and hours. This bore a horrible similarity to all the hours I had spent cradling Christopher, but I drew strength from those dark days, wanting to do my best for Henry as well and, above everything, wanting him to feel that he wasn't alone.

Before Princess Diana went to the London Lighthouse in Notting Hill – the first centre and hospice made especially for AIDS patients, in 1989 with a posse of photographers in tow – Princess Margaret had helped set it up, officially opening it in 1988. She went on to become the patron of the Terrence Higgins Trust, the UK's leading sexual-health charity. She didn't hold hands and stroke the patients, like Princess Diana did, because she wasn't tactile in the same way, but she made them laugh and told them stories.

The London Lighthouse opened just in time for Henry, who by then was rapidly declining. He was covered with purple blotches and had no hair left, due to Kaposi's sarcoma, a type of skin cancer. That was the problem with AIDS: the immune system became so weak that Henry was unable to fight even a cold, and while he got skin cancer, other people succumbed to pneumonia.

Characteristically, Henry took it all in his stride, always trying to stop me worrying, even though we both knew he was going to die. He managed to find peace through being a Buddhist, and when he'd been diagnosed in 1986, he had gone straight to Japan to a Buddhist monastery. I still have the postcard he sent me in which he wrote: 'I'm in the monastery, looking at Mount Fujiyama, and if I die tomorrow, I won't mind, because I've been to Paradise – I can see Heaven.' It was consoling that the religion made Henry feel comforted and less afraid of death.

When Christmas 1989 came, he desperately wanted to come home for the day, but I was worried his appearance might upset his son, Euan, who was still a toddler. The people at the London Lighthouse were fantastic and told me not to worry when I raised my concern. Having supported many patients in Henry's condition, they had a special team of make-up artists for this very reason. Henry came home wearing a turquoise hat and a lot of foundation. Too weak to stand or even really talk, he lay in the drawing room and we all had our Christmas lunch on trays. Euan opened his presents around him and kept saying, 'Daddy, come and play with me,' and Henry would reply, 'Daddy's very tired. You bring your toy to me.' Which Euan did. It was as lovely as it could have been.

May, not knowing what to give her brother as a present, decided on a fun cuddly toy – a bright green frog with a red and white striped night hat, which Henry loved, putting on the hat as he lay surrounded by us all. He had become really close to the twins: for sixth form, they had made the joint decision to go to different schools in order to gain some independence from each other, but they found it very difficult. Henry made an effort to support both of them, driving down to their schools to take them on days out. How we all got through Christmas Day I don't know. It was heartbreaking, but I put on a brave face, wanting to make it as ordinary as possible.

After Christmas Day, Henry's condition declined, and he was moved to St Mary's, Paddington, which had just opened a special wing for AIDS patients. Like all of the other very ill young men, Henry was moved into a room of his own. Most visitors would sit quietly with their loved one in private, but Henry had asked to be surrounded by a couple of dozen of his Buddhist friends. I found the visits increasingly difficult because each time I went I had to clamber through a crowd of people chanting: they were so involved in their trance that they were unaware of me. In his last weeks, I was never alone with Henry.

On the final visit, I was opening the door, preparing to wade through the Buddhists, when a nurse grabbed me firmly by the elbow, stopping me entering. She said, 'Lady Glenconner, will you come with me?' My heart sank. There was a special room where people went to grieve, and she was leading me there. I knew what was coming but even knowing did nothing to cushion the blow. She told me gently, 'Henry has just died.'

I don't know what I felt – a feeling of agony I can't put into words. Not only had my son just died, but I had missed saying goodbye to him by minutes.

I also felt pure anger. Anger that he had been so careless. I had warned him so many times to be careful but he just hadn't listened. Henry died eighteen months after he was diagnosed in January 1989. He was only twenty-nine.

The whole family was devastated. Charlie, who had always been jealous of Henry and had not been on good terms with him for a few years, had made up with him just before he died and now was kicking himself for past failings. I remember sitting in the kitchen at Hill Lodge with the twins while Charlie cried his eyes out. I'd never seen him cry like that and soon I was also comforting the twins, who had dissolved into tears too. They had only just turned eighteen and, on the cusp of developing an adult friendship with Henry, were heartbroken that they would never get the chance.

No one knew how to comfort me and the family, although both Princess Margaret and Princess Diana had eased the shame of AIDS through associating themselves with it and also did a lot for individual men and their families. When Princess Diana heard that Henry had died, she made an effort to comfort me personally by writing a letter of condolence. She had sat with and spoken to Henry at his bedside shortly before he died. She'd been there filming some of her meet-ings with the young patients on the ward to raise awareness. At the end of the filming, she had asked the nurses if there were any patients too ill to be there. When the nurses said there were two, Princess Diana visited both of them on her own, without the film crew. One of them was Henry.

'Oh, Ma'am,' he had said to her, smiling broadly, 'we've got something in common.' Princess Diana had looked surprised and asked him what it was. 'Well,' came Henry's reply, 'Barbara Barnes was my nanny before she came to look after Prince William and Prince Harry.'

In the letter she wrote she said it had been lovely to meet Henry, even though under sad circumstances, and said she wanted to tell me how brave she thought he was. She wasn't afraid to confront the situation head-on, which was a complete contrast to a lot of people we knew, who just simply didn't know what to say at all. Normally I found it hard to relate to somebody so openly emotional, so different from the mould I was used to, but when it came to dealing with Henry's death, she got it right.

Her acknowledgement of his bravery made me feel proud of him, which was a comfort, especially when I was faced with so many other people distancing themselves from us, then having to deal with the press, who behaved like animals. Having followed his story, they swarmed to the house after his death: Henry had become headline news. While he had wanted his story to be shared in the hope it would have a positive impact, for us in the direct aftermath, the reality was extremely difficult to deal with.

Every morning, a newspaper was posted through the door

with Henry's photo and huge, normally very blunt, headlines. And the press kept coming, the police seemingly unable to stop them, as they filled the street, ringing the doorbell all day and all night, stooping to an all-time low of hiding in the dustbins outside Euan's nursery school.

Wanting to protect Euan, we asked the local clergyman to come around wearing his cassock so that he could hide Euan under it and get him out of the house. It worked, the press just assuming a member of the clergy had come to comfort us, not realising Euan was being smuggled away from them. Instead of leaving us to grieve in private, the press hounded us in our family's darkest hour.

Determined not to let their behaviour affect me, and desperately trying to hold everything together for the sake of the other children, I shook it off and busied myself with the funeral arrangements. So, while members of the press were jumping out of dustbins and knocking at the windows and doors, I was trying to make sure Henry's last wishes were carried out. Because he was so tall, his coffin was very big, and when it came to the funeral, I couldn't help but emit a tiny smile because, as is Buddhist custom, it was covered with pineapples and other tropical fruit so it looked like a giant fruit salad as it came into the crematorium.

The months after Henry's death were very difficult. No one else could relate to what I was going through; no one seemed to know how to deal with me or with what had happened. Colin found it difficult, returning to Mustique, away from the press, and I went to Norfolk to get away from it all. When I went to the shops, the people who would normally say hello and spark up a conversation would see me and scurry away. I think they were terrified of saying the wrong thing or making me burst into tears. It was as though everybody was so scared of death, and AIDS was such a feared and reviled illness, they pretended it hadn't happened. I was from a generation that didn't have endless heart-to-hearts, we didn't share our emotions, and for the sake of the other children, I thought it was best to put on a strong front, get on with life and not dwell. Apart from at the funeral I don't think anybody saw me cry. Instead I went to church and prayed. After all, what else could I do? Nothing was going to bring Henry back.

My close friend Margaret Vyner understood I needed support and, knowing how devoted Henry was to Buddhism, she took me out to India to stay with Mitch Crites, our mutual friend who had got Colin out of trouble when he'd started a fight with an Indian shopkeeper several years before. I was absolutely exhausted and didn't want to go but Mitch re-assured me, telling me how healing India was. He told me, 'Death is a part of daily life and it isn't uncommon to see a body being cremated on a funeral pyre floating off on the river. The culture embraces death: they talk about it and they see it.'

I was so grateful to Margaret and Mitch because as soon as I arrived I knew it was the right decision – everything Mitch had said was true, and I felt a sense of relief straight away. They took me along to different temples: to Jain temples, which looked like they'd been made out of lace, and we watched the monks in devotion, wearing nothing but a feather fan over their groins. The nuns wore white garments, their bodies bundled up, so they looked like huge white meringues.

We went into one of these temples and found a family mourning a family member who had died, in the middle of a *puja*, a Hindu form of worship. They were bunched together, clapping and chanting, moving in rhythmic unison. Mitch went up to them and said, 'I've got a lady with me whose son has just died. He was a Buddhist. Do you mind if she watches you?'

'No, no, she can't watch, she must join in!' they said, opening their arms to me. I felt a huge sense of release when I was swept up in their *puja*, as they burned incense and chanted.

We carried on visiting more temples but I started to get worried: in Buddhism, it is believed that when the deceased has reached a certain level in their journey to nirvana, there has to be a Buddhist monk chanting a prayer at the precise time in this journey to help the person reach the next level. The process is the same for everyone and therefore, on a set day and time, a few weeks after the death, this prayer has to happen.

On that particular day, we were driving and hadn't found anywhere with monks to chant the prayer. I knew the time slot was a slim one, so I began to get anxious on behalf of Henry. We were in the middle of nowhere, driving down a long road in the desert, when Mitch said to me, 'Don't worry. I am absolutely certain we will find a monk.'

I didn't know why Mitch was so sure, since there was nothing but camels and palm trees, but then we saw a lone figure on the road. Mitch said, 'I think this is what we've been waiting for,' and stopped the car.

Mitch, who spoke Hindi, explained and the monk smiled

and took my hands at once, starting the *puja* for Henry. I couldn't help but feel it was a sign that this monk, the only person we had passed on the whole journey, was there for me, for Henry, and that Henry was all right. He was at peace.

With that, I felt so exhausted I almost collapsed. I think it was the grief, followed by an enormous flood of relief. I got back into the car and slept for hours. It was the most important trip of my life, which is why I think I found it so draining and yet, at the same time, I found this amazing strength. The strength has stayed with me and still makes me feel more able to cope when I think about Henry.

As the eighties came to an end, my life had changed considerably. Ever since Henry's diagnosis, swiftly followed by Christopher's accident, I had revaluated my priorities and focused on being a mother, then a wife, staying in England to be with Christopher far more than being with Colin.

Christopher was walking again, his recovery astounding. The first proper outing he had was three years after the accident when we went to a ball at Holkham. He wore black tie with an enormous smile, and I kept looking at him in disbelief, although the reality was that for most of the evening he leant on me. I didn't mind in the slightest, but because he is very tall and very heavy, I did wonder whether we would both suddenly find ourselves in a pile on the floor. In the end it took five years for Christopher to recover as much as he was going to.

During that time Mustique had changed too. The hedonistic carefree days of the seventies and eighties had been so successful that they had changed the island. Colin had sold more shares and slowly but surely had less and less say in the decisions of how Mustique was run. It was no longer possible for him to do it his way. Having clashed with so many people over his rigid opinions and the extreme way in which he conveyed them, Colin had left Mustique in 1987, selling The Great House to the heiress Christina Onassis's third husband, former KGB agent Sergei Kauzov.

Moving to St Lucia, he had invested in an undeveloped 480-acre estate that Henry had found before he died. Selling half of the land to developers, who built the Jalousie Plantation Resort, he kept the other half for himself, coming up with all sorts of ideas, wanting to create somewhere else as spectacular as Mustique.

As Henry had suspected he would, Colin fell in love with the place, which was between the pair of volcanic spires known as the Pitons, with land sloping to the sea, building the third and final Great House. Unfortunately, it was the least 'great' of them all. Although it had a vast main room on the top floor, with a domed roof, which was spectacular, the bedrooms were on the ground floor and were very gloomy. With the water tank on the terrace over the bedrooms, I was always nervous that it would burst above my head and I'd be drowned while asleep. I was never quite so connected to St Lucia because, over the years, Mustique had come to feel like home.

The twins, by then in their late teens, took after their father, loving the lifestyle the West Indies offered, as did Christopher, who craved independence, so Colin came up with a brilliant idea. Finding a cottage in Soufrière on St Lucia, he invited Christopher to move out there. Thrilled by his father's plan and desperate to start a new life, and have a bit more fun, he left England at once.

Colin's plan was a huge success. Christopher loved the set-up, never realising that Colin had hired two old ladies who lived next to the cottage Christopher was occupying, to keep an eye on him. He just thought they cooked for him and did his laundry, but in fact they followed him at a distance in case he fell over and made sure he had got into bed all right. It was the perfect compromise and meant I was hugely reassured. It was amazing to think he was able to live like that after all that he'd been through.

A state of normality returned and, as time progressed, the sadness of losing Henry became, very slowly, easier to bear. Although we had lost Henry, Charlie had managed, amazingly, to stay free from heroin and, although on prescribed methadone, was able to live a much more normal existence. The candle-making couple, Mr and Mrs Parsons, had given Charlie a new focus – the long and the short of it was that Charlie and Mrs Parsons, Sheilagh, had fallen in love.

We were all thrilled when, after her divorce in 1993, Charlie and Sheilagh got married in a London register office. Charlie, who took after Colin in his flamboyant dress sense, wore Tennant tartan trews and a leopard waistcoat, and drove to and from the ceremony in a bright pink Cadillac, past Buckingham Palace on the way home. They were quite a spectacle, especially when the traffic police assumed they were going to one of the Queen's garden parties. Corralled into a queue, Colin, absolutely furious, had to get out and explain, leaving the garden-party guests in their tea-dresses and suits with open mouths at the extraordinary car and its occupants.

The wedding reception was held at our house and we all danced reels to a ceilidh band. I just hoped that Charlie had many happy years in front of him and that maybe he would be okay. When Cody, their son, was born in 1994, everyone was thrilled. Although Charlie had been disinherited and Henry's son Euan would inherit Glen, Cody would inherit the barony, as well as the Caribbean assets.

For Charlie, the birth of his son changed his outlook on life entirely. Two days after Cody was born, he said to me, 'I have never in my life felt so happy, and I feel like I have suddenly realised what life is about.' To hear those words coming from Charlie was momentous. For years, I had never dared hope that he would get himself out of addiction, let alone become a happily married man and a father of a wonderful son. No one had, least of all Charlie. This was all down to Sheilagh, who had managed to keep Charlie on the right path.

But although he had turned his life around, it was too late. Charlie's happiness was to be short-lived because, when Cody was still a toddler, Charlie became ill and was diagnosed with hepatitis C, a direct result of the years of heroin addiction. All the family were worried but Charlie played it down. Sheilagh conveyed that it would be a rocky few months and that the doctors had been unsure whether he would stabilise, although as time went on, it looked increasingly unlikely.

When Amy rang him up a few weeks later to see how he was doing, he dismissed it completely, doing the little laugh he always did, assuring his sister that she needn't come all the way up to Scotland to see him. Colin, used to Charlie being up and down over the years, didn't come back from the West Indies so I went on my own and spent the weekend with Charlie, Sheilagh and Cody.

We had a really lovely time feeding the ducks in Edinburgh and walking round the garden at Holyrood, but I was in two minds about leaving, unsure exactly how unwell Charlie was. When I discussed with Sheilagh what I should do, she re-assured me, saying Charlie might go on for a long time and I should carry on living my life. When I explained I was supposed to be going to Morocco on holiday with Zannah and Nicky Johnston, she said how guilty Charlie would feel if I cancelled my plans, so I went.

None of us realised how quickly Charlie would deteriorate. Only a few days later, while I was in Morocco, I got the devastating phone call from Sheilagh telling me Charlie had died.

Once again, the family descended into grieving. Colin was riddled with guilt, having become less and less sympathetic to Charlie over the years. Christopher was distraught and May, even now, is full of regret for having cut their last phone conversation short and postponing a visit to see him that she and Amy had arranged.

As a mother, I hadn't thought there could be anything worse than burying one son until I was in the churchyard again, burying another. I've never seen Colin cry the way he cried at Charlie's funeral. It reminded me of Charlie's reaction when Henry died.

There were so many what-ifs with Charlie. Looking back, I question and doubt the choices we made: the things we noticed developing in his childhood but chose not to delve into or were unable to solve, the things we thought would be fixed by sending him away to hospitals, clinics and, later, to rehab. But even with the greatest help in the world, he was such a free spirit with such presence that I don't know if we'd ever have been able to stop him going down the route he chose.

Once again, when we needed privacy the most, the press was intrusive, this time because of their obsession with the old myth about 'the Tennant Curse', which had been entirely made up but revolved around the notion that family members died before their time in various dramatic ways. Now that two sons in the family had died young, the 'Tennant Curse' played into the reporters' hands perfectly, only adding to our anguish.

On the day of the funeral, the press were surrounding the church and appearing over the graves. There we were, mourning our sweet Charlie, only to have them banging on the door of the church, wanting to get their story. I suppose by then we had got used to them behaving so badly, but I still can't think of anything much lower than gate-crashing a funeral.

Over time, my stress levels began to lower, the sorrow eased, life turned a corner, but it was never the same again. To this day my heart almost stops whenever the telephone rings too late at night. I don't know what I would do with another death in the family. The twins had always been so proud of being a big family and having three older brothers, but as Christopher has had to remind us all numerous times, 'Although they're gone, the love continues.'

CHAPTER SEVENTEEN

The Last Days of a Princess

A LOYAL FRIEND all her life, Princess Margaret supported me throughout. She allowed me time away from the Household when my children needed me, and she always welcomed me back when I was ready. Over the years, she had spent so much time with Colin and me that our lives were completely connected. By the nineties, I had been a Lady in Waiting for over twenty-five years.

At my coming-out dance, I remember realising we had both grown up, our childhood days on Holkham beach long behind us, and then, in 1993, I had a similar realisation when Peter Townsend came to have lunch with Princess Margaret at Kensington Palace and I happened to be there. Suddenly, I was aware we were getting old.

They hadn't seen each other since he'd moved away in the 1950s, following the ultimatum she'd been given to choose between him and her royal life. I watched him from the window, now a very old man, as he got out of the car and slowly made his way into the house. I didn't go to lunch but afterwards, once he'd left, she asked me to sit with her. 'How did it go?' I asked her.

'He hasn't changed at all,' she replied. It was a touching response, given the forty years that had passed.

I had never really asked her much about their relationship but now I sensed she wanted to talk about him. 'Ma'am,' I said, 'when did you first fall in love with him?'

She didn't need much encouragement, launching into the story of the 1947 royal tour to South Africa. Every morning and evening she had gone for a ride, with the horses that had been brought on the Royal Train, accompanied by an Equerry to the King, Peter Townsend. They had fallen madly in love and, although it had happened long ago, the subject made her pensive. I felt sad for her, but just like with me and Johnnie Spencer, there was no way of telling whether we would have been happier had we married those men instead of our husbands. Not one to dwell on things, after a moment's pause, she moved on to a completely new conversation as though she wanted to draw a line under the topic, in exactly the same way my mother would have done.

That matter-of-fact attitude had served us both well, enabling us to laugh and have fun, living our lives and making the best of them, despite all the obstacles we had both faced. Some of the happiest times that Princess Margaret and I shared were on Mustique, and by this time we had been going every February for thirty years. But things had changed. With Colin on St Lucia and The Great House no longer mine and Colin's, I stayed with Princess Margaret at Les Jolies Eaux, although she had passed it on to her son David, who often rented it out during the high season. This meant we went at set times of the year and, as we had always done, swam together, collected shells and had drinks at Basil's Bar, watching for the green flash over the sea at sunset.

Although we were both only in our mid-sixties and I was in good health, Princess Margaret had been on a steady decline since 1985 when she had had part of a lung removed. It was when we were on Mustique in 1994 that she had her first official stroke. In the months before, I had noticed that during conversations when she was in full flow she would suddenly stop. Not for long, just a moment or two. At first, I thought perhaps she had been distracted or she didn't want to continue the conversation. It was rather odd, but I dismissed those moments because they lasted only a few seconds and she would seem perfectly fine, carrying on with the conversation almost straight away.

One evening, when we were halfway through dinner at our friends the Harding-Lawrences' – their house stands cut into the hillside as though built for a Bond villain – I heard a sudden intake of breath from Princess Margaret. Glancing across the table, I saw her slumped forward. Everybody got up and we carried her from the table to the drawing room where we laid her down on the sofa.

Fortunately, there was a wonderful doctor on the island called Dr Bunbury, who is still there today. He is much loved among the expat community, and Colin always said that some of the women came to Mustique especially to be ill so they could see him. Dr Bunbury came straight away and confirmed that Princess Margaret had had a small stroke. There were no obvious lasting effects – her speech wasn't slurred, her muscles hadn't stopped working – but she became gradually slower and the little moments I had noticed before, when she would suddenly lose her place, continued.

The following year while on the island, Princess Margaret scalded her feet, a story that was somehow leaked to the press, making headline news back in the UK. I wasn't on Mustique but Janie Stevens, another Lady in Waiting and a great friend of mine, was with her. After her usual breakfast in bed, Princess Margaret went to take her shower or bath and Janie waited for her to appear to help her dress. When there was no sign of her, Janie went outside in case Princess Margaret was there. Noticing the bathroom windows were completely steamed up, she rushed back inside and knocked on the bathroom door but there was no answer. Opening the door, she found Princess Margaret sitting on the side of the bath with her legs in the water, not moving as the steam billowed all around her.

Whether or not Princess Margaret had had a stroke at the time, no one knows, but she had been washing her hair in the bath with the overhead shower and had fumbled to turn the water off. Instead of turning off the hot tap, she had turned off the cold, and with something wrong with the thermostat, the hot tap ran hotter and hotter. Dazed, she didn't react to the boiling water, and although Janie managed to get Princess Margaret out of the bath, her feet were left in the most terrible condition, burnt so badly she was unable to walk.

Dr Bunbury instructed Janie on how to care for Princess Margaret, but when she had to leave, I flew from London to take Janie's place. Les Jolies Eaux had been rented out for the following weeks so we had to find somewhere else to stay. 'Do we really have to leave?' I said, worried because I couldn't find anywhere that was available at such short notice. 'Don't you think everybody would understand?' But, as was her way, Princess Margaret insisted she moved, not wanting to make a fuss.

In the end, I rang the Harding-Lawrences, who immediately offered their beach house, which happened to be just below Les Jolies Eaux. It was on a steep part of the hillside with steps going down to the beach and the ever-amenable Dr Bunbury organised a rickety out-of-service ambulance to drive her down to the new house.

When we arrived, she turned to me and said, 'I don't know the staff in this house. I don't want them to come into my bedroom so you will have to look after me.'

We stayed there for about ten days in the gloomiest of conditions. Outside the sun was as bright as ever, but Princess Margaret wouldn't allow the curtains to be drawn, staying in the dark for the whole time, which meant I had to fumble around as I changed her ash trays, cleaned her room and took the meals to her that had been left at the door by the maid.

Dr Bunbury had given me a bleeper, which I wore around

my neck, and whenever Princess Margaret wanted me, which was pretty much all the time, she would buzz it. A few times, thinking she was asleep, I took the bleeper off my neck, thrust it at John Harding, darted off down the stairs and jumped into the sea. While I swam John Harding would stand on the balcony and listen out for Princess Margaret's call. If she wanted me, he would wave frantically, and out I would get, rushing back up the stairs while wringing out my hair before seeing what the matter was. I was never sure if she timed it to exquisite perfection, waiting for me to have a quick dip but then summoning me back so I had to dash back up the steep steps, putting my clothes on as I skidded into her room, trying to catch my breath.

'Yes, Ma'am,' I would pant, 'do you need anything?'

'Where were you, Anne?' she'd reply, rather crossly.

'Just quickly having a swim, Ma'am. I hope you're all right?'

'Well, I wasn't.'

'I'm so sorry, Ma'am. I'm here now and not going anywhere.'

This went on for almost a fortnight. The Palace confirmed there had been an incident but claimed she was in high spirits, but that was far from true. She was very glum indeed and the only person who cheered her up was the lovely Dr Bunbury. The minute he left, she would say to me, 'Could you ring Dr Bunbury again? There's something I forgot to tell him.'

'He's only just left, Ma'am,' I would say. 'Do you think we could leave it for another half an hour or so?'

She did the same to me: as soon as I had done something for her and then left, she would call me back. In the end, I asked her whether she minded if I got into the other single bed in her room and we watched videos while she recovered enough to be moved.

She was thrilled and said, 'Oh, Anne, is this like boarding school?'

'Yes, Ma'am.' I smiled. 'Except we weren't allowed to lie in bed and watch films.'

Her feet weren't improving, but when I suggested we flew back to England to get proper hospital treatment, Princess Margaret refused. 'I'm not nearly well enough, Anne,' she said incredulously.

For the only time ever, I contacted Buckingham Palace and asked to speak to the Queen, who listened as I explained the situation and sought her advice. The Queen was wonderfully understanding, concerned and supportive, and agreed to talk to Princess Margaret. She successfully persuaded her to come home, and her household arranged for us to fly back on Concorde, where I set up a milk crate for Princess Margaret's feet to stay propped up.

I'd been through a long-haul flight with Princess Margaret in ill health before, taking her from Barbados, where she had had some medical tests, back to London. The whole of the first-class cabin had been emptied of people and the usual set-up had been swapped for two lone beds in the bare space. I'd held her hand for most of the journey and remember waking up in the middle of the night to the kindly, rather huge Barbadian doctor looming over her to check her vital signs while she slept. She couldn't have looked more vulnerable. Although she had recovered that time, I wasn't so sure she would this time, dreading what the doctors would conclude about whether she would be able to walk properly again.

Once we were back in London, Princess Margaret underwent intense treatment for the burns on her feet. One day she rang up and said, 'You'll never guess what they're doing to my feet. Come and have lunch and I'll show you.' So off I went, and after lunch I watched as leeches, which had come from Wales, were taken out of a bag and put on her feet. Fascinated by facts and not at all squeamish, Princess Margaret listened eagerly as the nurse explained that leeches had been used to treat wounds for centuries, dating back to the ancient Egyptians. 'The leeches naturally secrete anticoagulants, keeping the blood flowing so they can consume it. But that also helps wounds heal quicker so it's mutually beneficial,' explained the nurse, obviously impressed with the shining black leeches, which were bulging all the time. While Princess Margaret didn't mind in the least that the leeches were sucking her blood, I found myself feeling extremely glad they were not attached to me.

Wheelchair-bound, Princess Margaret continued her official engagements but didn't commit to as many, and her life as she knew it steadily dissolved. Instead of staying up late, laughing and joking until the early hours, after great long evenings of singalongs, she no longer wanted to socialise. Instead I would find her listening to Radio 3 on the wireless in her bedroom.

In the summer of 1999, I went up to Balmoral with her for her birthday, which coincided with the annual visit of the Prime Minister, who at the time was Tony Blair. I was asked to look after his wife, Cherie. She was wearing a crumpled trouser suit and didn't give the impression she was overly pleased to be there. When I asked whether she wanted to see her room, she replied, 'What for?'

I explained that every guest has their own maid who waits in the room to meet them to make sure everything is in order. Rather reluctantly, she followed me upstairs. When we were in her room, I explained that she would have breakfast in bed, because all the ladies do, and that Tony would join the men downstairs. She looked at me, confused. 'But Tony will have breakfast with me,' she said.

At that point, Tony appeared and remarked, 'Breakfast downstairs sounds really great.' Obviously trying to ease the tension.

Tony did go down for breakfast the following day, but directly afterwards I was extremely surprised to see him with Cherie, changed into Lycra running outfits and halfway up the glen, with their security detail behind. Every morning while they were there I would look out of my window and see two brightly coloured dots jogging up the hillside.

Cherie Blair cheered up over the course of the visit, especially when I took her to the shop, coming out with packets of Balmoral shortbread and fudge. This particular trip to Balmoral ended up making headlines when Cherie announced later that she was unexpectedly pregnant and divulging that she had forgotten her 'contraception equipment' so must have conceived during her stay. Princess Margaret and I enjoyed the commentary in the newspapers but her health continued to go downhill.

In the years that followed, Princess Margaret had one or two more strokes and then her eyesight started to fail. Very quickly she lost it almost entirely. Having loved being surrounded by men, she now refused their company, even Colin's, only feeling comfortable with a few female companions.

A few of us would regularly read to her and sometimes I would stay the night. Her taste in reading material was eclectic to say the least. On one visit, I arrived to find her extremely animated. 'I've got a new book,' she said excitedly. 'Would you read it to me? It's all about seeds.' My heart sank. A whole book about plant seeds. What could be more boring? I thought, but Roddy had given it to her, and not only was she thrilled but she was clearly genuinely interested. I got as far as a chapter on potatoes before saying, 'Ma'am, are you really interested in this book? Should I carry on? Isn't it rather boring?'

'Keep going, Anne,' she said, without missing a beat. 'It's *fascinating.*' So, on I ploughed through that beastly book, but not without her stopping me and questioning my pronunciation, which she was always correcting. This was a habit of hers.

When I finally got through the blasted book some days later, I began reading a book about different religions to her, which I much preferred. I was mid-flow reading about Hinduism, when she started to interrupt, asking me if I was sure such-and-such word were 'pronounced like that'. By then I'd been to India many times. 'Yes, Ma'am,' I replied, somewhat testily. 'Of course it is. As you know, I've been to India twenty-six times.' She knew I wasn't exaggerating about the number of times I'd been, but we both also knew I had no idea how to pronounce some of the words.

One day, the Queen came to tea with Princess Margaret.

I stayed in the drawing room so they could have some time together and she went off to the bedroom to find Princess Margaret. Quite soon after she had gone in, she reappeared.

'Oh, Ma'am, is everything all right?' I asked.

'No, it isn't,' the Queen replied. 'Margaret is listening to *The Archers* and every time I try to say something she just says, "Shh!"'

I wasn't surprised. Princess Margaret's defiant streak extended to her sister, despite her being the Queen. I had always noticed that she had a very subtle strategy for one-upmanship, which contributed to the bickering that went on between her and the Queen Mother.

I said, 'Let's go back up together.'

When we got into the bedroom, I said to Princess Margaret, 'Ma'am, the Queen is here, and she can't stay all that long. Would you like me to help pour the tea?' I switched off the wireless, made sure they both had a cup and left the room.

I visited Princess Margaret every day for several months. She wanted the company and we both knew she wasn't recovering. In fact, as the days progressed, it was clear her health was declining rapidly so I wanted to spend time with her and make sure she was as comfortable as she could be.

Over Christmas 2001, when I was in Norfolk and Princess Margaret was at Sandringham, I was contacted by one of the Queen's Ladies in Waiting because Princess Margaret was refusing to eat and seemed to have rather given up on life. I went at once and found Princess Margaret in bed, with the covers tucked right the way up to her chin – I could hardly see her. Deciding to be firm, just as she would have been, I ignored the dreary atmosphere and greeted her enthusiastically. 'Ma'am, *Antiques Roadshow* will be on in a minute. Let's go and watch it while we have some tea.' Her face lit up a little bit and she agreed to get out of bed. I wheeled her along the corridor for a change of scene and we settled down in front of one of Princess Margaret's favourite programmes. I stayed with her for the evening and managed to get her to eat a little bit of the tea, leaving her in better spirits.

When I went downstairs the corgis, dozing in the hall, barked as they saw me, which in turn summoned the Queen, who asked how the visit had gone. 'Ma'am, it went quite well. Princess Margaret did manage to eat a jam tart.'

'A jam tart!' replied the Queen, the emphasis reminiscent of Lady Bracknell in *The Importance of Being Earnest*, so surprised was she to hear Princess Margaret had agreed to eat anything.

After Christmas, Princess Margaret returned to Kensington Palace but as 2001 ended and the new year began, she declined further. I kept up my visits, reading to her and listening to the wireless with her, but on the evening of 8 February 2002, her Private Secretary, Viscount Ullswater (who had taken over from Nigel Napier), rang. He told me she had suffered another stroke that afternoon and the outlook wasn't good. I never saw her again.

Princess Margaret died early the next morning in King Edward VII's Hospital in Marylebone. In the aftermath of her death, I found myself extremely sad, lost in some ways without her in my life. We had been such good friends, spent so much of our lives together, that it was difficult to believe I wouldn't see her again. While I was relieved she was no longer suffering and was now at peace, her absence left an enormous hole in my life.

Princess Margaret's funeral took place in St George's Chapel, Windsor, on 15 February, fifty years to the day since her father's funeral in the same place. As well as being full of sorrow, I was apprehensive about the other guests. Not only would her ex-husband be there but so would Roddy. Considering the affair had sparked such scandal and the Royal Family had not approved of it at the time, I felt nervous in case there was an awkward atmosphere as a result. What also felt really strange was that Colin had refused to come. He had adored Princess Margaret, but he couldn't face the farewell and didn't want to risk appearing emotional in public.

I sat with the other Ladies in Waiting in the front of the nave, the rose-covered coffin already at the altar as the congregation arrived. Princess Margaret had chosen the music herself, and although I love singing and wanted to give her a good send-off, I could hardly sing a note.

At the end of the service, as the coffin was accompanied down the aisle, the Queen Mother, who was a hundred and one and in a wheelchair, managed to get up and stand, bowing her head as her daughter passed.

Eight sergeants from the Royal Highland Fusiliers – Princess Margaret had been their Colonel-in-Chief since the regiment's conception in 1959 – carried the tiny coffin, wearing red Erskine tartan and piper's plaids, and took Princess Margaret away. The organist eventually stopped playing, assuming people would have gone, but instead the whole congregation sat unmoving, in mournful silence.

When the congregation finally left the chapel after the service, we went to the wake in Windsor Castle where the Queen thanked me for all I had done for Princess Margaret. She acknowledged the positive impact Roddy had had on Princess Margaret and how glad she was that Les Jolies Eaux and Mustique had made Princess Margaret so happy. I was left feeling very touched by the Queen's words.

Very sadly, Princess Margaret's funeral was the Queen Mother's last outing. Less than two months later, she, too, died. Losing both of them in such a short space of time had a deep impact on me. All those happy weekends spent with both of them at Royal Lodge – the laughter in Whistler's drawing room, the Queen Mother, glittering in a crinoline dress, raising her glass over her head or lowering it under the table in her hilarious toasting game, and endless sing-alongs with Princess Margaret.

While the Queen Mother's final resting place had been reserved next to her husband, King George VI, in St George's Chapel, there was no such space for Princess Margaret. Desperately wanting to be buried with her beloved father, she was cremated so she could fit beside him. Her ashes were kept in the royal vault until the Queen Mother died, and when she was buried, Princess Margaret's ashes were put into the grave.

The months after her death felt very quiet without Princess Margaret. She really was an extraordinary woman: if someone was anxious about something, she would always see the problem in an entirely different way, from a new angle, which would often help in finding a solution. Even now, when I'm faced with a problem, I wish she was here to tell me what she would do. Right up to the end, she stayed interested in the world around her. Life has not been the same without her, especially when I go to Mustique.

Every time I visit, I can hear the years of our laughter ring out and I miss the many little routines we always had together. Whenever I sit at Basil's Bar, at sunset, I half watch for the green flash, but it's not the same without her. Les Jolies Eaux is now owned by a charming Canadian family, and while they have made some wonderful improvements to the house, the front looks just the same. On a visit in February 2018, I felt Princess Margaret's spirit around me, and I stood there for a while, thinking she might walk out of one of the rooms, or if I turned the corner, I would see her in her favourite place looking out to sea.

CHAPTER EIGHTEEN

Until Death Us Do Part

By the millennium, Colin had spent most of the previous forty years in the West Indies, returning to England less and less.

In 1983, when his father died, and he inherited the title 3rd Baron Glenconner, he became a member of the House of Lords, taking the Liberal whip, staying true to his family's Liberal roots. Over the years, he used his peerage to try to support the Caribbean and its people, seeking to cross boundaries, achieve equality and improve living standards. In 1992, he gave his maiden speech in the House and, without notes, started talking about the need to support the viable crops traditionally grown in the Caribbean. Having seen sugar cane swapped for sugar beet and the cotton trade become extinct – he pointed out that the clothes he was wearing were made from the last of the Sea Island cotton grown on Mustique – he stressed the need to support the dwindling banana trade. He was articulate and charismatic, and while the Chamber had been empty when he started, by the end it was packed. I was proud to be his wife.

When Colin was visiting England, shortly after he moved permanently to St Lucia in the early nineties, he saw an advertisement for an elephant for sale at Dublin Zoo and spontaneously bought it, organising its shipment to St Lucia at once. 'What shall we call the elephant?' he asked the twins, as he happened to be in the car with them on another of his trips, this time to Brighton Pavilion. Amy happened to look out of the window as the car passed a BUPA medical centre. Seeing 'BUPA' and thinking it sounded like the trumpeting noise an elephant makes, she said, 'What about "Boopa", Dad?'

'Brilliant!' Colin replied.

Colin and I went back to St Lucia in time for Boopa's arrival, which was a big event because she was the first elephant to come to the Caribbean. Everybody flocked to the beach when she arrived on a ship importing bricks, and I watched as she got off, interested in her new surroundings, not startled by the huge crowd of people who had flocked excitedly to the port.

Many of the young men on the island wanted to be her keeper and were bustling and waving to try to get Colin's attention as he surveyed the crowd. Among them, he saw a boy with very big ears and picked him on the spot. 'Boopa will feel very much at home with you,' he said. The boy was delighted, grinning from ear to ear.

The boy's name was Kent. He was very friendly, and immediately bonded with Boopa, who settled in well, enjoying being allowed to walk free, making her big personality known when she started helping the fishermen by dragging the little fishing boats in with her trunk.

At night she was put into a wooden outhouse to keep her out of harm's way. Knowing that elephants need company, Colin tried to get another. He went to Africa with Christopher and the twins to buy a pair, which were shipped to St Lucia, only to be denied entry. Having allowed Boopa ashore, officials had decided one elephant was enough, so the new elephants made their way back to Africa, leaving Boopa still in need of a friend. In the end we settled for pigs and, although it might sound like an unlikely combination, Boopa bonded with them instantly.

The twins delighted in having a pet elephant, riding her sometimes with Colin, and spent a great deal of time following her about. I was very fond of her too. Suddenly there she would be, swinging her trunk through the kitchen window, waiting for me to give her a banana.

One day, when Colin was having another of his birthday parties, this time on a yacht called *Sea Star*, someone killed one of Boopa's pig friends for its meat. When Colin heard about this, he knew the danger Boopa might have put herself in, because she was aggressively protective of the pigs. He went ashore to find the culprit, hoping Boopa's instincts hadn't backfired on her. The next thing I saw from the boat was a man running for his life along the beach, with Colin

291

chasing after him, his stick in the air. It was like a Charlie Chaplin silent film. The man got away and Colin's temper cooled once he realised Boopa hadn't come to any harm.

Colin made quite an impression on St Lucia: this tall Englishman, with his flamboyant mood swings, who owned an elephant and strode around in his signature white kurtas and white pyjama trousers. Having worn all sorts of different, normally brightly coloured outfits, his fashion had changed after my friend Margaret Vyner and I returned from a holiday in India. Margaret and I had tried on all the beautiful women's clothes and decided they looked dreadful on us, so had kitted ourselves out with the men's things. When Colin saw us, his arms shot up and he said, 'Exactly what I want! Brilliant!' And before we knew it, he had gone off to India to get a whole new wardrobe of clothes he'd wear for the rest of his life.

As he settled into his new ventures on St Lucia, the children visited him regularly, becoming closer to him as they grew up. In the late nineties Amy, who was in her twenties, decided to go and live with Colin, who was thrilled by the decision, saying to me, 'It's the right time for Amy. She needs me but, more importantly, I need her!'

They had a strong relationship. Although he wasn't tactile, he would show his affection in subtle ways: if Amy was dressed up for something, she would ask him, 'Do I look all right?' And he would invariably tweak something or add something to her outfit before giving her the nod of approval. He was proud of her skills as a specialist painter and gilder, especially when she was commissioned to restore an Indian temple, and admired her for being down to earth and easygoing. Like him, she enjoyed engaging with the local community, often going off to cock fights with Kent in an effort to fit in.

They also had the same quick wit. When Colin had bought a restaurant in the middle of the two volcanic mountains known as the Pitons he asked Amy, 'What shall we call it?'

Without hesitation, she replied, 'Bang Between the Pitons?'

'Brilliant!' Colin exclaimed, delighted by the clever name.

Colin had thrown a huge launch party for Bang Between the Pitons, which Princess Margaret had officially opened, and she and May adorned the cover of *Hello!* magazine.

Over the years, Amy came and went, as I did, and Colin became more and more reliant on Kent for pretty much everything. Kent devoted his life to Colin, who in return was generous, giving him two hotels and paying him well. Occasionally, Kent would leave Colin for a few hours, having to get away to do some shopping or something for himself, and Colin would go berserk with anxiety. Although he had improved since the early days of our marriage, when he used to keep me awake all night, lying in a foetal position on the floor, crying, he still was very highly strung.

On one particular occasion, Colin became hysterical under the most embarrassing circumstances: he had taken me and Kent to Italy and organised an evening in Verona to see *Nabucco*, one of my favourite operas. I was really touched by this because while I love the opera Colin didn't particularly enjoy it.

After a difficult drive there, with Colin flipping a few times, convinced we were going the wrong way, Kent, who was mad about football, went off to watch a match on television instead.

We arrived at our seats in the arena, which unfortunately were very uncomfortable, and Colin quickly declared, 'Well, I'm going to leave at half-time. I can't possibly sit on these seats.'

Having been so excited about the evening, I was determined to have a good night so I went off to see if we could get slightly more comfortable seats. After pleading that Colin was unwell, we were very kindly moved to much better seats nearer the front, so I could finally settle down, next to Colin, and anticipate a marvellous evening. It was going well until halfway through the Chorus of the Hebrew Slaves in the opera's third act when, to my absolute horror, Colin started to wail and scream beside me. 'Colin, what *is* the matter?' I asked.

'I wish Kent was here,' he wailed.

'Honestly, I don't think Kent would enjoy it, but *I* am here.'

But he continued to wail, 'No, no, I want Kent!'

By this time, more and more of the audience were turning their heads in our direction. Seeing the rug over Colin's knees, I grabbed it and threw it over his head, hoping it would shut him up. To my amazement, he didn't tear it off and, with his wails now considerably muffled, the audience turned their attention back to the stage. Shrinking into my seat, I hoped the saga was over, but the worst embarrassment was yet to come. When the chorus finally ended, the conductor turned to the audience and announced, 'Under the circumstances, I think we will have to have that again.'

I was utterly mortified as the chorus began again. My only solace was that the rug had finally done the trick and Colin had calmed down – although perhaps it would have been better if he had left at the interval.

For all of our married life, Colin felt he needed somebody on hand all the time, to solve problems and calm him down. I had been that somebody for decades, but after Christopher's accident, my priorities changed and Kent replaced me. I just wasn't prepared to spend every minute of the day doing things for Colin any more. It was a job, a paid job now: I no longer felt it was my job as his wife.

Instead of looking after Colin, I stayed in England so I was not too far from Christopher and was delighted when he fell in love. Once he had moved back to London, still with terrible balance, he adopted a clever ploy of asking to be assisted over the zebra crossing near his house by passers-by. He would wait until a pretty girl came along and ask to borrow her for a moment, so was rather disappointed when a much older woman volunteered. Reluctantly, Christopher crossed the road and the woman struck up a conversation, asking where he was going. When Christopher answered, the woman told him that her daughter lived right next to him and promptly introduced them. Her daughter, Anastasia, a half-Greek highly intelligent lawyer, fell in love with Christopher and they got married, having two beautiful daughters, Bella and Demetria.

But after being happily married for a time and raising a family, the marriage had started to fail, and one day Christopher rang me up and said, 'Anastasia's got fed up with me and told me to leave. Can I come and stay with you?' So he came to stay in my farmhouse in Norfolk, neither of us knowing how long he would be there, wondering if Anastasia would change her mind or whether their marriage was over.

Because my house is in a small village and walking long distances can be hard for Christopher, I got him a tricycle so he could get around. It was a strange image seeing a grown man cycling off down the country lane on a trike, but it meant he could get to the pub easily so he didn't care what he looked like. Over the years, he had become completely at ease with how he was and took the attitude that if someone was going to give him a hard time about it, they weren't worth knowing.

I was worried in case he fell and couldn't get up, but didn't want to be an overbearing mother of a middle-aged son, so I would just say, 'Do come back by half past eleven or give me a ring so I know you're all right.'

One night half past eleven came and went and there was no sign of him. My mind started darting around, worried he had had an accident, imagining him stuck in the middle of the road or in the ditch, unable to get up. I got out of bed, put a coat over my nightie and drove to the pub. When I saw his tricycle outside I was furious, realising he must have just forgotten to phone me. I stormed in and started yelling at him: 'How dare you? What do you think you're doing? You had me so worried!' Shocked at my entrance, he didn't have time to respond to my wrath as I dragged him out of the pub.

The next day when I had calmed down, he said, 'I'm sorry I didn't call you. I met the most brilliant woman.'

'But what about Anastasia and the children?' I said.

The truth was that, although they had loved each other, their lives were too imbalanced, too unequal. They decided to divorce, but amicably, and he stayed a big part of their daughters' lives. As for the brilliant woman he'd met in the pub – he married her. Although I had been sad his first marriage hadn't worked out, both Colin and I were terribly glad he'd met someone else who clearly adored him. Johanna became part of the family and Christopher was thrilled that she got on so well with both Colin and me. He settled down for good, conveying his absolute joy at being able to reassure both of us that we needn't worry about him because he had Johanna, who would always be there to take care of him.

Suddenly, in my mid-seventies, I found myself completely independent. With Kent looking after Colin's every need and Johanna supporting Christopher, the twins grown-up, and my days as a Lady in Waiting sadly gone, I could finally relax. I had a real love of travel so I embarked on spontaneous trips all over the world with friends, some of whom were almost as eccentric as Colin.

One of them, Mary Anna Marten, was a remarkable lady I'd known for years who sadly died in 2010. She would ring me out of the blue and ask if I wanted to go on holiday. The strangest trip we ever took was to Russia. Before we left, Mary Anna, who had a substantial figure, said, 'The food is simply disgusting in Russia. I've ordered a leg of Parma ham from Harrods to be delivered to you. We'll split the cost. One can always eat Parma ham, any time of the day or night.'

Two days before we were due to leave, a Harrods van trundled up. The delivery man rang the bell and put this enormous parcel into my arms. It weighed an absolute ton. I don't quite know how we got it through Customs but we lugged it with us as we travelled to where we were staying in Moscow. The room was boiling and tiny, so I decided to put the leg of ham on the windowsill.

In the middle of the night, we woke up to the most dreadful noise of whirring and beating wings. Opening the curtain, I was greeted by every single bird in Moscow, busy devouring our Parma ham. The next day we cut off the bits that had not been savaged, took it with us and went off to a park, where Mary Anna had arranged to meet someone. I discovered she was meeting a hit man, which, of course, horrified me. She had only told me there was an ulterior motive for the trip when we were already on our way.

Able to speak a bit of Russian, and convinced that her daughter had inadvertently married a Russian spy, Mary Anna had arranged to talk to a man to discuss 'getting rid' of her son-in-law. I sat nervously on one park bench, while she sat with this shifty-looking man a few benches along, as I wondered whether we would be arrested. When she came back, I said, 'Well, what happened? Have you hired a hit man?'

Mary Anna replied, 'Actually, I don't think it's going to work quite as I hoped. There are one or two difficulties.'

I was unbelievably relieved when she gave up on the idea and even more relieved when we left Moscow altogether. We flew south to Samarkand, where Mary Anna wore brightly coloured kaftans and a great deal of jewellery. People would gather round her wherever she went and we eventually realised that everybody thought she was an incarnation of Catherine the Great. People tried to touch her, thinking she might bring them luck, and more people would follow suit, creating a stir. I was used to people behaving in this manner when I had been with Princess Margaret, although it wasn't quite the same, but as Mary Anna walked, I followed, brushing the arms away from her as she sailed along with all these people.

She was always full of surprises. On the way home it transpired that a lot of people on the plane had gippy tummies. Mary Anna had just the solution. Out of her bag came a bottle of medicine no longer available over the counter called Dr J. Collis Brown's Mixture, which contains morphine, and she went up and down the aisle dispensing spoonfuls of it. By the end of the flight everybody was knocked out. I said to her, 'That was fortunate. Do you always have that in your bag?'

'Yes, darling, I do,' she said. 'You never know when you might need it.'

That was typical of Mary Anna. A trip with her was never short of incident – I might have had lots of dramatic things happen to me, but I had never considered hiring a hit man.

When I wasn't off travelling the world with friends, I spent more and more time in Norfolk, finding a good balance between excitement and a more peaceful existence. I was delighted when, in 2005, May got engaged to Anton Creasy, a friend she and Amy had both known for years.

Eddy, the Earl of Leicester, very kindly insisted that the wedding should take place at St Withburga's, with the reception in the state rooms at Holkham. I was really touched by this because Holkham was such a part of us all, and since I had got married there in 1956 I was so glad that my own daughter was able to do the same.

I helped with the flowers, just like my mother had done for me, and May wore my tiara and looked absolutely beautiful. Eddy gave a speech, and then Colin stood up and, without having prepared anything formal, spoke eloquently and affectionately, injecting his characteristic enthusiasm, ending the speech perfectly with a humorous toast.

Shortly after they got married, May and Anton decided to move out to St Lucia to be with Colin because by then Amy had decided to continue her adventures, going off to the Dominican Republic. Unfortunately, when May and Anton tried to help Colin run his businesses (not only Bang Between the Pitons, but also a hotel), he found it hard to give the reins to Anton. After several clashes, May and Anton decided to return to their life in England.

In his seventies, Colin still had the same tendency to lose his rag in a spectacular fashion. One day he was supposed to meet the minister of tourism at a restaurant on the cliff edge in St Lucia, but the minister didn't appear. Colin waited and waited, and eventually the cook came out and said that the kitchen would close after five more minutes. Colin completely lost it and went the whole way along the cliff edge, chucking one table after another into the sea. Then he drove straight to the airport, arrived in London without any luggage or his keys, and knocked on the door of our house. I hadn't been expecting him and when I opened the front door he was covered with what I thought was blood.

'Colin, what's happened? Are you all right?' I exclaimed, imagining he'd been in the most terrible accident.

'Anne,' he replied crossly. 'It's not blood, it's ketchup.'

When he told me that the ketchup had spilt all over him as he had picked up the tables and thrown them off the cliff, I couldn't help but laugh, which didn't go down well but by then we had been married for over fifty years and his short fuse no longer alarmed me.

Although Colin's moods were often extreme, especially from an English point of view, out in the West Indies people didn't seem so affected by them. They simply accepted his blend of bad temper and incredible generosity.

Colin had always had protégés, trying to advance the careers of young men, and Kent became Colin's last major 'project' in the belief that, one day, he could run things for him. The only problem was that Kent was illiterate. Thinking he would be able to solve this, Colin sent Kent to London to an adult literacy centre. After a few months, Colin got a phone call. 'I very seldom fail,' said the director, 'but I have with Kent. I'm sending him back to St Lucia.'

Colin kept me regularly updated with everything that was going on, talking to me on the telephone for hours when we weren't together, telling me all about his successes and failures when we were apart. One day in late 2009 he rang me up and asked me if I was sitting down. 'What is it, Colin?' I asked, dreading whatever he was about to say.

'Marvellous news!' he said. 'I've got a new son.'

'What are you talking about?' I said, aghast.

'A letter came from out of the blue and now I've met him: somebody called Josh Bowler. I had a one-night stand with his mother before we were married. He's been married three times so I have four new grandsons,' Colin continued, sounding delighted.

He always got frightfully overexcited about everything, but it never lasted very long. I tried to be suitably enthusiastic and gave a house party at Glen for Josh and his family, introducing him to everybody to make him feel welcome. Colin opened his arms to him, taking him back to St Lucia with him to show his new son the island he so loved.

Within about three days, he was on the telephone again. 'I can't stand it any longer, Anne!' he shouted, as if he thought I couldn't hear him all the way from St Lucia.

I wasn't surprised, and found it rather difficult myself that Josh had turned up after all that time.

By then Colin had prostate cancer but he was adamant that nobody should find out. He always had the idea that people didn't want to buy land or do business with someone who looked ill or old. So, he had two face lifts and kept his illness to himself, at first not even telling me.

I'd suspected he was ill for a while because he had lost so much weight, but he didn't confirm anything until he took a turn for the worse in the summer of 2010, while in Trinidad with Charlie's widow Sheilagh and their son, Cody, in search of a rare bat. Sheilagh called me and I went straight out to St Lucia to look after him and stayed for several weeks. As he recovered slowly, we enjoyed our time together. I was glad to be looking after him and he was relaxed and loving.

With commitments in Norfolk, I went home with the intention of coming back to St Lucia a week or so later with Amy, who was planning to live there permanently.

On 27 August 2010, three days after I'd left him, Colin died. When he had called out in the night to Kent, Kent had driven him to hospital but Colin then had a massive heart attack and was dead by the time they got there. Kent was inconsolable when he rang to tell me.

I was left completely shocked, finding the news hard to comprehend. Only a few nights before we had spent the evening recalling our lives together, and Colin had been uncharacteristically loving, talking about how he thought we had been a good team. 'It wasn't all bad, was it?' he had asked me before I left him for the last time, as though he was trying to make amends for the harder times we had gone through.

As I flew straight back to St Lucia to organise the funeral, I found it hard to imagine a world without him. Colin was a uniquely difficult and brilliant man in equal measure. But somehow, despite his endless affairs and histrionics, there was an overriding loyalty, a friendship that bound us together, no matter what. He was right: we had made a good team and I knew I would miss him terribly.

Christopher and the twins were devastated and it was particularly hard for Amy. The last time she had seen Colin, he had said goodbye to her before getting into a taxi, only to stop the vehicle and get out to give her another hug. Perhaps he had had a premonition, especially considering it was very unlike Colin to be tactile, but, of course, Amy hadn't known it would be the last goodbye. Not only had she just lost her father, but she had also just lost her future. Instead of flying to St Lucia to start her new life, she was flying there to attend her father's funeral.

May, too, was heartbroken. She had often been on the receiving end of his impatience, but their relationship had improved, and their last meeting, in the Portobello Hotel, had been a huge success, Colin remarking how much he had loved spending time with her.

Christopher had had perhaps the easiest relationship with his father, whom he described as a 'demigod', so was devastated but, once again, he rallied round, supporting the rest of us, reminding us that although Colin was gone the love would continue, just like he had done when Henry and Charlie had died.

All I could think about was when we had all been together as a family nine months to the day before Colin had died, staying with my friend Josephine Loewenstein. It had been Josephine's idea to commission a statue and she had arranged for a huge bronze to be made by the sculptor Philip Jackson of Colin in his signature clothes, hat and cane. It was unveiled on Mustique in recognition of all Colin had done for the island. Colin was thrilled, and afterwards we all went to the lagoon and sat on the beach in a line with our legs stretched out, our toes in the water. And now, less than a year after that happy day, and less than a week after I had seen him, I was back to bid my final goodbye.

The funeral was a spectacular St Lucian affair, far removed from the traditional English services that I was used to. Colin would have enjoyed it. There wasn't a hint of black anywhere. Inside the big white church, the atmosphere was distinctly Caribbean. There was a carnival atmosphere and the whole thing was redolent of Colin's endless parties. He had always loved grand entrances and the funeral was his big exit. It had begun with his lying in state in The Great House a few days before, after he was moved from the Lazarus Funeral Home, and now he arrived at the church in a beaten-up old pick-up truck, which had been crudely converted into a hearse, complete with a neon cross on the roof.

He had chosen 'Lord of the Dance' as one of his sending-off hymns, but instead of people standing stiffly and solemnly, the congregation swayed to the music. Kent was in floods of tears so I held his hand and swayed along with him. Outside, crowds of people had surrounded the church and were singing too. When Bryan Adams sang 'He Was A Friend Of Mine' inside the church, the congregation joined in and they raised a framed photograph of Colin above their heads.

The heat hit us as the doors of the church opened at the end of the service. I followed the coffin, draped with the St Lucian flag and with Colin's hat on top of it, as it was taken to the graveyard. I had inadvertently picked the heaviest coffin because it had been the only one that wasn't decorated with gold or silver or with ghastly handles. Euan, Henry's incredibly tall son, who clutched a bunch of Scottish heather, had to crouch to balance the coffin, while the rest of the pall-bearers, including Cody, puffed and sweated, surrounded by local people in colourful fancy dress and painted faces. They had practised earlier that morning, around the pool, using sun-loungers, which weren't nearly as heavy.

I stood between the tombs, next to the plot Colin had chosen. The final party was in full swing, but this time without input from the ringmaster himself. And then, as if this wasn't all odd enough, suddenly, from behind the other tombs, came all these people with their faces painted white, wielding scythes. The grim reapers came up to me and beckoned. 'Come, Lady, Come, Lady, Mr Tennants' wife. You must dance with us.' Horrified, I said no, but they just took me along anyway. And before I knew it, I was weaving in and out of the tombs, half dragged, half dancing. As they danced, they let go of dozens of black balloons, which floated up over the sea. It was utterly bewildering and exhausting, but it was the local tradition so I went along with it.

Eventually Colin was interred, as the local gospel choirs sang 'Swing Low Sweet Chariot', and we all went back to the wake at The Great House, which was filled with rows and rows of tiny little cakes covered with bright pink icing – enough to mistake it for a confectionery shop. It looked more like a birthday party than a funeral. The sound of steel bands and singing, of banshee-like wailing, of clapping and drumming, of every note in every octave being played in one form or another, filled the hot Caribbean air. In the surrounding villages, while the local people sang and danced to mark the passing of 'Mr Tennants' as they called him, I thought of him with love, his death finally beginning to sink in.

I stood, clutching a vodka tonic, underneath the pink and white streamers, making small-talk with government officials, policemen, soldiers, magistrates and locals. Everybody from the island seemed to be crammed into Colin's beloved home. Only then did Kent tell me he had wanted Colin to have a state funeral, which was not unknown for grand people on the island, but apparently I had organised it too quickly. When I heard that I had a flash of regret – Colin would have been disappointed that I had inadvertently denied him a police escort.

On St Lucia it is customary for a will to be read quickly so that night I waited for the lawyer. I was apprehensive and a little worried about it, as Colin's lawyer had warned me that he didn't have the latest will, telling me: 'I believe Lord Glenconner made a new will seven months ago with a lawyer from Soufrière.'

My heart sank when the new lawyer turned up. There was something shifty about him – he barely kept eye contact and was very fidgety. I stood with my daughter-in-law, Sheilagh, whose son Cody was the heir presumptive. The lawyer scrabbled around in his briefcase and got out a single piece of paper. He looked down at it and then read aloud: 'I hereby leave everything to Kent Adonai, and I trust he will carry out my wishes towards the family.'

I thought my heart was going to stop.

Afterwards I found Kent, who had been told by the lawyer, and as calmly as I could, I said, 'Well, Kent, I hope you will carry out Lord Glenconner's wishes to us all.'

He looked at me, shrugged his shoulders and said, 'I don't know what Lord Glenconner meant.'

I knew then that my worst fears had come true and that we truly stood to lose everything. The surreal wake was nothing compared to the feeling that ran through my blood in that moment and afterwards.

Later that night I stood on the balcony of the house that no longer belonged to us. Normally, in the Caribbean, the night sky is filled with stars but that night the sky was completely black. As I stood there, my entire married life flashed before my eyes. Fifty-four years. Five children. A marriage filled with Colin throwing as many tantrums as he threw parties. And now, after all I'd been through – this. This last attention-seeking gift. It was such a terrible humiliation. And to do it to our children . . . I despaired. Going against everything my mother had always taught me, I let emotion take over and I screamed and screamed and screamed into the pitch-black night.

CHAPTER NINETEEN

Whatever Next?

IT TOOK A long time for the dust to settle. Friends were horrified by the will and encouraged me to contest it.

In the UK, primogeniture law normally means the majority of an estate is handed to the heir, who in this case was Cody, Charlie's son. Incidentally, this was the same law that had prevented me from inheriting Holkham as a daughter. This time, it dismissed me for being a wife, but that was not what I minded. I had accepted long ago the reality for me as a woman, but I had expected Colin to leave me and the children the chattels and for Cody to inherit Colin's estate.

The only thing the family had left was Glen, which was in trust to Henry's son, Euan. Colin's huge fortune had dwindled over the years but on his death he still owned land and hotels on St Lucia, but everything that belonged to him, whether sentimental or valuable, he had left solely to Kent.

The reality was that Kent immediately put the contents of The Great House up for sale, including a lot of things that belonged to me. He had been approached by the lawyer, who had shown him outstanding bills that needed to be paid, and when it had been suggested that an auction would raise enough money to settle the debt and more, Kent agreed. I found this out through a friend, who rang up shortly after the funeral and said, 'Your silver bed is on the front cover of Bonhams' catalogue.'

I contacted Bonhams and told them they couldn't sell things without the owner's consent. They were apologetic but reluctant to stop the sale so I flew back to St Lucia to see what was going on. When I got to The Great House, everything had been packed up and the people from Bonhams were in the process of organising shipment to London for the auction.

In the end I came to an agreement with Bonhams, who assured me the money made from the sale of items I owned would be mine.

The auction went ahead, and I was glad to see that Colin's iconic hat and cane were bought by the Mustique Company. Kent raised more than enough money to pay off the debts, and I got the proceeds from the sale of my silver bed.

Once the auction was over Cody and his mother disputed the will. In the end it took seven years to resolve. While Kent kept a huge amount of land and money, about half of Colin's estate was handed to Cody.

If I think about it now, I still find it impossible to tell whether Colin intended to leave us all with nothing. It is entirely possible that he decided to do it on purpose, as some sort of horrible stunt, which would secure his reputation as a memorable eccentric. It is also possible he didn't understand what he was doing in the last few months of his life, when he had become frail and vulnerable. I will never know for sure. It was hard not to dwell on this question, hard not to feel betrayed, not just for myself but for our children.

Obsessing about this would have driven me mad so, instead, I made a decision to move on. I was in my late seventies when Colin died and I realised time was of the essence for me too. Determined not to be cast down, I turned my attention to the future.

It's now been almost ten years since Colin died and nearly twenty since Princess Margaret died. Christopher is fifty-one and the twins are forty-nine. No longer do I hop between a life in the West Indies, Glen and big houses in London. I am back in my farmhouse in Norfolk, the place that feels more like home than anywhere else. I owe a lot to my father's sound judgement all those years ago when he told me I should buy a house of my own due to Colin's flaky character. If I hadn't bought it, I have no idea where I would be now.

There is a family saying that the Cokes come back to Norfolk and, since I can see the boundary wall of Holkham Hall from my window, it must be true. Norfolk is a great draw especially because I love being by the sea. Glen was lovely in its own way, and hills and mountains are beautiful, but I always felt slightly closed in there and, like Mustique,

I could never see the weather coming, the unpredictability governing a sense of unease.

I surround myself with my children, grandchildren and great-grandchildren, and my life is no longer full of endless parties, dinners at Kensington Palace and royal tours. Although my days now might seem rather pale in comparison, at the age of eighty-seven I am very happy, doing whatever I feel like doing.

Instead of endless extravagant fancy-dress parties, I socialise with my many kind friends in Norfolk who live nearby, like Patricia Rawlings, who gives wonderful long lunches, and Tim, whom I met through my sister Carey, and his husband Menno. I was 'best man' at their wedding and have enjoyed evenings with them that go on into the night, sometimes involving singalongs around the piano. In the summer we sit outside drinking Tim's world-class Bloody Marys and it was he, as well as my cousin Tom and his wife Polly, who gave me my two eightieth-birthday parties – days when I felt quite spoilt and completely relaxed, quietly relieved that Colin wasn't looking over my shoulder. I still spend time at Glen. Henry's wife, Tessa, sadly died in 2018, but I stay with Bill, whom she went on to marry, and Euan with his flame-haired children William and Ruby. I visit Cody in Edinburgh – and finally David and my darling sister Sarah, near Perth.

I still go abroad, to Mustique most years to stay with Josephine Loewenstein and catch up with another great friend, Georgie Fanshawe. I also love to go to Turkey to stay with Ömer Koç. Ömer is the son of one of Turkey's most successful businessmen, Rahmi Koç, whose former wife,

Çiğdem Simavi, was a friend of mine and used to invite Princess Margaret and me on her boat, *Hallas*, every year. There was always a small group of us, including Rupert Everett whom I've known all his life, I having been his mother's bridesmaid, and Nicky Haslam, also a great friend. Princess Margaret would always have the master cabin, which had a four-poster bed. The bed was too high for her to get in and out of it so I would heave her in at the end of each evening, leaving her with a bell. She would ring it in the night if she needed to go to the bathroom, whereupon I would come and help heave her back out and in again.

Ömer is the same age as Henry would have been, and when I met him, just after Henry's death from AIDS, he was so sympathetic and kind to me. We struck up a close friendship, and nowadays he invites me on his yacht every summer with a group of friends, including Christabel and Jools Holland. Christabel and I love swimming so every day we set off together. Ömer is so conscientious that he organises a little boat to follow us around just in case we get into trouble.

It was through Ömer's mother that I met Bettina Graziani, the eccentric former supermodel, business partner of Hubert de Givenchy, and the fiancée of Prince Aly Khan, the socialite son of the Aga Khan. A few years ago, she invited Tim and me to stay with her in Paris. Ever since my honeymoon, I've always been wary when I'm invited to Paris, but I brushed off the absurd thought – I was almost eighty and was going *without* Colin.

Even in her eighties, Bettina was excessively glamorous. She had tea ready for us when we arrived, all set out in her supremely elegant flat in the rue de Grenelle, scented by Rigaud candles and masses of fresh flowers. The evening started off like a Parisian dream: we drank champagne in front of the fire before Bettina took us out to dinner at Brasserie Lipp. Afterwards, when we had assumed we would go home, she took us to a party given by the boyfriend of an ambassador, who was entertaining in the ambassador's absence.

A butler in a white coat let us into a hall lined with bird-cages full of brightly coloured finches, and on into a hot, rather dim room full of people sitting about wrapped around one another. Briefly and languidly, they looked us over and then looked away again.

Bettina led me and Tim through the interconnected rooms, and as we walked, we passed some of the guests and looked at each other, appalled, realising we were at an orgy. There were men in drag mincing around, and women very skimpily dressed, and some people oiled up wearing nothing at all. We passed a bedroom, and on the four-poster bed, a couple of lesbians were writhing around. They took an interest in me, so I clung to Tim, whispering urgently, 'Tell them we're married!'

I don't think being married would have made much difference, especially as everybody was high: the bathroom was full of bowls of cocaine, the glass-topped table by the basin criss-crossed with lines. Tim and I sat on a sofa, close together, rather helplessly. Meanwhile, Bettina seemed oblivious to the difference between the first part of the evening and the second, finally taking us home at three in the morning.

When Tim and I returned to Norfolk, we were both rather glad. I haven't been back to Paris.

The best trips have undoubtedly been with my friend Margaret Vyner. Together we have gone to India many times and we always have great fun, although we have wound up experiencing some rather unforeseen things. Once we were at a hill station and decided to cross the Deccan desert. The hotel owner was rather surprised when we mentioned our plan. 'That's very brave. Be very careful,' she said, her eyebrows raised, probably thinking it rather strange to see two such adventurous old women. We set off, thinking nothing of her concerns, focusing more on the peculiar taxi we found ourselves in, which was decked out in red velvet and had a chandelier. Somewhat relieved when the taxi pulled up at a wood, though surprised to see trees in the middle of the desert, we started gathering our things. 'No, no,' said the taxi driver, in no uncertain terms. 'You stay here. Do not get out. Bad ladies in the wood. Bad, *bad* ladies in the wood.' Before we could say anything, he jumped out of the car and disappeared among the trees.

It turned out it was a prostitute stop where all the lorry drivers came. I suppose the taxi man thought if we got out the other men might think we had joined the woodland prostitutes. Eventually he came back, obviously having had a marvellous time spending the money we'd given him for the journey on the 'bad ladies'. Off we went again with the chandelier swinging, but by nightfall, we still hadn't reached the smart hotel we had booked. It was getting late and we had no choice but to find a place to sleep in a tiny town, not wanting to risk driving in the dark. The taxi driver took us to the only hotel in the area, which was absolutely filthy. In all my time in India, this was the only hotel that was so dirty we had to use the field instead of the bathroom if we wanted to go to the loo. It had an odd atmosphere, emphasised by a bell that kept ringing outside our room, and every now and then somebody would bang on the door. It was while we were discussing these peculiarities that the penny dropped: we'd gone from an outside brothel, to an inside brothel. The men were given half an hour with the ladies and then the bell would ring. All that was missing was the call, 'All change.'

It was so appalling we had to find it funny. Luckily, we always travel with a bottle of vodka, which often turns out to be completely necessary. Margaret tracked down the taxi driver to get a mixer and returned with a huge jug of fresh cherry juice, which was the most delicious thing we'd ever tasted. We put a chair under the door handle so no men would stumble into our room and drank ourselves into a lovely stupor as the bells rang and the doors banged around us.

The next day, we arrived at the hotel, which was frightfully smart, and I'm sure nobody would ever have guessed where we'd been the night before. Yet again, there I was going from one extreme to another. We couldn't help but laugh. After all, I've grown used to the unexpected, the shocking and the peculiar.

Most of the time, though, I spend my days poking around in the garden, and up until very recently I still enjoyed sailing from the creeks of Burnham Overy Staithe. I still help run the boathouse. Some of the most fun I've ever had is here in Norfolk – the sailing clubs celebrate all Nelson's victories, of which there were quite a lot. On the two-hundredth anniversary of Trafalgar we were all told our tiny boats could fly the white ensign and the Bishop of Lynn came down to do a blessing, throwing his ring into the water. So the creeks were full of enthusiastic people dressed up in sailor hats.

Everyone, including me, was rather merry on Nelson's Blood, a cocktail of red wine and brandy. This is the traditional tot given to sailors because when Nelson died his body was kept in a barrel of brandy to preserve him during the voyage home, the contents drunk by his crew when they came ashore. There is a photograph that shows just how jolly I was, with my hand rather rudely on top of somebody's head, clinging on for balance, as I waved excitedly at the camera.

When I'm not on the water, I enjoy walking next to the creeks and over the dunes, my thoughts inevitably turning to the days of building sandcastles and having picnics with my children, and going back further in time to when I was a child, playing with my Ogilvy cousins and with Princesses Elizabeth and Margaret. Holkham beach is still as beautiful as ever, attracting thousands of visitors each season, and is apparently consistently voted the most popular beach in England.

The Royal Family liked Holkham so much that my father gave them a beach hut, although it wasn't really like those garden sheds painted in a pastel shade squeezed between others that dot the seafront, and was more of a summerhouse. This one stood alone towards the far end of Holkham beach and had a big room, a veranda all the way round it and a small kitchen. The Queen Mother would come down to the beach hut in the summer at teatime and bring the corgis for a walk along the dunes. Below the hut to the far side, there was, and still is, a nudist beach.

The Queen Mother's protection officers weren't too happy with the proximity of the naturists and would often be heard saying, 'I don't think you should go down to the beach today, Ma'am, because there are some nudists out there. It might be a bit embarrassing.'

To which she would reply, 'Embarrassing? For whom? I'm longing to see them. Perhaps the corgis will nip their bottoms.'

And off she would go with the corgis. The nudists always seemed to be oblivious of her, the men too busy absorbed in their sport – everything dangling about – and the big-bosomed women sitting in the dunes, knitting. The protection officers learnt to accept that there was no question of the Queen Mother not heading in their direction.

The nudist beach was of perennial interest. A few years ago, Prince Charles and the Duchess of Cornwall invited me to Sandringham during the flower show, and in the evening there was a dinner party with guests from the world of entertainment. I had a great conversation with Dame Judi Dench, who told me how much she loved swimming, so I invited her to the beach for a swim. The next day, the Duchess of Cornwall and Judi Dench arrived with some other friends and, despite the grey, windy weather, everybody got into their swimming costumes and jumped into the sea. I only went up to my knees but Judi Dench was intrepid, rushing into the choppy water grinning broadly.

When everybody got out of the sea, I told them about the nudist beach, relaying the story of the Queen Mother and her corgis. Well, of course, just like the Queen Mother, they all peered into the fog, and at that moment a man wearing only a towel and a rucksack came walking along the dunes. Recognising the Duchess of Cornwall, he said hello. The Duchess struck up a conversation with him and discovered he was a nudist (albeit partially dressed at the time), so everybody piled in and asked him questions. Eager to engage, he told us all about how liberating it was, how he loved being part of the elements, close to nature. At the end of the conversation, the Duchess asked whether he lived and worked locally. 'Yes,' he said happily. 'I'm headmaster of a school nearby.' When he left, we fell about laughing. Being a headmaster and a nudist somehow didn't seem to go together.

Holkham Hall still stands, rather glumly in the grey winter fog, magnificently when the sun shines. After Eddy died in 2015, his son, Thomas, became the 8th and current Earl of Leicester. Following tradition, just like my father, he was commissioned into the Scots Guards after going to Eton and became an Equerry to the Duke of Kent. He lives at Holkham Hall with his wife Polly and their four children and, together, they continue the Coke legacy. The estate is flourishing.

As the house is open for visitors, attracting thousands of people a year, sometimes I slip in. Whenever I go, I see the visitors who have come from all over the world staring up the marble staircase where I stood for my coming-out dance in my parachute dress, and for my wedding in my Norman Hartnell dress. On they go, busy with chatter and interest, often talking about the film *The Duchess*, starring Keira Knightley and Ralph Fiennes, because much of it was shot at Holkham.

But while they see the dark red silk damasked walls and the splendid gold-decorated ceilings, I see Tommy Kinsman setting up his band, to the delight of the Queen Mother, and Princess Margaret being spun around the room by Billy Wallace. In the state bedrooms, I don't just admire the four-poster bed, but am reminded of Lord Stair, who always slept there. As I walk through the corridors, I see the childlike forms of Princess Margaret and I pedalling our trikes, hearing our laughter carry down the halls, and the doorways where we'd jump out at the footmen. As the visitors snap away with their camera phones, little do they know that they are capturing the spot where the Queen used to stand as a little girl, scolding me and Princess Margaret for getting up to mischief.

But what I love more than anything is when the house is all shut up to visitors and when the family are away because I feel it is part of me again. I look at the top middle window on the left-hand side – my old bedroom – and think of my teenage self, sitting at my desk scribbling letters to my friends or daydreaming about Heathcliff, from Emily Brontë's *Wuthering Heights*, as I looked into the park.

Recently a little note, written by Carey to me when we were children, was found in the attic by one of Tom's children. It was a touching reminder of the times we shared together because, very sadly, Carey died in May 2018, aged eighty-four. I was so sad when she died, remembering so vividly what she was like when she was a golden-haired little girl shouting, 'Cowardy custard!' and teasing me no end. This catchphrase was such a huge part of our childhood that our cousin James Ogilvy mentioned it fondly in a reading at her funeral.

No longer being able to reminisce with Carey, and with Sarah being that much younger, my early childhood secrets and memories are wrapped up in the house and grounds, binding me to Holkham for ever. My parents and Carey are buried in the churchyard at St Withburga's, which stands in the middle of Holkham park above the lake, surrounded by a herd of fallow deer. This was my father's absolute favourite place in the world and when he died, in 1976, the game-keepers carried his coffin all the way up the hill, from the house to the church. One day I will be buried there too.

Although my father's death marked the end of the line for our particular branch of the Coke family, my children and grandchildren are our legacy. None of my direct descendants will become the next Earl of Leicester, but my high-spirited family is alive and well, ready, like me, to cope with whatever life throws at them.

Amy has travelled the world and settled back in East Anglia, with May and Anton just down the road with their two daughters, Honor and Greta. Christopher is still happily married to Johanna, who has become a significant part of my life too, because they now live just down the road from me.

I took Christopher to a lecture the other day and thought, God, I'm lucky – he's just sitting here beside me, enjoying life. There's nothing wrong with his brain or his mind. He's such an asset, and I often think about what might have happened, so relieved there is a happy ending. I don't think anyone can ever know how they will react under terrible circumstances until something catastrophic happens but, thank goodness, I didn't listen to the doctor who told me to go home and forget about him.

While I am so proud of my three children, it's still painful to think about Henry and Charlie. I am now twice as old as Charlie was when he died, and three times as old as Henry. The pain of losing your children never goes away. But I try not to dwell on the sad things in my past, instead concentrating on the present, trying to make the most of my life. Fortunately, I still have great friends who share this attitude and we have continued to travel the world on great adventures.

The eighty-seven years I've lived on this earth have been many things, good and bad, but above all, extraordinary. I have had to adapt continuously throughout my life but now I can relax and, perhaps surprisingly, I have no regrets. I am very much at my happiest and intend to live to a hundred, although still always wondering, 'Whatever next?'

ACKNOWLEDGEMENTS

I WOULD FIRST like to thank Tom Perrin for asking me to write this book and for encouraging and helping me along the way.

Hugo Vickers has also been a source of wise advice and encouragement – he was invaluable in finding out obscure facts about my Hardwicke grandfather. Hugo also introduced me to Hannah Bourne-Taylor who became indispensable, holding my hand throughout and putting in order and sorting out my memories as we sat for hours together.

I would also like to say how much I appreciated everyone from Hodder and Stoughton and Zuleika. Firstly, Rowena Webb: nothing was too much trouble for her; and secondly, Juliet Brightmore, who had the difficult task of choosing the photographs with me. I would also like to mention Lucy Hale, Eleni Lawrence, Rebecca Mundy, Rebecca Folland, Hazel Orme and Ian Wong. A very big thank-you to Simon Elliot who rightly insisted I should have an agent and found me the charming and efficient Gordon Wise.

Lastly, the two most important people in supporting me that I would like to thank are Johanna Tennant, my daughter-in-law, who became my go-between arriving each morning with messages, reading the first draft and checking up that I was alright, and my best friend Tim Leese who encouraged me and provided wonderful suppers for us through the writing of this book. And, of course, I would also like to thank my daughters Amy and May and my son Christopher for their invaluable contributions.

PICTURE ACKNOWLEDGEMENTS

Inset pages 1–16

Author's collection:

1-3, 5 below right, 6 above, 7, 8 above right/centre right/ below left, 9 above left and centre right, 11, 12 above, 13-14, 15 below left, 16 above left and below left.

Additional sources:

Alamy: 4 below, 5 centre left. ©Armstrong Jones: 5 above right. Associated Newspapers Ltd/Solo Syndication dmg media: 4 above right/Daily Sketch 30th May 1953. © Daily Express/Ted Bath: 15 centre right. Getty Images: 4 above left, 6 below/Slim Aarons, 10 above and below/Litchfield, 12 below/Anwar Hussein. Trustees of the Glen Settlement: 8 above left. PA Images: 9 below left. Shutterstock: 6 centre left/Leon Schadeberg, 15 above left/Mike Forster/Daily Mail, 16 centre right/Albanpix.

Chapter openers 1–19

Author's collection:

2: With my sister Carey, right. 3: Stock checking at the

Holkham Pottery. 6: Colin, in his 'gathering of the clans' tartans, with Rob Roy. 7: Colin's house on Mustique, 1980. 8: Colin with Princess Margaret, Mustique early 70s. 9: With Christopher and twins May and Amy, 1970. 11: Invitation to Colin's 50th Birthday Party, Mustique, 1976. 13: With Princess Margaret, Kensington Palace. 14: With Charlie, 1976. 15: Christopher and Charlie, 1986. 16: With Henry in India. 17: Princess Margaret. 18: Our 50th wedding anniversary, 2006.

Additional sources:

1: Holkham, photo Gareth Hacon. 4: On the way to the final dress rehearsal for the Coronation, 1953/TopFoto. 5: At our engagement reception, 1955/TopFoto. 10: Lady in Waiting to Princess Margaret, arriving at the ballet in London, 1980/ Shutterstock. 12: Lady in Waiting to Princess Margaret, Australia, 1975/Getty Images. 19. At home, 2019, photo Hal Shinnie.